The Healing Promise

Richard Mayhue

HARVEST HOUSE PUBLISHERS
Eugene, Oregon 97402

THE HEALING PROMISE

Copyright © 1994 by Harvest House Publishers
Eugene, Oregon 97402

Library of Congress Cataloging-in-Publication Data

Mayhue, Richard.
    The healing promise / Richard Mayhue.
       p.   cm.
    ISBN 1-56507-182-4
    1. Spiritual healing—Biblical teaching.   2. Healing in the Bible.
    I. Title.
    BS680.H4M38   1994
    234'.13—dc20   94-6870
                                                         CIP

Printed in the United States of America.

94 95 96 97 98 99 00 01 – 10 9 8 7 6 5 4 3 2 1

To Dad and Mom—

who now enjoy perfect health,
spiritually and physically,
in the presence of our Lord Jesus Christ.

Foreword

Everybody dies. Everybody gets sick. Everybody has been injured. Avoiding these pirates of peace and pleasure is a lifelong enterprise for everybody. Because they mean pain, suffering, debilitation, and separation, we all pursue triumph over them. Eliminating death, sickness, and injury from life would bring bliss! No disease, no disaster, and no death would mean no fear, no anxiety, no dread. A life like that would be Utopian. People would do anything and pay anything for it.

If someone had the power to heal all disease, eliminate all injury, and end all death, the world would surely make that person the object of their love and adoration. Right? Wrong. Jesus had the power and demonstrated it, but His enemies injured Him and then killed Him. Amazingly, they wounded and murdered the One who came to end their pain and death forever! Such is the irrational selfishness of man.

Jesus brought the healing promise of God, and it was clear to see that He could fulfill it. He banished disease from Palestine. The prospect of physical healing drew people to Him and His apostles by the thousands. And they were not disappointed, for they were healed. This massive demonstration of both the power of God over the effect of sin and the compassion of God for the experience of suffering clarified the reality that God was offering healing to those who came to Him. Just what that healing gift involves, both now and in eternity, is the purpose of this important and encouraging book.

You are highly privileged to read this treasure and come away with the richness of God's healing promise.

John MacArthur
Pastor-Teacher
Grace Community Church
Sun Valley, California

Preface

Twenty years have passed since healing advocate Hobart Freeman prompted my first interest in this subject while I attended seminary in north-central Indiana. That led eventually to my writing *Divine Healing Today* in the early 1980's. Since 1985, new books on healing have appeared at an unprecedented pace, accompanied by a fresh generation of people promoting healing ministries. The time has now arrived for me to update and significantly expand my material in this new book—*The Healing Promise*.

I am not writing to debunk every healer on the scene. Were that my intent, the book would be quickly outdated, since a new group will undoubtedly arise before long. Rather, I intend to develop a biblical model of healing by which we can test anyone who claims to heal—past, present, and future. With this approach we can minister biblical truth and protect Christians from the pain and anguish that come as a result of unbiblical teaching and practice. At the same time we can positively and correctly understand God's healing promises in Scripture.

It is not my desire to be bombastic or sarcastic, nor to treat other believers ungraciously. But I must interact with the biblical and contemporary issues in the teachings and writings of those leaders whose ministries have a high degree of impact on people today. The greater good of protecting the church of Jesus Christ from painful error requires the lesser risk of offending others unintentionally in our pursuit of truth.

I have tried to avoid focusing on the lunatic fringe as though they established the norm; I also have not dismissed all healing claims as works of Satan. Above all, I have prayed that this book would not appear to put God in a box or in any way unbiblically limit our omnipotent Lord.

I deeply desire to make a positive biblical contribution toward understanding how God works in the physical affairs of the human race, especially in the lives of Christians. To help accomplish that goal, some of the designed features in *The Healing Promise* include:

1. Seeking Scripture to understand God's will in the matter of healing.

2. Setting Scripture above experience when interpreting claims of healing.

3. Seeing God's hand in our health and healing at all times.

4. Exposing outright fraud or false doctrine.

5. Interacting with those who have also written on healing.

6. Equipping Christians to biblically deal with sickness in their own life, in their family, in the body of Christ, and in the world.

7. Allowing God to be God.

I have prayed that God would use *The Healing Promise* as a ready reference tool for pastors and laypeople who must continually minister to the sick and suffering. It is also intended to equip the saints for understanding the issues of life and death, and to be effective in ministering to those who now suffer. Portions of this material can encourage and strengthen the sick because through it they can better understand the truth of God's Word and the direction of God's will. My chief objectives include 1) glorifying God in all His majesty, 2) honoring God in His ministry to the church, to both the healthy and the ailing, and 3) letting God's Word be the final arbiter in these issues.

Without the gifted help of devoted friends and family members, *The Healing Promise* would still be a pile of illegible notes. My wife "B," my son Wade, and my secretary Cindy Kranich all labored furiously on the computer to keep endless streams of rewrites moving forward.

Elaine Bersoza, John Metcalf, and Dennis Swanson lent their invaluable computer and transcription expertise to the project. Jim Stitzinger and The Master's Seminary library staff tirelessly helped me obtain a seemingly never-ending supply of books and articles written on healing. Terry Holley and Lance Quinn alerted me to some key books that I otherwise would have missed.

André Kole, one of the world's renowned illusionists, John and Patricia MacArthur, friends for 15 years in ministry, and Joni Eareckson Tada, champion extraordinaire for the handicapped, have all significantly enriched me personally as well as *The Healing Promise*, for which I thank them and the Lord.

Eileen Mason, Steve Miller, and Barbara Sherrill at Harvest House Publishers have given me the kind of opportunity and encouragement that most writers dream of but rarely experience.

Even though *The Healing Promise* has unquestionably been a team project, I must stand accountable before God and to the church for its content and conclusions. I can only pray that our Lord will be pleased to use it in effective ministry to the body of Christ.

Richard Mayhue

Contents

PART 4:
A Christian's Response to Sickness

Part 1
A Perspective for Today

1

God's Healing Promise

Gᴏᴅ heals! Let's acknowledge that up front. To say anything else rejects the biblical witness to God's majesty and unending power. To deny healing would be to deny God's promise and would be to call God a liar.

This precious truth has not been lost on the great hymnwriters of the past. Listen to their grand declarations:

> Praise, my soul, the King of heaven,
> To His feet thy tribute bring;
> Ransomed, healed, restored, forgiven,
> Evermore His praises sing. . . .[1]

> Out of my bondage, sorrow and night,
> Jesus, I come, Jesus, I come;
> Into Thy freedom, gladness and light,
> Jesus, I come to Thee.
> Out of my sickness into Thy health,
> Out of my want and into Thy wealth,
> Out of my sin and into Thyself,
> Jesus, I come to Thee.[2]

More Questions Than Answers

But to believe and sing this truth in worship doesn't always mean that we understand it. To overstate or understate this truth is to misconstrue it, and not to fully understand this truth means we can easily misuse it.

The subject of divine healing raises many important questions. Consider this sample:[3]

- Does Christ heal today as He did on the pages of the Gospels?

- What is the relationship between Satan and sickness?

- Can Satan imitate divine healing?

- Are we showing a lack of faith when we visit a doctor for help with an illness?

- What is the relationship of sin and sickness to divine healing?

- Is medical care a last resort or the first line of defense for Christians?

- Has something gone wrong when godly people are chronically ill?

- What is the role of faith in divine healing?

- Why does God heal some people and not others?

- Can non-Christians experience divine healing?

- Is an emphasis on miraculous healing more suited to mission contexts where medical resources are not readily available?

- How is God healing today?

- Is it always God's will to heal?

- Will He heal me? Or a friend? Or a family member?

Toward Biblical Answers

I have always been impressed with Reuben A. Torrey's little volume *Divine Healing*, originally written in 1924.[4] The situation in his day parallels what we now experience 70 years later in the 1990's:

> The subject of divine healing is awakening an unusual interest in all parts of our country at the present time. Much is being said in favor of it, even by persons who have been opposed to the doctrine in times past; much is being said against it on every hand. The land is being flooded with religious adventurers who are taking advantage of the widespread interest in this important subject to deceive and rob the people.[5]

Dr. Torrey modeled the approach that we are now using in *The Healing Promise*. He stated:

> A book is greatly needed that considers with utter impartiality all that God has to say on this subject and that has but one aim: to discover exactly what God teaches on this very important subject, and *all* He teaches.[6]

Dr. Torrey's wise counsel demands that we thoroughly inspect the Scriptures. Our purpose will be to discover *all* that God has prescribed. Only through the thorough study of God's Word can we expect biblical answers to our questions.

Both doctrine and experience are essential elements in healthy Christianity. An authentic experience of God's truth always issues from His Word as the source. Few areas of current interest are more confused than divine healing, because God's priority of first *understanding truth* and then *interpreting experience* has too often been reversed or ignored.

The Challenge of Understanding

Someone has observed that the Bible is a literary pool in which a child can wade but an elephant can swim. For example, John 3:16 reads rather easily. However, the Ethiopian eunuch needed Philip to interpret the far more difficult Isaiah 53 (*see* Acts 8:31).

The Old Testament prophets wanted to know what person or time the Spirit of Christ within them indicated. They struggled to reconcile the sufferings of Christ with His glories to follow (1 Peter 1:10-11). Even Peter had to strain. He noted that some of Paul's letters contained prophetic teachings that were hard to understand (2 Peter 3:15-16).

The theme of divine healing offers the same challenge. Joni Eareckson Tada learned a great lesson while she sifted through personal doubts. Listen to her well-stated discovery:

> Often we have questions about issues like this which require more than just simple answers, but we don't have the patience to hear those answers out. Sometimes in the past, my own attitude has been, "Don't give me any detailed theological stuff. Just answer my question." Then, because I refused to take the time or mental energy to hear and consider the answer, I would go away assuming no answer existed.[7]

God's Healing Promise

The Bible does contain a healing promise. Many have misunderstood it. Look at 1 Peter 2:24 carefully:

> He Himself bore our sins in His body on the cross, that we might die to sin and live to righteousness; for by His wounds you were healed.

Can you see it? *"By His wounds you were healed."* What does Peter mean? How does this apply to you and me in this life? If it applies physically, then why aren't all Christians healed? Has God's Word failed? Has God lost His healing touch? Are the Scriptures mistaken?

Two foundational truths help get us off to a right start in understanding Peter and divine healing. First, every human being, when conceived, possesses a congenital spiritual defect—a sin disability that needs to be healed. Second, Peter addresses our need for spiritual restoration in 1 Peter 2:24 with his discussion of Christ's provision of salvation's healing.

Let me dissect 1 Peter 2:24-25 for us. Then, when we reassemble it, you will be able to understand the whole because we have first identified the parts. Our text explains five elements of salvation:

1. The *fact* of salvation (verse 24a):
   "He Himself bore our sins in His body on the cross . . ."

2. The *purposes* of salvation (verse 24b):
   ". . . that we might die to sin and live to righteousness . . ."

3. The *means* of salvation (verse 24c):
   ". . . for by His wounds you were healed."

4. The *need* for salvation (verse 25a):
   "For you were continually straying like sheep . . ."

5. The *result* of salvation (verse 25b):
   ". . . but now you have returned to the Shepherd and Guardian of your souls."

First Peter 2:24 has everything to do with spiritual healing, which the Bible calls salvation. In fact, 1 Peter 2:18-25 means just the opposite of what most healing advocates teach. Peter argues that since Christ physically and spiritually suffered for our spiritual healing (verses 21-24), then we should be willing to physically suffer in this life at the hands of men (verses 18-21) because we have already received God's healing promise for eternal salvation (verses 24-25). *Peter actually validates the divine purpose in human suffering rather than eliminates it.*

Unless we begin with this eternal salvation perspective, we will never biblically understand how God works in the physical affairs of mankind in this life. The good news is that Christians are securely saved. The other news is that not all of salvation's benefits will be received until our bodies have been raised from the grave. After God initiates our salvation, all Christians still sin, still suffer ill health, and eventually will die.

Half-Truths[8]

Tragically, this wonderful truth of eternal salvation (our spiritual healing of which Peter writes) has been seriously mistaught by many people today. Their teachings have taken various forms but almost always contain a mixture of truth and error. Half-truths about divine healing fuel the injurious errors of our day.

Let me alert you to some of these more frequent half-truths so that you can be prepared for them.

1. Because God wills that Christians enjoy His bless-ings, sickness shows that you are out of His will.

2. Sin is the root cause of sickness; therefore you must resist sickness as you would sin.

3. Since Christ died for your sickness and your sin, you can be freed from both.

4. If you had enough faith, you would be healed.

5. What you confess is what you possess; so talk sick-ness and you will get sick; talk health and you will get well.

6. All adversity comes from Satan; so sickness, like Satan, should be rebuked.

7. If you only knew the secret fact of God's healing power, you could be healed.

8. Since Christ and the apostles healed in their day, Christians can heal today.

9. Since sickness is from Satan, nothing good can come from sickness.

10. Since God wants you well, never pray, "Thy will be done" in regard to healing.

11. Since sin is the cause of sickness, if you are sick, then you have a pattern of sin in your life.

12. God has healed you, but the devil is not letting the symptoms leave.

Thousands of people could testify how painful these half-truths can be. Dr. C. Everett Koop recalls a particularly brutal episode.

We hired an investigative writer to look into some of the cults and into faith healers specifically. Our investigator traveled to a Southwestern city where a healing campaign had been advertised some weeks in advance. . . .

Among those who applied for healing was an elderly Christian gentleman who lived out on the prairie. His vision was becoming dim, and he most likely was developing cataracts. The only lighting in the little cabin where he lived was a kerosene lamp. He was a devout Christian, read his Bible daily—or tried to—and had all the faith necessary for healing, if faith indeed does secure healing. His major complaint was that his sight had deteriorated to the point where he could no longer read his Bible.

On the night of his appearance before the healer, the old man was brought up in the atmosphere of a side-show. The faith healer said, "Well, Pop, you can't see anymore. You've gotten old, you can't even see with your glasses. Your vision is failing." Then he reached over and took off the old man's spectacles, threw them on the platform, stamped on them, and broke them. He then handed the elderly gentleman a large-print Bible, which, under the lights necessary for television in those days, enabled the gentleman to read John 3:16 out loud, to the astonishment and applause of the audience.

The elderly gentleman praised God, the healer praised God, the audience praised God, and the old man went back to his dimly lit cabin and could not *find* his Bible, because his glasses were destroyed. The man went back to the healer but was told the most discouraging thing a godly man like that could possibly hear: "You didn't have enough faith, or the healing would have stuck."9

Help Is on the Way

If understanding how God works today is this complex, how can a sincere Christian ever know for sure what to receive and what to reject? How can a Christian avoid the abuse and embarrassment suffered by that dear old gentleman? First, by knowing something about prominent, highly visible Bible teachers and about their teachings. Hank Hanegraaff, who has written *Christianity in Crisis*, served us all well by analyzing the Faith movement of our day.10 Much of the error taught about divine healing comes from this movement.

The second way to learn the truth about divine healing is to learn the truth of Scripture itself. In one sense, *The Healing Promise* complements *Christianity in Crisis* by focusing primarily on the Scriptures. This book helps develop a biblical model and biblical theology of healing. By possessing both a knowledge of false teachers and their false teaching coupled with a knowledge of the truth, every sincere Christian should be well-equipped for discernment.

Growing numbers of pastors have become increasingly alarmed over the vast amount of false teaching on divine healing that goes out on tapes, over radio and TV, and through

Christian publishing. We echo the sentiments of Paul, who feared for the Corinthians almost two millennia ago:

> I am jealous for you with a godly jealousy; for I betrothed you to one husband, that to Christ I might present you as a pure virgin. But I am afraid, lest as the serpent deceived Eve by his craftiness, your minds should be led astray from the simplicity and purity of devotion to Christ (2 Corinthians 11:2-3).

A well-known pastor speaks for all of us who fear for the sake of Christ's flock, the church.

> I have had the privilege of leading some in our flock to Christ, introducing them to the joy of knowing God and walking with Him, and my heart is linked with them in their spiritual growth. But I agree with Paul: *I am afraid for many of them.* The thought of their being led astray greatly concerns me. I don't know of a pastor worth his salt who doesn't struggle with that same fear; namely, that his parishioners' "minds should be led astray from the simplicity and purity of devotion to Christ." Though I am not normally a worrier, I am more than slightly concerned over what people do with their pain, their brokenness, and especially their need for relief. Why? Because there are so many unbiblical and erroneous answers being offered which will only deceive, disillusion, disturb . . . and bring greater confusion.[11]

Does God heal today? Most certainly! How? In what ways? Whom does He heal? Read on for a biblical explanation.

Part 2
Faith Healing

2

Contemporary Confusion

Larry and Alice Parker wanted God's best for their family of six. But their oldest son suffered from diabetes and regularly received insulin injections. When Daniel Badilla held special services in their Barstow, California, church, the Parkers "walked the aisle" with 11-year-old Wesley. They sincerely sought a healing miracle.

The preacher pronounced Wesley healed. Larry joyfully entered "Praise God our son is healed!" into Wesley's insulin log. But Wesley's next insulin test indicated differently. Yet by faith the Parkers claimed the healing and blamed the unexpected insulin results on Satan.

Shortly afterward, Wesley began to suffer the nausea and severe stomach cramps that predictably indicate low insulin. Larry and Alice postponed medical treatment and sought God's continued healing power through prayer. In spite of their sincere faith, Wesley fell into a coma and died three days later. *Newsweek* magazine reported the tragedy nationally.[1]

Healing Explosion

During the last three decades of the twentieth century a

renewed worldwide interest in healing has emerged in both secular and Christian circles. Many circumstances have caused this interest to rage like a mighty river, potentially wreaking havoc in the lives of those who seek relief in these "healing waters."

First, the information explosion in recent times has recreated the Dark Ages in reverse. During those cruel times of intellectual poverty, uneducated people did not possess enough knowledge to believe. Today, however, the available knowledge more than doubles every decade, and people do not know what to believe.

Second, a new wave of existential thought has joined the data deluge. Belief in miracles creates a surging reaction to liberal theology with all its spiritually deadening effects. This wave has overflowed biblical boundaries at points and flooded people's thinking with presumption disguised as faith.

The late Francis Schaeffer explained such thinking with extraordinary perception:

> One can also see a parallel between the new Pentecostals and the liberals. The liberal theologians don't believe in content or in religious truth. They are really existentialists using theological, Christian terminology.[2]

Third, "experiential Christianity" is the ultimate judge of truth today.[3] This mindset can be found within many age groups and denominational organizations, and the common denominator that unites them is *experience*. In this view, God's reality cannot be expressed apart from experience, and experience can override biblical teaching.

Fourth, sickness runs rampant in our society. A popular periodical reported that the health-care industry billed record increases in payment for medical services over the last decade. This has forced the United States to consider adopting a government-directed health-care plan.

Each year the medical profession makes phenomenal advances in the raging war against disease. Yet an increasingly sick society, bent on instant cures, is willing to turn to whomever can offer the quickest and least expensive path to relief.

Although various Pentecostals and charismatics have focused new attention on divine healing, no two groups agree in every detail. Their messages frequently include the promise of God's complete and immediate healing if the afflicted person responds with full faith. Such a person, who has no hope from doctors and lies helplessly incapacitated without God's intervention, feels irresistibly drawn toward this last-ditch, beckoning prospect of health.

The following brief overview provides an important historical perspective on the faith-healing phenomenon in America over the last century.[4]

The Healing Century[5]

The names F.F. Bosworth,[6] A.J. Gordon, Aimee Semple McPherson, and A.B. Simpson stand out among the prominent personalities associated with healing in the past. Because of their popularity, they became household names.

After 1940 a new generation came along.[7] Among those promoting healing were Allen, Angley, Branham, Hagin, Kuhlman, Osborn, and Roberts. Their ministries ranged from hospitals to healing cloths.

Oral Roberts built the "City of Faith"—an impressive medical complex on the Oral Roberts University campus in Tulsa, Oklahoma.[8] Medical, dental, and nursing students were to be trained there. (The medical center was never finished and ended up being sold.)

Faith healers T.L. and Daisy Osborn also operate out of Tulsa. The Osborn Foundation sends a small piece of burlap to the readers of its magazine. The respondents must write out "the special miracle needed from God" and mail it with the piece of cloth to the foundation. Printed on the envelope provided is Acts 19:11-12: "And God was performing extraordinary miracles by the hands of Paul, so that handkerchiefs or aprons were even carried from his body to the sick, and the diseases left them and the evil spirits went out." Underneath that the Osborns have written, "After 3 days and 4 nights of fasting and prayer, we'll return this same cloth to you."

Streams of literature have been written to promote faith healing. Such publications circulate widely and usually contain all sorts of promises and procedures.

For example, Dr. Hobart Freeman wrote, "When genuine faith is present it alone will be sufficient, for it will take the place of medicine and other aids."[9]

William Caldwell provided an unusual claim:

> In order to receive healing, it may not be necessary for you to read this book through to the end. Rather, just take the first nugget of truth that applies to your situation and act upon it.[10]

Oral Roberts announced:

> I have a feeling that the mass healing of an entire audience is nearer than we think.[11]

The Changing Landscape

During the 1980's the players changed radically. Few healers remain in the spotlight today who also stood there in the 1940's through the 1970's. The various elements in this new generation of healing defy compartmentalization because of their diverse overlaps; they cannot all be considered as one movement because of their varying uniquenesses.

However, at least two distinct strands seem to stand out. On one hand we have adherents to a "health-and-wealth" theology preaching a prosperity gospel whose results come by way of Positive Confession. The teachers of this gospel make up what is commonly called the Faith movement. Then on the other hand are those who believe that signs and wonders should be evidenced in our time because the kingdom of God is now present. The health-and-wealth teachers tend to have little formal education in Scripture and view God as prospering those people who show sufficient faith. The signs-and-wonders teachers are generally well-educated and appeal to the glory and kingdom purposes of God as the basis for supernatural intervention. The former generally blame failure on man's lack of faith; the latter explain inconsistent results as consistent with the present kingdom will of God.

First let us consider those who espouse a health-and-wealth theology. Paul Yonggi Cho,[12] Morris Cerullo, Kenneth and Gloria Copeland, Paul and Jan Crouch, Kenneth Hagin, Marilyn Hickey, Robert Tilton, and Benny Hinn rank among the more influential representatives.[13] This movement focuses first on man and then afterward on God to supply mankind's need of health and wealth.[14]

The Positive Confession element of the Faith movement has cultic origins.[15] A careful study of Satan's two attacks on Job's spiritual integrity—the removal of his wealth (Job 1) and the removal of his health (Job 2)—highlights the true basis of name-it-and-claim-it theology.[16] Satan theorized that without health and wealth, Job would curse God. Job's righteous response to God, however, proved Satan and the health/wealth movement wrong (Job 42:5-6).

The Third Wave

The second major group has been called the Signs and Wonders movement[17] or "The Third Wave,"[18] or has been identified with John Wimber's Vineyard movement.[19] Visible personalities include Jack Deere,[20] Wayne Grudem, Kevin Springer, John Wimber, and C. Peter Wagner.[21]

These vignettes taken from John Wimber's book *Power Healing* give an idea of what he believes about healing.

Stories like Naaman's are not confined to biblical times. Several years ago a young man from the Anaheim Vineyard Christian Fellowship was in a cafe, sitting near an elderly gentleman who suffered from severe palsy of his hands. The older man was shaking so much that he kept dropping his food as he tried to eat. The young man, full of compassion, walked over and grabbed the man's hands, then said, "Jesus will heal that." The shaking stopped immediately. Everyone in the cafe looked on in stunned silence. Then the young man said, "Now Jesus will heal your heart just as he healed your hands." Within a few minutes the older gentleman was praying a prayer of repentance and faith in Christ.[22]

Several years ago I received a call from a distraught father. He was sobbing and could hardly talk. "My baby is here in the hospital," he said, "and they have tubes from machines attached all over her body. The doctors say she will not survive the night. Would you come?" I told him I would come to the hospital. After hanging up the phone I prayed, "Lord, are you calling this baby to you at this time?" I sensed the Lord saying no. I walked into the hospital with the knowledge that I was a representative of Christ, a messenger who had a gift for that baby girl.

When I entered the baby's room, I sensed death, so I quietly said, "Death, get out of here." It left, and the whole atmosphere in the room changed, as though a weight were lifted. Then I went over and began praying for the girl. After only a few minutes I knew she was going to be healed, and so did her father. Hope came into his eyes. "She is going to be okay," he said. "I know it." Within twenty minutes she improved greatly; several days later she was released, completely healed.[23]

In sum, raising of the dead was a dramatic and infrequent event in the New Testament, but something that I believe is possible still today.[24]

Benny Hinn

No one involved in healing ministry today approaches the

visibility and recognition accorded to Benny Hinn.[25] His recent books have been bestsellers; he also appears as a regular guest on the Trinity Broadcasting Network. Hinn intimates that he has taken up where Kathryn Kuhlman left off.[26]

Because of his unusually widespread influence and because he has attempted to express a theology of healing in *Lord, I Need a Miracle*, it becomes particularly important to examine what Benny Hinn teaches. This brief analysis will compare what Hinn believes about healing with what the Scriptures teach. You can then make up your own mind about Hinn's teaching credibility (*see* Acts 17:11).

1. Benny Hinn does not pray "Lord, Thy will be done."[27] Jesus Christ did (Luke 22:42).

2. Hinn believes that God always intends for believers to be healed.[28] In contrast, the Bible teaches that some of the greatest saints had physical infirmities from which they were never healed, including Jacob and Paul.

3. Hinn teaches that believers should command God to heal.[29] The Bible teaches we are to ask (1 John 5:14-15).

4. Hinn suggests that miraculous healing from God is gradual.[30] Healing by Christ and the apostles occurred instantly.

5. Hinn teaches that faith on the part of the sick person is essential to healing.[31] Lazarus and Jairus' daughter could not have exercised faith when they were raised from the dead.

6. Hinn writes that we must do our part before God can heal.[32] The Bible teaches that God is sovereign.

7. Hinn believes that Christians should not be sick.[33] The Bible teaches that Christians can be sick and all will eventually die.

8. Benny Hinn implies that a person's healing can be lost and that the healed person must do certain things to keep the healing.[34] Nowhere in the Bible do we find such teaching.

Amazingly, Hinn not only contradicts Scripture on the subject of healing, but he also contradicts himself. Hinn wrote in 1992:

> This recalls the day years ago when I heard Kathryn Kuhlman prophesy in her own inimitable way that the day would arrive, before the coming of the Lord, when the power of God would be so great that everyone would be healed. "There will not be one sick saint in the body of Christ," she declared.
>
> With her customary drama, pointing of finger, and hand on hip, she asked, "Could it be today?"
>
> Of course, she never saw it come, but it will come. The Holy Spirit has convinced me of that.[35]

Later, in a 1993 interview, *Charisma* magazine asked Hinn, "You've mentioned some other changes in your theology. Have you changed your view of healing?" Compare his 1993 answer to what the Holy Spirit allegedly told him in 1992:

> Huldah Buntain, the missionary to India, was in our church recently, and she talked about how her husband, Mark, died. The story broke me up because I realized some of the greatest saints on earth have gotten sick.
>
> Jacob walked with a limp. Elisha died a sick man, though the power of God lingered on his bones. Even the apostle Paul had an infirmity—although we're not sure what it was. Why didn't God heal them?
>
> You know, my father died of cancer. Sadly, in the past, I stated publicly: Had my father known then what I know now, he wouldn't have died. How cruel! I'm not going to say that about anyone again.

Yet I still believe that healing is promised to all of us as children of God. The Word of God is clear on that. Psalm 103 says: "Bless the Lord, O my soul, and forget not all His benefits: who forgives all your iniquities, who heals all your diseases."

So I believe with all my heart that healing is a part of our inheritance as believers. It's a provision of God's covenant with us. But now I have come to realize that God is sovereign, and there are things I just don't understand.[36]

Either the Holy Spirit spoke correctly in 1992 and Hinn has chosen to correct the Spirit in 1993, or the Spirit didn't speak what Hinn alleged in 1992 and he has resorted to damage control in 1993.

Our Challenge

The Christian community must come to grips with the fact that it is extremely rare when a reported healing begins to match up with the biblical model. When God miraculously healed through the prophets, Christ, or the apostles, these qualities, among others, characterized the healing:

1. It was immediate.
2. It was public.
3. It took place on ordinary, unplanned occasions.
4. It included illnesses that were untreatable by the medical community.
5. It was complete and irreversible.
6. It was undeniable, even to detractors.

Taking contemporary healing a step further, most of today's reported healings look little different than reported healings from the cults and other world religions. John MacArthur makes this point.

The gift of healing . . . has been claimed through the centuries by Christians and pagans alike. Historically, the Roman Catholic Church has led the way in claiming the power to heal. They have boasted of healing people with the bones of John the Baptist, or Peter, fragments of the cross, or even vials of Mary's breast milk. Lourdes, a Catholic shrine in France, has supposedly been the site of countless miraculous healings. Medjugorje, in Yugoslavia, has drawn more than fifteen million people in less than a decade. They come in search of a miracle or healing from an apparition of the Virgin Mary, who supposedly appeared to six children there in 1981.

Oriental psychic healers say they can do "bloodless surgery." They wave their hands over afflicted organs and say incantations. Supposedly people are cured.

Witch doctors and shamans even claim to raise the dead. Occultists use black magic to do lying wonders in the healing arts. Mary Baker Eddy, founder of Christian Science, claimed to have healed people through telepathy. Satan has always held people in his dominion by means of counterfeit healings.[37]

If contemporary healings look little like those in the Scriptures and much like those of false religions, then there must be explanations for these experiences other than the power of God. Are these ministries of God or of man? Charles Swindoll answers the question for us.

Now the critical question: Do I believe God has placed His healing powers in a few "anointed individuals" who claim to do divine healings? I say, unequivocally, I do not. In fact, I don't think I have ever ministered to any more disillusioned souls than those who had been promised healing by an alleged "healer" and then were not healed.

In this day of the resurgence of so-called divine healers, my convictions may not represent a popular position. I realize that. In no way does this mean, however, that I do not believe God has the power to heal ...and, on unique occasions, He does do so. I believe that with all my heart. The problem comes when attention is focused on a person who claims healing powers, or on the series of emotionally overpowering events that surround a so-called healing service. If those "divine healers" are authentic and "anointed" miracle workers of God, why aren't they out going floor-to-floor in hospitals and emergency wards? Why don't they prove the truth of their ministry there...humbly...unobtrusively...free of charge? Then I would have reason to believe they are servants of the living God in whose lives the Spirit is consistently pouring out His power to heal.[38]

Contemporary Confusion

After surveying what is being taught and written in the name of Christianity, we can see why a state of confusion about divine healing rests over the church. Questions like these perplex many people: Is it real? If it is not real, how can I explain some of the apparent healings? How does it work? If it does work, why should I ignore or deny a good thing? Why the sudden appearance and increase of healing if it was possible all along? Is it biblical? Why am I sick? Should I quit taking medicine? Why haven't I been healed? Why are some leaders in the healing movement sick? Why do all people in the healing movement die? Which offer of healing is biblically valid?

Maybe you have asked some of these questions yourself. No doubt many of these same inquiries agonized the hearts of Larry and Alice Parker. When people's lives could be at risk, we must have the sure Word of God, not the theories and reported experiences of men. Remember, even though Larry and Alice had placed their full faith in God, Wesley still died.

A lawyer in Indiana shared with me this letter that he received from Larry Parker. Years had passed since Wesley's death. During that time Larry struggled for the truth, and found it only as he sought full scriptural counsel. He wrote:

> I am writing this letter with the hope and prayer that somehow I can share with you a lesson that I have learned at great expense. It is only by the grace of God, and the never-failing, all-encompassing love of Jesus Christ our Lord that my wife and I have been able to come through this trial. . . .
>
> We wanted to see our son healed, but went about it the wrong way. It was during our trial for involuntary manslaughter and felony child abuse that my wife felt she could tell me what the Lord had shown her. She told me that our love, because it was lacking, failed Wesley, and that God's word says, "Love never faileth" (1 Corinthians 13:8).
>
> I knew then that we had allowed what we thought was faith to cause us to forget to love. As we prayed for Wesley and saw him in obvious pain, our love for him wanted to give him the insulin that we knew would stop his suffering. However, we felt that would be a lack of faith, and would cost him his healing. We learned that our actions were contrary to what the Scriptures say. God's Word says that love is greater than faith (1 Corinthians 13:13).
>
> The trouble lies with the fact that we confuse faith and belief. We think that if we believe hard enough, the healing will take place. We tie healing to some ability on our part to believe enough, i.e., to have enough faith.
>
> To withhold medicine, especially life-giving medicine, is a very presumptuous act on our part that actually hinders the Spirit of God from His work.
>
> My prayer is that you will consider these thoughts at length, for they have come at an incomprehensible price that no one would voluntarily pay.[39]

I am deeply moved by Larry's honesty, not to mention the excruciating pain he suffered. The issue could not be more real, for the lives of loved ones are at stake. God can, has, and does heal, but always for His own purposes, in His own way, and at His appointed time. We cannot force God to heal nor can we humanly manufacture a genuine healing experience.

Tragically, our world offers very convincing counterfeits of the real thing. Even more tragic, in our eagerness to see God work, we as Christians sometimes flock to anyone who claims a miraculous healing. In doing so, we trivialize genuine divine healing—we accept man's deceitful illusions in place of God's divine intervention.

3

Are Faith Healers for Real?

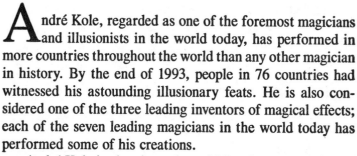

André Kole, regarded as one of the foremost magicians and illusionists in the world today, has performed in more countries throughout the world than any other magician in history. By the end of 1993, people in 76 countries had witnessed his astounding illusionary feats. He is also considered one of the three leading inventors of magical effects; each of the seven leading magicians in the world today has performed some of his creations.

André Kole is also the author of *Miracles or Magic?* This fascinating book reveals the difference between divine power and man-made magic. Most importantly, Kole is a committed Christian who has used his talent for over 30 years to share the reality of Jesus Christ with millions of people through his ministry with Campus Crusade for Christ International.

One of André Kole's special interests has been to study the techniques used by faith healers who resort to illusions to make audiences think they are witnessing miraculous healings. For this reason and with this emphasis, I have asked André to write this unique chapter.

41

Illusion or Reality?

Years ago, as a professional magician and a skeptic, I was challenged to investigate the miracles of Christ from a magician's perspective. At that time I took great pride in the fact that I had never been fooled by any other magician, so I had no intention of being deceived by any form of first-century trickster, if that was all that Jesus was. During the months following the challenge I made that investigation; and after eliminating every possibility of the use of some form of mesmerism, hypnosis, or other means of trickery, I came to the place where I had to agree with the great religious leader Nicodemus, who, in the third chapter of the Gospel of John, said to Jesus, "No man can do the miracles that thou doest except God be with him" (verse 2, KJV). Like Nicodemus, I could no longer question the authenticity of Jesus Christ.

As a magician and illusionist, I discovered that Jesus Christ is no illusion; rather, He is a reality and it is possible to know Him in a personal way. I also discovered that He is the one who makes life worth living.

Since making this discovery over 30 years ago, I have devoted the major portion of my time traveling throughout the world performing and sharing my personal faith in Christ, and helping people discern the difference between illusion and reality.

As an illusionist/magician, I define the art of illusion/ magic as "the use of natural means to create a supernatural effect." There is nothing supernatural taking place; it is only the illusion of the supernatural. It would be good to keep this definition in mind whenever the term "magic" or "illusion" is used in this chapter. One may wonder what this kind of magic (illusion) has to do with Christianity and physical healing and why I would be invited to write this chapter. The fact is that much of what appears to be taking place in many faith-healing services today is not divine healing, but magical trickery. Often what people see and think is supernatural is simply the illusion of the supernatural.

One of the problems I encounter in discussing whether faith-healing and other phenomena are real or fraudulent is that most people underestimate what can be accomplished through trickery. My own inventive career may be a good illustration of this. For many years I have created illusions for the world's greatest magician, David Copperfield. I have collaborated with him on accomplishing such tricks as levitating over the Grand Canyon, visibly dematerializing through the Great Wall of China, making the real Statue of Liberty disappear, and causing an 80,000-pound passenger car from the Orient Express to levitate and disappear in midair. Some of my most recent accomplishments have included devising ways to make the pyramids of Egypt seem to disappear and apparently levitating the entire Washington Monument to a height sufficient for a line of people holding hands to walk from one side to the other under the raised monument. As incredible as these illusions may sound, remember that there is nothing supernatural involved. I could explain to anyone how we accomplish these illusions, and in a matter of minutes he or she could understand how we do them.

It is easy for scientists, theologians, and most other people to be fooled by a magician because they do not think like magicians, and they do not understand all of the psychology and trickery we use in order to fool the audiences. At the same time, it is hard for most people to believe that deception and illusions could play any part in religious healing services. Many Christians just cannot believe that anyone would stoop so low as to use trickery and deception in what is being presented as a sacred, religious healing crusade.

The Great Faith-Healing Act

All of us, whether Christian or not, have a curiosity and desire to see and experience the supernatural. We want to believe that what we are seeing is real, and therefore we let down our guard when it comes to spiritual discernment.

The fact is that when anything, no matter how ridiculous or incredible it may be, is presented in a serious or sacred manner in an atmosphere where honesty is taken for granted, even the most intelligent and spiritually discerning person can be taken in by a clever sleight-of-hand demonstration of trickery and deception.

In recent years many of the more blatant methods used by faith healers have been exposed in books, investigative television shows, and even movies such as the Steve Martin film *Leap of Faith*. The methods portrayed in the film were accurate and were based on some of the techniques exposed by James Randi, myself, and a few others.

In 1987 James Randi wrote his book *The Faith Healers*, which exposed the tricks used by the leading faith healers of recent years.[1] James Randi is a professional magician whom I have known for over 30 years. He is the only person I know of who has spent more time than I have investigating and exposing the tricks used by faith healers.

Although Randi claims to be an atheist, I would have to say that at least he is an honest atheist in regard to his investigating and reporting of the faith healers concerned. Because of my recognition in the magical profession, he has demonstrated a great deal of respect for me, and he expressed the opinion that I am one of the few Christians he has met whom he believes has any integrity. In fact, during the preparation of his book he contacted me to ask my advice from the Christian perspective. I believe this was a sincere effort on his part to separate his non-Christian bias from the reporting of the facts of the fraud and deception we both knew were true.

Let's look now at some of the deceptive "magic" techniques used by so-called healers. Some are crude in their methodology, while others are extremely sophisticated. In the next few paragraphs I will describe the methods that rely on what I call "gimmicks"; and after describing these techniques, I will discuss the much more subtle methods that permeate much of the "healing" that is being claimed today.

Healing Illusions

The Word of Knowledge. Some healers claim that they are given supernatural knowledge about individuals in the audience. This knowledge may include phone numbers, addresses, names, and sicknesses. Unfortunately for the three television preachers whom Randi investigated, careful research showed that all three had their wives or "front men" walk through the auditorium prior to the meeting and collect information about individuals through the guise of striking up casual conversation. During this time, data were gathered regarding names, illnesses, physical descriptions of the people, and the locations of their seats. At other times, "prayer cards" were passed out so audience members could write down their names and prayer requests. These were then collected and used as information during the "word of knowledge" portion of the program.

Peter Popoff was exposed on *The Tonight Show* as receiving his information from his wife through a small radio receiver in his ear. She would simply collect the information on the prayer cards and relate it through her transmitter from a mobile television studio trailer outside the building.

Leg Lengthening. This trick has been used quite extensively by various healers over the years; and as Randi has pointed out, it is simply done with a combination of two techniques. First, the person with the "short leg" is brought on stage and seated on a chair which is facing across the stage but angled slightly toward the audience. As the legs are horizontally straightened out by the "healer," the shoe on the foot farthest from the audience is pulled off a bit, giving the illusion that the leg closest to the audience is shorter. At the same time, the legs are swung slightly away from the audience. Since the legs are swung but the rest of the body stays pointing in the same direction, the leg closer to the audience appears to be shorter than the other. To perform the "miraculous" lengthening, the "healer" simply pushes the loose shoe back onto the foot and manipulates the legs so that they are aligned to the same length.

The Wheelchair Scam. The "healing" of someone confined to a wheelchair can bring cheers from the audience, as witnessed in a healing campaign which I attended in Phoenix a few years ago. As the healing evangelist's team ministered to a woman reported to have lung and liver cancer, she rose up from her wheelchair and walked around the floor to the cheers and applause of the other attendees. To all eyes, it appeared that a dramatic healing had taken place. But was that reality or only an illusion?

Following the convention, the religion editor of a local newspaper followed up on this so-called healing. The editor found out this "healed" woman could walk without her wheelchair before the "healing." Although she had planned not to use the wheelchair at all after the meeting, a follow-up interview a few days later found that she was still using it, although she mentioned "hardly at all." A few months later, my office attempted to follow up on this woman to see how successful her healing was. The letter sent to her came back with a note on the envelope stating "deceased."

Another not-so-subtle wheelchair scam has been used by W.V. Grant and others. During Grant's meetings, the person "healed" jumps out of the wheelchair and pushes Grant around the floor in it. Once again we ask, Is this illusion or reality? Interviews with those who were "healed" in this way have shown that the wheelchairs were provided for them at the meeting. In other words, these individuals had walked in under their own power, and some had never used a wheelchair before in their lives!

Let's take a look now at various methods that work on a psychological basis rather than those that use gimmicks such as transmitters and receivers.

The Benny Hinn Phenomenon

In 1990 and 1991, many people who knew of my research started asking me about Benny Hinn.

The faith-healing performance that Benny Hinn and many others have presented through the years is basically an illusion act. In this act, the illusion is created to make it appear that dozens—or even hundreds—of people are being instantly and miraculously healed by God right before the eyes of the thousands of people who attend these Miracle Crusades and the millions who watch by television. The truth is that apart from certain psychosomatic illnesses that will respond to the suggestions of a faith healer, Christian or non-Christian, very few people are ever healed of anything. This faith-healing act will be discussed in a moment.

Some of what Benny Hinn does seems wonderful and appears to honor the Lord. There are also many people who claim they came to Christ in response to the evangelistic part of Benny's program. It is also a fact that many people are made to feel better and are genuinely helped, even though they are not healed. An associate of one of the best-known faith healers of our time once confided to me that "while no one has ever been healed of a physical problem, he [the faith healer] nevertheless makes them feel better and spurs them on to bigger and better things in life."

The problem with this kind of rationalization is that many unhealed people experience devastating guilt and depression, and even attempt suicide, when their individual healing is *not* realized. The cruel illusion has been created that "if they had enough faith, they would be healed."

One major reason people are vulnerable to the healing illusion act is that they have such a great desire to escape pain and sickness that they are willing to go to almost any extreme to escape the pain, no matter what the cost. Unfortunately, many times illusion is more enjoyable than reality. This is one reason why so many people become addicted to drugs or alcohol—they want to try to escape reality.

In the Broadway play *The Man from LaMancha*, the main character makes this statement: "When illusion reigns supreme, it quite overwhelms reality." Benny Hinn is a tremendous personality, and the most difficult challenge in dealing with an issue like this is the willingness and the ability to separate our emotions and positive feelings for the person from the facts.

Exposing Faith Healing

To understand the facts and the apparent results of the faith-healing "performance" it is first essential to understand the difference between faith-healing and divine healing. The two are not the same. Faith-healing can be done by anyone, Christian or not. Divine healing is something that only God can do. Let's examine both types of healing as we press toward finding the truth.

Christians have a difficult time distinguishing faith-healing from divine healing because the word "faith" is automatically associated with Christianity. However, faith-healing is a universal principle that works no matter who uses it, whether Christians or non-Christians are involved. Faith and trust in any designated person or object, or simply faith in faith alone, is the sole criterion for understanding the concept of faith healing.

The Placebo Effect

One of the main elements that makes the faith-healing act work is the "placebo effect." When medicine was primitive, doctors, not knowing what to do, often prescribed sugar pills, a salt solution, or colored water. There was no medicinal value to these items, yet many patients experienced relief after the "medicine" was applied. This form of treatment is called the "placebo effect."

Doctors say that up to 70 percent of all illnesses could probably be cured by a placebo. The placebo has no proven benefit in itself; it works simply because the person expects it to work: He starts thinking in terms of recovery rather than sickness. The placebo is an illusion, but since our lives are shaped by our perceptions, the placebo works. It is the power of the mind over the body. But as we will see later, the placebo effect will only work for certain illnesses and is ineffective as a cure for many diseases.

Throughout history, various objects, substances, plants, foods, and potions have been popular placebos. Currently, many people involved in the New Age movement believe that certain crystals have the power to heal various diseases. The fact is that the same people who would be helped by believing in the crystals would be equally helped if they believed a piece of bubble gum had the same healing power.

Years ago I investigated the psychic healers of the Philippines for *Time* magazine. It appeared that these healers could miraculously reach through the skin of the body with their bare hands (without instruments) and remove diseased organs. My investigations exposed that they were using sleight of hand to perform fake operations by using animal parts from a chicken, cow, or goat. However, many of the patients who believed the operations were genuine were actually healed. The healing, then, came not as a result of the operations (which were fake), but rather because of the powerful psychological effect these fake operations had on the patients. The results of these fake operations are good examples of how the placebo effect works, which in turn contributes much to the apparent success of the faith-healing act.

Faith-healing can be done by practically anyone—even a cat! It is reported that people from several countries have made trips to Blackburn, England, to visit a faith-healing cat. Dozens of former disease victims attest to the cat's incredible healing power by the laying on of its paws. People come seeking relief for everything from hiccups to heart disease. Leora, the cat's owner, claims, "It's the power of God acting through my cat. . . . God has given him the power to heal!"[2]

The Self-Limiting Factor

To be thorough in our treatment of faith-healing, we must recognize what is called the "self-limiting factor." That is, after a certain period of time, the body simply heals itself of many or most illnesses such as the common cold, measles, mumps, chicken pox, and flu. Many times these diseases just need to run their course, but they can make faith-healing appear to work as the illness subsides.

Psychic Technique

In addition, my investigations of faith-healing throughout the world have shown that the psychological techniques used in America are not unique to American Christians. The same placebo and psychological phenomena can be found around the world. Evidence of this can be illustrated by examples of faith-healing deception which I investigated during a visit to Russia.

Kashpirovsky and Chumak, who have nothing to do with Christianity, have become psychic-healing superstars through their television appearances in the former Soviet Union. They claim to heal broken limbs, scars, blindness, and even AIDS through their healing powers. Followers put tubes of cold cream and jars of water in front of their television sets. Later they rub the cream on themselves or drink the water "energized" by these healers, and afterward thousands of letters are received that testify of healings.

Another new Russian healing star is Gennady Rootzko. He says he is a pupil of the Tibetan monk Lakh-do, who lived near Saint Petersburg (which is Rootzko's native city), that he knows 16,997 languages, that he can read thoughts, that he has several contacts with UFO-nauts, that he is the one who must "save the ill world," and that he can heal all illnesses. Rootzko, in his shows, usually makes some gestures with his hands, similar to Tai-Chi-Chuan exercises, and chants something he calls "Tibetan singing." He also works with various placebo suggestions and stage-hypnotist techniques that supposedly make thousands of people "become free of their illnesses." In the cities of Saint Petersburg, Riga, and Kiev, Rootzko has gathered a tremendous following. Kiev's Republican Stadium hosted two appearances with 100,000 people at each performance, and The Palace of Sports held 10 shows with 30,000 people at each event.

Remember, these "healers" are using the simple hypnotic and suggestive techniques of *faith*-healing, not *divine* healing. These techniques work anywhere in the world, whether they are used by a Christian like Benny Hinn or a non-Christian like Rootzko, Kashpirovsky, or Chumak. For this reason we must be cautious to not view these healings as divine.

Drama and Expectations

Much of the supposed success attributed to faith-healing is due to the preconditioning and manipulation of the crowd in preparation for the healing portion of the performance. Benny Hinn, for example, is a master showman and a master at crowd manipulation. Having been in show business most of my life, I have a great admiration for him in this area. He knows exactly how to prepare his audience psychologically, which is vitally important in the success of the faith-healing act.

It is critical to note that probably 90 to 95 percent of the audience has already seen Hinn on TV or attended one of his services, so they know what to expect and how they are to act. Everyone I talked to at the Benny Hinn Crusade had been to one or more of his previous crusades. Several had been to *every* crusade. Three of the people I talked to had just returned from his crusade in Israel.

The setting and atmosphere in the crusades could be likened to the entire auditorium being the stage and each of those in attendance being an actor. Everyone, with very few exceptions, wants to have a part in the act. It is a religious psychodrama where people come to live out their expectations.

I could also compare a Hinn crusade to an orchestra and its conductor. If you want to be a part of the orchestra, you play along with the conductor. If you don't want to play the same music the conductor does, then you can't be a part of the orchestra.

Benny Hinn is the conductor, and everyone wants to be a part of his orchestra. He starts out his performance with beautiful, inspirational music that is unsurpassed. Then he gets the *entire* audience involved in singing, raising their hands, clapping, and so on.

Over the next two to three hours, every phase of the performance is orchestrated to give Benny absolute social and crowd control—to the point that the audience will go along with almost anything he would say or do. This is a key element in bringing about the "success" of the faith healer's results.

The Test for Divine Healing

How can we tell if the results of a miracle-healing crusade are divine healings or just the psychological results one would expect from the faith-healing act? The best way to find out is to examine the types of diseases that are healed.

Diseases can be categorized into one of two types: *functional* or *organic*. So that we can better understand the difference between the two, I have asked Dr. Eric Chico, a medical doctor and colleague, to provide us with a simplified definition.

> A *functional* disease is one associated with a change in function of a bodily organ or tissue without any tissue damage. An *organic* disease is one associated with a demonstrable change in a bodily organ or tissue.
>
> Therefore, in dealing with functional diseases such as high blood pressure, addictions, low back pain syndrome, or most headaches there is no demonstrable tissue damage, yet the organ or tissue is certainly not functioning as it should. By contrast, organic diseases such as broken bones, paralysis from severed nerves, congenital malformations, or coronary artery disease evidence a very clear change in the tissue. Medical science can demonstrate these changes through the use of X-ray evaluation, nerve condition studies. . . .
>
> Symptoms are indeed present in both. The difference is whether there is demonstrable tissue damage or not. It is the difference between a painful arm being caused by sprain/strain or caused by a broken bone.
>
> One additional point we need to understand is that in all diseases, both functional and organic, there exists an emotional component. It is this emotional component

that elicits a true physiologic response such as seen in the placebo effect. This response, along with the fact that many symptoms are very much subjective, is responsible for patients experiencing decreased pain with a broken bone, decreased insulin requirements in diabetes, decreased frequency of chest pain or pressure episodes in coronary artery disease, etc.

Also, in the highly festive and emotionally charged atmosphere of a faith-healing service, the brain can be stimulated to release endorphins into the nervous system which science says are pain suppressants "200 times more potent than morphine." This is why people can honestly say "the pain is gone" and sincerely believe they are healed—until the effect wears off hours or days later.

It is important to understand that the symptoms of an organic disease, such as pain, can be helped and relieved through some of the psychological principles that make faith-healing work. However, the mere removal of the pain is far different from the actual healing of the disease causing the pain.

Here is a good way to illustrate the difference between a functional and organic disease in nonmedical terms: If a computer showed that two plus two equals five, chances are good that the computer has a functional problem—that is, it was incorrectly programmed. However, if a rat crawled into the computer, chewed some of the wires, and caused the computer to malfunction, the cause would be an organic disorder.

The reason it is essential to understand the difference between a functional disease and an organic one is that this is the key to discerning whether or not divine healing is taking place today. Perhaps the single most important observation ever made about faith-healing is that it has never healed an *organic* problem, such as a broken arm. Faith-healing is only effective in bringing about a certain amount of healing with *functional* diseases.

The illusion and deception of the faith-healing act, then, is the implication that *all* kinds of diseases are being miraculously healed. The limited results that faith healers have with functional diseases are what fool people and give apparent credibility to the illusion that divine miracles are taking place. This is the lie that needs to be exposed.

Which Healings Are Valid?

Many contemporary faith healers claim to have thousands of documented cases of healings. However, since doctors also claim to have thousands of documented cases of healings, the real issue is not how many cases there are but *what is the true source of those documented healings?*

Through my investigations over the past 30 years I have discovered that various cults, false religions, witch doctors, psychic surgeons, and New Age healers *also* have an abundance of what they call documented cases of miraculous healings. All of these so-called documented cases of healing appear to be just as valid and convincing as any case the Christian faith healers have been able to produce.

But do any or all of these documented cases meet the biblical criteria of a truly miraculous healing? Absolutely not. To truly qualify as a miraculous intervention by God, the healing should match the model Jesus gave us for all cases of divine healing in the Bible.

Whenever Jesus healed someone, it was always 1) instantaneous, 2) 100 percent successful, 3) without any recovery period, 4) permanent, and 5) done apart from any major medical attention that could possibly have taken credit for the healing in any way.

It is also significant that almost every case of healing reported in the Bible which was described in any detail was an *organic* healing. In each of the three cases where there was a short time delay, the total healing was still completed within a matter of minutes—not the days, weeks, or years which faith healers use to justify the absence of an instantaneous healing and still call it a miraculous, divine healing.

It is absolutely essential to adhere strictly to the *biblical model* for divine healing in order to clearly distinguish between a miraculous healing (one which truly qualifies as a genuine miracle) and all other documented cases of so-called miracle healings in the world today.

I have been told by a medical doctor that there are 53 illnesses that are psychosomatic in nature. All 53 illnesses are functional diseases and would potentially be responsive to psychological, faith-healing techniques. When such a healing takes place, it could appear to meet most, if not all, of the biblical criteria associated with a divine healing. Therefore we cannot tell if the healing was a result of faith-healing practices or divine intervention. However, if an organic disorder, such as a broken leg, is instantly and completely healed without any medical attention, it would be difficult for anyone to question whether it was a miraculous divine healing. A broken leg simply cannot be corrected by a psychosomatic, placebo-type of healing.

To qualify for a genuine case of divine healing, then, all that is necessary is this:

1. Adequate medical documentation to prove that the organic disease was present immediately before the miracle took place.

2. Adequate medical documentation to prove that the organic disease was no longer present immediately after the miracle took place.

To have a qualified and impartial evaluation of any cases brought to my attention, various members of the Christian Medical Society have volunteered to assist me or at least help find the appropriate medical experts to review the submitted cases in light of the biblical standards mentioned above.

In Search of Evidence

Oral Roberts

In 1986, when Oral Roberts was the best-known faith healer in America, Dr. Jon Askew, a doctor friend of mine who knew one of the directors of Roberts' City of Faith Hospital, arranged for us to meet together. I flew to Tulsa to meet with Oral Roberts at the City of Faith, which is on the campus of Oral Roberts University. We spent several hours together, during which I shared with him my concerns about the illusion of faith-healing. I asked if any of his doctors could provide medically documented evidence of an organic disease that was miraculously healed through Roberts' personal ministry. He called the doctors together for a meeting and told them of my request. They stated that no one had any documentation affirming the miraculous healing of an organic disease. The doctor friend and I continued to keep in contact through the years, but no one at the City of Faith was able to provide any case they felt qualified as the divine healing of an organic disease.

Kathryn Kuhlman

Along with Oral Roberts, Kathryn Kuhlman was the best-known faith healer in the United States before Benny Hinn. During the height of Kuhlman's popularity as a faith healer, a medical doctor by the name of William A. Nolen followed up on people who were supposedly healed through her healing ministry. He had a genuine desire to see if real healing miracles were taking place or if they were simply the type of healings you would expect from the typical placebo and psychological results of faith-healing.

Dr. Nolen summarized his findings in a statement I would like to quote:

> Kathryn's lack of medical sophistication is a critical point. I don't believe she is a liar or a charlatan or that

she is, consciously, dishonest. I think that she believes the Holy Spirit works through her to perform miraculous cures. I think she sincerely believes that the thousands of sick people who come to her services and claim cures are, through her ministrations, being cured of organic disease. I also think—and my investigations confirm this—that she is wrong.

This problem is—and I'm sorry this has to be so blunt—one of ignorance. Kathryn Kuhlman doesn't know the difference between psychogenic and organic diseases. Though she uses hypnotic techniques, she doesn't *know* anything about hypnotism and the power of suggestion. She doesn't know anything about the autonomic nervous system. Or, if she does know something about these things, she has certainly learned to hide her knowledge.

There is one other possibility: It may be that Kathryn Kuhlman doesn't *want* to learn that her work is not as miraculous as it seems. For this reason she has trained herself to deny, emotionally and intellectually, anything that might threaten the validity of her ministry.[3]

Benny Hinn

Recently in the course of my research on faith-healing, Benny Hinn graciously agreed to meet with me. A time was scheduled, and what was just to be a luncheon meeting ended up lasting for many hours.

During our afternoon together, I came to Benny in love and with a sincere desire as a fellow Christian to confront him with some things that I thought were not right. I want to make it very clear that it is not my intention to attack Benny's character or motives in anything I say. After spending time with him and watching a number of his interviews on television, it is my opinion that Benny is a sincere man who wants to serve and honor God in all that he does.

After several hours of discussion with Benny regarding the differences between faith-healing and divine healing and the fact that about one-third of all diseases are organic, I told him that if divine healing were taking place in his meetings, we should expect about one-third of all the healings to be of organic disorders and have the same characteristics as divine healings in the Bible.

Near the end of our time together, a portion of which Benny graciously allowed me to tape, Benny said, "André, I see you as a friend, and maybe together we can do something for the Lord, to bless the work of the Lord. When it comes to the healing ministry, God has called me to the healing ministry. I believe in the healing ministry. I believe the miracles are genuine. Yes, some are psychosomatic. We all know that. When people come on the platform, I don't ask them, 'Was your sickness psychosomatic?' I wouldn't ask that. It's not my place to ask that. It's my place to pray for them and believe God with them for the miracle. Maybe you'll never see eye to eye with me on miracles and on healings. But I think we're both after the genuine and the real, and not the phony. And I will gladly work with you on that. Let the miracles speak for themselves. Let those healings speak for themselves. I would more than gladly give you those names or any names you want for you to go check them out thoroughly."[4]

Although Benny directly admitted in this statement that he is aware that various healings he sees through his ministry are psychosomatic, for the next several months he appeared on various nationally broadcast television programs and requested the help of millions of people to provide him with documentation of cases of divine healing to include in a book he was planning to write to prove to the skeptics that divine healings were taking place, not just psychosomatic ones.

All of us who were interested in this subject eagerly awaited the publication of this landmark book. A year-and-a-half later a book of only 166 pages and just ten cases was published.[5] There was absolutely no documentation provided for any case included in the book.

It was also obvious from the text of most of the cases that the healings did not match the biblical model Jesus provided for a genuine, divine healing. I personally investigated two of the cases and found that they involved extensive medical treatment and surgery prior to the healing—treatment which also included a lengthy recovery period. All of this significant medical information was omitted from the book. My findings coincided with the findings of those who took the time to investigate other cases included in the book.

Benny Hinn quotes the well-known faith healer of the past, Smith Wigglesworth, who said, "The day will come when a man without legs will be carried down the aisle and we will see legs grow right before our eyes. People without eyes will have eyeballs instantly pop into their sockets." All I can say is that when this type of organic healing finally does take place, then there will be no question about the reality of genuine, divine healing at the hands of the faith healers.

As I stated earlier, most of us have the desire to see and experience the supernatural. When Benny Hinn or anyone else creates the illusion that this is happening in their services, they create a trap for themselves because this is what people come to see. So the illusion must be continued to keep the people coming.

Dr. C.M. Ward, a spokesman for the largest charismatic denomination, affirmed that this trap is a more widespread problem than we might think. He said, "The biggest problem we have with our Assemblies of God ministers is to get them to resist the temptation to manipulate their audiences to make it appear that miracles are taking place. Everyone comes expecting this and the ministers feel they have to produce this effect or their people will think God is not blessing their services anymore."

The Wait Continues

Benny faithfully promised time after time to work with me to prove to me and the world that divine, organic healing miracles are taking place every day and by the hundreds in his Miracle Crusades. He faithfully promised to start sending me documented examples immediately.

At one point I said, "Benny, I don't mean to be unkind, but I think I should mention that for 35 years every Christian faith healer I have contacted has made the same promises you have, and I never heard from them again." Benny replied, "You will hear from me. I'll supply you with those names right away. I will get them to you. I'll have my secretary immediately send them to you. We'll start feeding them to you by next week, by Monday."[6]

After a month had gone by, I contacted Benny to remind him of his promises to me and requested documentation for several of the cases he had presented on his television shows, but there was no response then or any time since.

Of course, there is no question that God can totally and instantly heal any person of any disease at any time, anywhere. I have never once questioned this fact. However, this does not seem to be God's standard operating procedure for our day, in spite of much wishful thinking. Genuine cases of divine healing are few and far between (as you will discover later in this book), and they do not take place according to the faith healers' desires and formulas.

I would like to close this chapter with one final excerpt from my conversations with Benny Hinn.

> BENNY: André, I look at you as a very sincere person that really wants to find out the real thing, and I would very much like to join my hands with you and do it together. Now when it comes to healings, do they really happen? Are they for real? This is where you and I need to sit down and really talk, and I need to show you those cases. This is the one area I want to join hands with you on.
>
> ANDRE: I really would appreciate seeing some documented cases.
>
> BENNY: I would love to supply them.

ANDRE: And if we can't find any?
[long pause]

BENNY: Well—we'll discuss that then.[7]

After patiently waiting for more than two years for Benny to fulfill his promise to provide the documentation for at least one case of divine healing, I am inclined to think that the "then" has now arrived.

4

Understanding Reported Healings

The *National Courier* carried the story of a girl who apparently had been born physically normal. Later her parents noticed that she moved her legs in a strange way, so they decided to seek a medical diagnosis.

An orthopedic surgeon took X-rays and discovered that the ball of her left hip joint was out of its socket. The parents later took her to a church where they requested an anointing service for the child.

After the service, the parents returned to the specialist for confirmation of the healing. X-rays were taken for a second time and showed that the ball was back in its socket. The doctor announced that surgery wasn't needed. His concluding remark to the parents was, "I guess your religion works."[1]

Dr. Jerome Frank, distinguished professor of psychiatry at Johns Hopkins University, estimates that there are more patients treated by healers who are not licensed medical doctors than by those who are.[2] Those people reason, "Since my religion works, why should I go to an expensive professional?"

A Call for Discernment

Because "religion works," reported healings extend way beyond the boundaries of Christianity. Restored health is not limited to the domain of the church. Christians don't monopolize the field of apparent healings. What works for non-Christians can also work for Christians, even though it clearly does not come from God. This means we must responsibly sort out authentic healings directly from the hand of God from those real or thought-to-be-real healings that have other explanations.

Carefully consider the following acknowledgment:

> "Miracles" are common in tribal religions where the shaman, master of ecstasy, performs spectacular feats amid hysteria and rapture. In folk Islam, folk Buddhism, and folk Hinduism, various specialists practice the miraculous; some are magicians, others are medicine men and witchdoctors, and still others deal in the manipulation of the spirits that haunt the air. All of them routinely report wonderful successes at healing through their magical ministrations. In high Islam we even find saints and sadhus who perform magic works of resurrection, along with fakirs and dervishes whose talent is limited to ecstatic healings. But here, too, reports of healings are commonplace. . . .
>
> Two things are noteworthy about the claims of healing in folk religions and cults. The first is that their reports are numerous and plausible. The second is that they are done in a spiritual context utterly different from and hostile to the Christian gospel.[3]

After 20 years of ministry, I am well aware that almost everyone has either personally experienced restored health or knows of someone who has regained his or her physical well-being in such a way that it can't be explained by prevailing medical norms. It is not my purpose here to say that these people have fabricated a healing or that Satan instigated their recovery. Let's accept the fact of unusual recovery; but at the same time, we must also ask some reasonable questions of the experience in order to discern the true from the fake, the Christian from the non-Christian, and the miraculous from the providential.

Explanations for Reported Healings

In an attempt to understand reported healings, we should always ask, "Could this be explained by ... ?" In the following discussion I have listed 12 possible answers to this important and practical question. Let's begin with the most obvious.

God Healed

That God could have directly intervened and healed is a very legitimate possibility. Biblically, nothing prevents God from reaching down directly to restore a person's health. To say anything less would be to limit God in ways that He does not limit Himself. This does not require, however, that the healing be miraculously instant.

Our charismatic, Pentecostal brethren might be surprised to learn that noncharismatics *do* believe that God can and does heal. Two of America's most respected noncharismatic pastors express this directly. First, John MacArthur writes:

> Does God heal? I believe He does. I do not automatically discount all claims of supernatural healings just because some are false. But I am convinced that dramatic, miraculous, immediate intervention by God is quite rare—and never dependent on some supposedly gifted person who acts as an agent of healing.[4]

Now listen to Chuck Swindoll:

> Back in the late 1950's I became close friends with a man who had been a fellow Marine. Our friendship

deepened as time passed, even though miles separated us. I was ministering in the state of Massachusetts, and he lived in Texas. Then one day I received a call from him.

"I need your prayers as I've never needed them before," he said in a rather grim voice. My immediate response was: "What is it?"

He said, "I have been diagnosed as having cancer of the tongue. . . . The doctor says I have this malignant tumor. It is clearly evident in the X-rays. I just want you to pray that God, if it is His perfect will, will do a miracle." I assured him we would certainly pray with and for him.

As soon as I hung up the phone, I walked down the stairs to a little place in our basement where I would often go for quietness and prayer. Cynthia prayed with me for a while, then left to care for our children, who were still small. I stayed for almost an hour, and as I prayed, God's "unidentified inner prompting" gave me an unusual sense of reassurance. I did not hear any voice. I did not see any vision. But I had an unusual feeling of confidence and a sense of peace about my friend's situation. I read several Scriptures, prayed for perhaps 45 minutes, then left it with God.

Two or three days later my phone rang again. I heard the voice of my friend on the other end of the line. By then he was in Minnesota, calling me from the Mayo Clinic.

"I have great news," he said.

I smiled to myself. "Well, what is it?"

"I have seen several specialists, and my wife and I have just met with our attending physician. He is baffled, Chuck. He tells us there is no cancer."

"Hey, this is great!" I replied. "Tell me what they said."

"Well," he responded, "actually they put me through all the tests again and took more X-rays. They don't believe I brought the correct X-rays with me, because the X-rays they took disagree so much with the ones I brought. I now have before me two sets of X-rays. One shows the cancer in the tongue as it was in Dallas. The other X-rays, taken here in Minnesota, are clear—no cancer." And with a touch of humor he continued, "So we had a remarkable flight from Dallas to Minnesota. Somehow, in some miraculous manner, the malignant tumor is nowhere to be found."

It was not only miraculous, it was also instantaneous, and it remained permanent. He never again had a problem with the pain or the growth in his tongue. My friend was a middle-aged man and had many wonderful years in front of him, which he lived to the fullest. His subsequent death—many years later—was brought on by an unrelated disease.

I can't explain what happened. He couldn't either. I have no powers within me that produce healing in anyone else. The God I know is the same God you know, and I simply trusted Him and prayed for His will to be done. The Spirit of God healed my friend sovereignly and silently. And best of all, God got all the glory.[5]

Medical Treatment Worked

Most people who go to faith healers and claim to be healed have also been to doctors. They have had medicine, and some have even had operations. In spite of that, they often fail to include the doctor when giving credit for their healing.

Jesus recognized the importance of doctors. He said that it is not those who are healthy who need a physician but those who are ill (Mark 2:17). He related the story of the good Samaritan, who used oil and wine as the basic medicines of the day (Luke 10:30-37). He chose a medical doctor (Luke the beloved physician) to be one of Paul's companions and to write two books in the New Testament.

Healers sometimes malign the medical profession. They cite Mark 5:26, where we read about a certain woman who could not be helped by doctors but was healed when she touched Jesus' cloak. Mark was not being derogatory about the medical practitioners of his day. He was simply acknowledging that the woman had been to doctors but could not be cured. He draws no conclusions, and nowhere else in Scripture does our Lord defame or denounce the medical profession. Never do the Scriptures teach that consulting doctors and using medicine demonstrates a lack of faith in God.

One area of medical treatment we do not want to leave out is the field of natural medicine, which includes everything from herbal remedies to botanical drugs.[6] Before the advent of the modern medical age, natural medicine provided "healing" means for millennia. Even today, throughout much of the Third World, folk medicine remains the state of the art. Not surprisingly, much of it works.

Healing Capacity of the Body

This is probably the one most-often overlooked explanations for reported healings. Our bodies are incredible pieces of machinery. God created them with such marvelous design that they have the capacity to heal themselves of many physical problems. We might call this natural/divine healing.

To make the point, consider the conclusions reached in this interesting article:

> As a protest to soaring rates for malpractice insurance, doctors in Los Angeles went on strike in 1976. The result with no doctors around? An 18 percent drop in the death rate. That same year, according to Dr. Robert S. Mendelsohn, doctors in Bogota, Colombia, refused to provide any services except for emergency care. The result was a 35 percent drop in the death rate. When Israeli doctors drastically reduced their daily patient contact in 1973, the Jerusalem Burial Society reported that the death rate was cut in half. The only similar drop had been 20 years earlier at the time of the last doctors' strike.[7]

We have all suffered a superficial cut. The broken skin developed a scab and healed. We have recovered from colds, the flu, and numerous other physical problems without medical aid. God's involvement through His creative order of our bodies should not be ignored in our explanation of restored health.

This feature article was headlined in a recent national periodical:

> The best medicine for a surprising number of ills, including some forms of heart disease and cancer, may be: Watch and wait. While no one suggests that sick people should stay away from doctors' offices, evidence is growing that for a number of conditions, high-cost specialty care often makes no difference in the long run and may even hurt more than help. Hard data are slowly convincing doctors and insurance companies of the merits of nonmedical healing, such as diet and exercise. The most intriguing studies suggest that some worrisome medical problems often go away on their own when doctors simply monitor the conditions—a deliberate, seemingly hands-off approach that advocates dub "watchful waiting."[8]

Spontaneous Remission

The medical field recognizes as unusual, but nevertheless real, spontaneous cures and regression of diseases for no apparent medically diagnosed reason. This seems to be particularly true of cancer.[9]

Dr. Verna Wright reports:

> There are striking spontaneous remissions even amongst cancer sufferers on rare but well-documented occasions. I am at the moment writing a book with another doctor on rheumatic diseases. I was very distressed some while ago to learn that my colleague was

unable to write at the moment because of an attack of multiple sclerosis. There were speech difficulties, difficulty in writing and general illness. In fact, some years before in South Africa, there had been an initial episode which had cleared up completely, but this time it was of considerable severity. I was absolutely delighted a few months later to learn that all these symptoms had once again cleared completely and my colleague was able to deliver the expected part of the book only a little behind schedule. We must appreciate that there is a natural variability in disease.[10]

Emotionally Induced Illness

Doctors agree that stress can have a severely debilitating effect on the body. Kenneth Pelletier wrote these significant words:

> Medical and psychological problems caused by stress have become the number one health problem in the last decade. One standard medical text estimates that 50 to 80 percent of all diseases have their origin in stress. Stress-induced disorders have long since replaced infectious disease as the most common maladies of people in the post-industrial nations.
>
> During recent years, four disorders—heart disease, cancer, arthritis, and respiratory diseases such as bronchitis—have become so prominent in the clinics of the United States, Western Europe, and Japan that they are known as "the afflictions of civilization." Their prevalence stems from poor diet, pollution, and most important, the increased stress of modern society.[11]

Emotionally induced illnesses frequently can go into reverse. Removing the stress helps to remove the physical symptoms caused by that stress. For instance, Psalm 32 reveals that the cause of David's physical distress was guilt over his sin with

Bathsheba. When David confessed his sin and regained peace of mind, he was restored to physical health. However, not all emotionally induced illnesses are reversible. For example, you may get rid of your stress but retain the resulting ulcer.

Psychogenic Illness

Doctors have confirmed that a psychogenic illness can falsely register an apparent physical infirmity in the mind. We normally call that a psychosomatic illness. Therefore, a change of mind can often cause a change in physical well-being.

William Nolen, a world-renowned surgeon, tells of an amazing case of pseudocyesis (false pregnancy) that he encountered as a young Army doctor. He treated a 35-year-old woman who had been married 12 years and had all of the signs of pregnancy.

He followed the pregnancy for seven months and all appeared normal. But in the eighth month, an associate discovered that the woman actually had a false pregnancy. After that, it took only a short while for the patient's body to return to normal.[12]

Dr. Verna Wright comments:

> This is well illustrated by an incident that happened at Liverpool, where I trained. There was an asthmatic sufferer who was allergic to roses and always went into an asthmatic attack if she visited a rose garden. She came into the consulting room of my chief, who happened to have a rose on his desk, and she promptly had an asthmatic attack. It was in fact a plastic rose. It is clear that the psychological aspect of disease should not be underestimated.[13]

Misdiagnosis

An illness sometimes can be diagnosed wrongly. As a result, the prescribed treatment for the mistaken illness is ineffective. The patient may then go to a healer, who supposedly heals a diagnosed disease. Thus the healer is credited with healing an ailment which in reality the person never had.

During April 1991, investigations at the University of California in San Francisco reported a survey of the most serious errors of 114 internal medicine residents at three major United States medical centers.[14] Thirty-eight out of the 114 physicians named "diagnostic error." Misdiagnosis is far more common than we might imagine.

Under such circumstances, the conclusion reached by the patient is very misleading: The doctor is heralded as a brilliant diagnostician but a poor practitioner, and the faith healer is billed as being superior to the medical profession.

Misleading Report

Often an alleged healing is embraced by people because of a convincing but misleading report. That is, the sincerely given testimony just does not match the facts as they actually occurred. George Peters, a former professor of missions at Dallas Theological Seminary, provides a vivid illustration. Having heard many stories of healings that took place during an Indonesian revival (written about by Mel Tari in *A Mighty Wind*), Peters decided to go to Indonesia to interview the people and find out firsthand what had happened.

He talked to people who were "raised from the dead" and questioned those who had been healed. His findings were published in the book *Indonesian Revival*. One portion of what he wrote deals with people who were raised from the dead. He writes:

> The reports from Timor that God raised some people from the dead have startled many American Christians. I do not doubt that God is able to raise the dead, but I seriously question that He did so in Timor. In fact, I am convinced that it did not happen. Let me explain.
>
> I visited a man who is known in the community as having been raised from the dead. I met a woman who

reported that her infant daughter of four months had been raised. I talked to the woman who was said to be responsible for having brought back to life two people, and to the man who claimed to have been instrumental in raising two people from the dead, a boy of twelve and a man forty to forty-five years old.

In my questioning, I kept the sentiments of the people in mind. Absolutist beliefs will not respond to questions of doubt. I was also aware of the fact that their word for death may mean unconsciousness, coma, or actual death. I also knew of their belief in the journey of the soul after death from the body to the land of the ancestors.

I had to explore the experiences of these people while they were in the state of death, how far they had "traveled," so to speak, between death and resuscitation. It became apparent that death takes place in three stages, according to their beliefs. In the first stage, the soul is still in the body; in the second stage, the soul may be in the home or immediate community; and in the third stage, the soul takes its flight to the beyond and the land of the ancestors. Not one of the dead persons believed his soul had completely departed to the region beyond. That is the region of no return.

Those who claimed to have experienced resuscitation and immediate restoration were people who had died suddenly. Several children who had died after suffering prolonged illnesses had more gradual restorations.

I noted several interesting facts regarding the experiences reported during the state of death. One man told me that his soul had been so near his body during his state of death that he was able to hear people come near to his body. However, he was not able to speak or move. He was able to relate experiences during his state of death. After some questioning, his wife added, "My husband was not absolutely and totally dead." This led to some further probing and lengthy discussions. The mother whose infant daughter was raised was quite sure that her soul had not left her body, for she had been dead only about half an hour. An older man was able to describe his condition after dying. While dead he had promised God that if he could ever live again he would confess his sins and pay back the money that he had stolen from an evangelist. He was sure that this theft had caused his sudden death, and so was the evangelist who brought him back to life. Thus the stories went. Two younger boys, one four and another eight, were not able to recount their experiences while dead. However, they were sure that they had not yet left the earth.

I shall leave any judgments about these miracles to the reader. I went away satisfied that according to *their usage* of the word *death* and their concept of death, they had experienced resuscitation. According to my concept of death, no such miracles happened; I learned again the value of seeing words and concepts from the people's point of view and interpreting them according to their mentality and understanding.[15]

Those people were either unconscious or in a comatose state. They had not yet reached the point where their life processes were irreversibly stopped—from which point no human being can return unless God supernaturally intervenes.

Reports (however sincere the reporter) may not accurately portray what took place. What *seemed* to happen through secondhand reports was not what *truly* happened. *Firsthand* reports can also be out of sync with reality. Dr. Wright chronicles this not-uncommon occurrence.

Patients often fail to understand the nature or the degree of seriousness of their condition. Let me give you an example from an Anglican church which placed a good deal of emphasis upon the healing ministry. A lady from this church who suffered from abdominal pain told the church prayer group that she was going into [the] hospital the following week for extensive surgery. Naturally they prayed for her. She came out of [the] hospital some fourteen days later and reported to the group that the operation had revealed that the disease had entirely disappeared, and they praised the Lord for this great deliverance.

It so happened that there was a surgeon in the congregation, a man clearly sympathetic to the healing movement, or he would not have been there. With the patient's permission he obtained sight of the medical notes and discussed them with the surgeon who performed the operation. He found that the surgeon had been extremely reluctant to operate and had only been persuaded to do so because of great pressure from the patient and her general practitioner. He opened the abdomen and rather as he anticipated he found nothing but a rather mobile colon. He therefore sewed the lady up again and her abdominal pain disappeared, but she soon began to suffer from migraine with increasing severity. Note the difference of perspective: to the healing group this was a miracle. Did they not have the testimony of the patient? She suffered from abdominal pain and extensive surgery was going to be necessary to rectify it; they prayed for her, the surgeon operated, and nothing could be found. But from the surgeon's perspective a very different story emerged, and we may feel that it was significant that this lady's symptoms soon changed from abdominal pain to migraine.[16]

Placebo Effect

The "placebo effect" describes the patient improvement that occurs after receiving medicine or undergoing medical treatment which has little or no documented or demonstrable medical value. In the July 1993 issue of *Clinical Psychology Review*, Dr. Alan Roberts, director of medical psychology at

Scripps Clinic and Research Foundation, reported the findings from a study of 6,931 patients who received treatments that later were medically discredited. Unbelievably, almost one-third of the former patients reported good results from their treatment and 40 percent reported excellent improvement.[17]

Dr. Payne comments:

> What is remarkable is that it works! The effect is so consistent and strong that medical research is sometimes considered invalid unless a placebo is administered to one group of patients along with another group who receives the actual medication. Not uncommonly, the placebo group does as well, and sometimes better, than those who receive the medication. Further, the placebo can actually cause physiologic ("real") changes! For example, blood pressure can be lowered, intestinal ulcers healed, and migraines relieved.[18]

Faith healers often prove to be no more and no less than "spiritual placebos." This one factor alone would easily account for many of the reported healings at so-called healing meetings, although only a small fraction of those who attend ever claim to be healed. Most leave with their hopes dashed because the "placebo effect" did not work for them. The unhealed pay the price in disappointment and doubt, while the faith healer continues to herald his "miraculous" triumphs.

Mass Hypnosis/Hysteria

When a John Wimber team conducted meetings in Leeds, England, five Christian doctors—including one of England's leading psychiatrists—were in attendance. They became so incensed at what they all agreed was the attempted induction of hypnosis that they filed the following report.

> There was an hour's repetitive chorus singing which began the proceedings. A fair amount of reeling and

writhing commenced at the start of the singing. No space was found for a Scripture reading as such. The congregation was at no time called to prayers of confession of sin and repentance. "Hold out your hands. Feel heat coming through you. Your eyelids may feel heavy. You may feel like falling; some persons may scream. It is all right. You can see the Holy Spirit resting on people, the power of God resting on many." . . .

[V]olunteers were then put into trance while hands were laid on them. They were not unconscious and would, we were assured, hear what was said to them. They remained thus for many minutes with assorted shakings, tremblings, smilings, fallings, swayings and utterings. . . .

Throughout the building other individuals proceeded to fall into trance. The audience was told that the Holy Spirit might lead some persons to scream or to breathe very deeply. As one expected from hypnotic states these things happened more or less at once. Uncontrollable laughter, crying, groaning, shrieking and sobbing, together with the murmurings of many who wished to minister some spiritual comfort to the affected brethren, made it more difficult to follow any more the official progress of events.[19]

The team of doctors then wrote:

Hypnotic trance with suggestion is a powerful psychological tool. It has many uses. Psychosomatic disorders and physical symptoms related to neurosis are very likely in the short term to respond to this treatment. Relief of pain as in dental extraction or childbirth is relatively commonplace with hypnosis. In the Wimber team's meeting we saw no change that suggested any healing of organic, physical disease. Given the concern of many attenders to be of use to their neighbours some very helpful suggestions were undoubtedly made during the numerous trance states.

The hypnotic state, though conscious, is not what Scripture means by self-control, the mind of Christ in us or mind renewal. To describe these trances, their visible or audible features, or any healings experienced as the perfectly legitimate result of hypnosis—to describe this as the plain work of the Holy Spirit is a deception.[20]

Deliberate Deceit

I am reluctant to discuss this reason because it may sound cynical, but I will document it. The Christian community needs to admit that there have been cases of deliberate fraud.

The example I am about to share first appeared in the *National Courier*. Later, *Moody Monthly* published a follow-up report about the *National Courier*'s subsequent retraction when it became apparent that the facts had been falsified.

> Last fall the *National Courier*, a biweekly tabloid published by Logos International, launched a testimonial series on miracles. One of the first stories was about faith healer Alice Pattico, who claimed she had been healed in a 1974 Kathryn Kuhlman meeting from breast and brain cancer and addiction to painkilling drugs.
>
> She said her breasts, which had been removed in surgery, were restored, and that God had filled thirteen holes that had been drilled in her head in 1973 to administer laser beam surgery. She and her husband provided the *Courier* with doctors' letters to document her claims.[21]

More recently faith healers W.V. Grant and Peter Popoff have been thoroughly exposed by James Randi as frauds.[22] Popoff received electronic transmissions from his wife Elizabeth as the supposed "word of knowledge"—not from God, as he claimed. Grant rented wheelchairs, put healthy people in them, and then later allegedly healed them.

Please be warned and beware. The people who hurt most are those whose last hope is the faith healer or the one who is told Jesus wants them well now. In their desperation they go to the meetings but are not healed. Then they are left with no hope at all.

Satanic Involvement

Is Satan ever involved in healing? Second Corinthians 11 indicates that Satan disguises himself and his "apostles" as angels of light. They appear and act as though they are from God. They come as close as they can to the real article while actually being false.

> Such men are false apostles, deceitful workers, disguising themselves as apostles of Christ. And no wonder, for even Satan disguises himself as an angel of light. Therefore it is not surprising if his servants also disguise themselves as servants of righteousness; whose end shall be according to their deeds (2 Corinthians 11:13-15).

Satan can actually hurt people in his attempts to imitate God. Job is the most familiar biblical illustration. Remember also the lady who was afflicted for 18 years, probably by Satan through demons: "This woman, a daughter of Abraham as she is, whom Satan has bound for eighteen long years, should she not have been released from this bond on the Sabbath day?" (Luke 13:16).

On at least four occasions the Scriptures credit Antichrist and the false prophet with the satanic power to perform signs (2 Thessalonians 2:9; Revelation 13:3-12; 16:14; 19:20). It is impossible to know for sure how real or perceived these powers might be.

However, not even good angels are given creative power. Since Satan and his demons are evil angels, we can reasonably conclude that with regard to miraculous healing, which would require creative power, neither Satan nor demons can actually heal. Nonetheless, they are masters at deceitful perceptions, attempting to convince people that they can do things that in reality they cannot.

A Reasonable Approach

The next time you hear of a reported healing, don't jump to instant conclusions. Make sure you have all the facts. Think through all the possibilities and their various combinations.

Dr. William Nolen, a world-famous surgeon, set out to investigate faith-healing. His findings are recorded in *Healing: A Doctor in Search of a Miracle*. Consider Nolen's thoughts, which demonstrate that similar conclusions about healing can be reached even though the subject of faith-healing is approached from two different perspectives—medical and theological.

> Two years ago I began looking for a healing miracle. When I started my search I hoped to find some evidence that someone, somewhere, had supernatural powers that he or she could employ to cure those patients that we doctors, with all our knowledge and training, still label "incurable." As I have said before, I have been unable to find any such miracle worker.
>
> What I've learned . . . is that we don't need to seek out miracle workers if we're ill. To do so is, in a way, an insult to God.
>
> Our minds and bodies are miracle enough.[23]

Nolen arrived at the same conclusion as did the psalmist about 3000 years ago: We are fearfully and wonderfully made.[24]

> For Thou didst form my inward parts;
> Thou didst weave me in my mother's womb.
> I will give thanks to Thee, for I am fearfully and
>   wonderfully made;
> Wonderful are Thy works,
> And my soul knows it very well.

My frame was not hidden from Thee,
When I was made in secret,
And skillfully wrought in the depths of the earth.
Thine eyes have seen my unformed substance;
And in Thy book they were all written,
The days that were ordained for me,
When as yet there was not one of them
(Psalm 139:13-16).

Part 3
God's Healing
Ministry

5

Before the Cross

A prophet's wife died to illustrate a point made in her husband's preaching (Ezekiel 24:18).

Dipping seven times in the Jordan River healed a visiting general of incurable leprosy (2 Kings 5:14).

An invading army 185,000 strong was put to death as they slept one night (Isaiah 37:36).

By placing his hand inside his shirt, a prophet found his leprosy cured (Exodus 4:6-7).

Insanity suddenly struck a renowned world ruler. Seven years later his full health returned, and he resumed his international prominence (Daniel 4:33-34).

Although her womb was closed, it suddenly opened at age 90 (Genesis 21:1-2).

What do all of those unique events share in common? Every one illustrates God's direct involvement in the physical affairs of people in the Old Testament (Isaiah 64:8).

Ezekiel's wife died to illustrate the spiritual death of Israel. God healed the pagan Naaman. Sennacherib's Assyrian army expired at God's will. Moses learned that God's ways are

not man's ways. God removed and later reinstated King Nebuchadnezzar of Babylon. Sarah conceived and bore Isaac to
100-year-old Abraham. These events stand so unique that no
one could have guessed or predicted them (*see* Isaiah 55:8-9).

Fortunately, the Old Testament also records God's under-
lying explanation for these unusual events.

> The LORD said to him, "Who has made man's
> mouth? Or who makes him dumb or deaf, or see-
> ing or blind? Is it not I, the LORD?" (Exodus
> 4:11).

> See now that I, I am He, and there is no god
> besides Me; it is I who put to death and give life. I
> have wounded, and it is I who heal; and there is
> no one who can deliver from My hand (Deuteron-
> omy 32:39).

> Behold, how happy is the man whom God re-
> proves, so do not despise the discipline of the
> Almighty. For He inflicts pain, and gives relief;
> He wounds, and His hands also heal (Job 5:17-18).

> The One forming light and creating dark-
> ness, causing well-being and creating calamity; I
> am the LORD who does all these (Isaiah 45:7).

> Who is there who speaks and it comes to
> pass, unless the Lord has commanded it? Is it not
> from the mouth of the Most High that both good
> and ill go forth? (Lamentations 3:37-38).

What testimonies! By His own declaration, God assumes
ultimate responsibility for health or sickness, for life or death.

I think you will be more than a little amazed at what we see
in the following summary of Old Testament healing experiences. From the time of Abraham (about 2200 B.C.) until the
time of Isaiah (about 750 B.C.), only 20 specific healing incidents appear in the Old Testament record: five in the time of

Sin-Related Sickness

Some physical affliction came because of personal sin, although the person afflicted was not always the sinner.

Surprisingly, when affliction was most appropriate, God occasionally withheld it. After Aaron led the nation into idolatrous worship, for example, the Lord smote the people, but not Aaron (Exodus 32:35).

On other occasions the one who sinned received God's physical chastisement. Miriam received leprosy for questioning Moses' leadership (Numbers 12:1-15), and Korah died in his rebellion against Moses (Numbers 16:1-50).

Even a person who did not sin sometimes became the subject of God's affliction. The most prominent example involves the child born out of David and Bathsheba's immoral relationship (2 Samuel 12:1-23).

Unexplainable Sickness

The Old Testament contains many cases of unaccountable illness. They seemingly have nothing to do with sin or even a known disease.

Consider Mephibosheth, for example. His nurse dropped him as a baby, and he remained lame for life (2 Samuel 4:4). Another occasion involved the death of the Shunammite's son (2 Kings 4:18-37). That incident had a pleasant ending because Elisha then raised the son from the dead. And Daniel turned ill more than once after receiving prophetic visions (Daniel 7:28; 8:27).

Satan Involved

Only the well-known Old Testament episode of Satan afflicting Job indicates that Satan could be an agent for sickness (Job chapters 1 and 2).

Saints Were Sick

Believers were not immune to physical infirmities. Isaac (Genesis 27:1) and Jacob (Genesis 48:1) became sick and later died.

Job was severely smitten with boils (Job 2:7). Read Job 2:13; 3:24; 7:5,15; 13:28; 16:8; 19:17; 30:17,30 and 33:21 to see how seriously ill Job became. But in the end God healed him (42:10).

Healed by God

Healing Methods Varied

God not only afflicted but He also healed. And no one can accuse the Lord of having one favorite healing technique. The means of healing varied widely and numbered almost as many as the actual healings themselves. Healing methods ranged from God's direct intervention, to human prayer, to some of the most bizarre methods imaginable.

For instance, Moses prayed that Miriam would be healed of leprosy (Numbers 12:13). After spending seven days outside the camp, Miriam was healed and she returned to join the assembly again (Numbers 12:14-15).

Nebuchadnezzar was healed seven years after God afflicted him—just as God had promised (Daniel 4:28-37).

The Syrian general Naaman emerged after seven dips in the Jordan River to discover that his leprosy had departed (2 Kings 5:1-14). And a healing occurred among the Israelites in the Judean wilderness (Numbers 21:4-9).

Certainly no Old Testament norm emerged as a healing method that God consistently favored. As a matter of record, rarely did any two instances follow the same pattern and even more rarely did healing occur in the context of the nation gathered for a tabernacle or temple service.

God Healed Unbelievers

It was not necessary for a person to have a saving relationship with God to be healed. Most notable are the healings of a Syrian general (2 Kings 5:1-14) and a Babylonian king (Daniel 4:28-37). God sovereignly healed whomever He wanted.

God Restored Life

In the entire Old Testament, only three people received restoration to life from the dead. The widow's son at Zarephath was healed through the hand of Elijah (1 Kings 17:17-24). Elisha raised the Shunammite's son (2 Kings 4:18-37). The third instance remains unforgettable:

> And Elisha died, and they buried him. Now the bands of the Moabites would invade the land in the spring of the year. And as they were burying a man, behold, they saw a marauding band; and they cast the man into the grave of Elisha. And when the man touched the bones of Elisha he revived and stood up on his feet (2 Kings 13:20-21).

Needless to say, that qualifies as a one-of-a-kind resuscitation!

Summing It Up

This is the revealed record before the time of Christ's cross:

- Saints suffered.
- God afflicted.
- Healing methods varied widely.
- Unbelievers recovered.
- Sinners went physically unpunished.
- The innocent were struck down.
- Satan proved insignificant.
- Resurrections were rare.
- Faith requirements are never directly mentioned.

So what can we conclude from these facts? Basically this: God's special interventions during the 2,000-plus years starting with Job and Abraham (about 2200 B.C.) and ending with

Christ fall shockingly short of most people's expectations. The Old Testament gives infinitesimal attention to healing in comparison to everything else addressed from Genesis to Malachi. God afflicted more than He healed. His healings were few and far between. And when God did choose to heal, His methods defied predictability.

What then can we learn for today? If we set aside the highly unusual, one-of-a-kind circumstances out of the 20 incidents of Old Testament healing, we are left with eight healings. A careful look at these do reflect some interesting observations which we will return to at the conclusion of this book.

Consider this summary of the eight and how healing was effected in each:

1. Genesis 20:17—Abraham prayed for Abimelech's household.

2. Genesis 21:1—The Lord took note of Sarah.

3. Genesis 29:31—God opened Leah's womb.

4. Genesis 30:22—God remembered Rachel.

5. 1 Samuel 1:12-16—Hannah prayed for herself.

6. 1 Kings 13:6—The man of God prayed for Jeroboam.

7. 2 Kings 20:3—Hezekiah prayed for himself.

8. 2 Chronicles 30:18—Hezekiah prayed for Israel.

On three of the above occasions, God healed without any human prompting. Twice God answered the prayer of the afflicted. Three times God healed in response to someone else's prayer. Certainly, the commitment of one's self to resting in the sovereign will of God and to interceding personally on behalf of the afflicted defines the Old Testament pattern by which we can compare today's healings.

Of course we cannot reach final conclusions about God's present healing involvements until we look at the complete biblical record. So in the next two chapters we will see how God worked in people's lives throughout the pages of the New Testament. Then we can compare the full biblical record with recent claims and personal needs to see how we should respond and what we should expect.

6

Jesus and the Multitudes

❖

A well-known collection of records begins with these words:

> Here they are! The largest, the longest, the deepest, the highest, the fastest, the fattest, the oldest, the newest, the most startling ... the most spectacular ... the most incredible ... packed with fantastic facts and fully documented fascinating figures ... here it is.[1]

What book is it? The *Guinness Book of World Records*. Believe it or not, an introduction to Christ's healing ministry reads with even greater superlatives:

> There are also many other things which Jesus did, which if they were written in detail, I suppose that even the world itself would not contain the books which were written (John 21:25).

Webster's *New International Dictionary* defines *unique* as "being without a like or equal; single in kind or excellence."

No other word so accurately portrays Christ's healing miracles. At no other time in human history have so many people been healed from such a multitude of diseases in so short a time as during Christ's three-year public ministry. History has not repeated itself. Christ's truly unique healing ministry remains unequaled.

It is no wonder that the Jews marveled at Jesus' healing ministry for, "nothing like this was ever seen in Israel" (Matthew 9:33; *see also* Mark 2:12; Luke 10:24; John 9:32). Look at the following accounts for yourself; I think you will agree.

The Healing Ministry of God Through Jesus[2]

		Matthew	Mark	Luke	John
1.	Multitudes	4:23-24	1:39	—	—
2.	Leper	8:2-3	1:40-42	5:12-13	—
3.	Slave	8:5-13	—	7:2-10	—
4.	Woman	8:14-15	1:30-31	4:38-39	—
5.	Multitudes	8:16-17	1:32-34	4:40-41	—
6.	Demoniac	8:28-34	5:1-20	8:26-39	—
7.	Paralyzed man	9:1-8	2:1-12	5:17-26	—
8.	Little girl	9:18-19, 23-26	5:21-23, 35-43	8:40-42, 49-56	—
9.	Woman	9:20-22	5:24-34	8:43-48	—
10.	Blind man	9:27-31	—	—	—
11.	Demoniac	9:32-34	—	—	—
12.	Multitudes	9:35	—	—	—
13.	Multitudes	11:2-5	—	7:18-22	—
14.	Man	12:9-14	3:1-6	6:6-11	—
15.	Multitudes	12:15-21	3:7-12	—	—
16.	Demoniac	12:22-23	—	—	—
17.	A few people	13:54-58	6:1-6	—	—
18.	Multitudes	14:13-14	—	9:10-11	6:1-3
19.	Multitudes	14:34-36	6:53-56	—	—
20.	Gentile girl	15:21-28	7:24-30	—	—
21.	Multitudes	15:29-31	—	—	—
22.	Demoniac boy	17:14-21	9:14-29	9:37-43	—
23.	Multitudes	19:2	—	—	—

	Matthew	Mark	Luke	John
24. Blind men	20:29-34	10:46-52	18:35-43	—
25. Blind/lame	21:14	—	—	—
26. Demoniac	—	1:21-28	4:31-37	—
27. Deaf man	—	7:32-37	—	—
28. Blind man	—	8:22-26	—	—
29. Multitudes	—	—	5:15	—
30. Multitudes	—	—	6:17-19	—
31. Widow's son	—	—	7:11-17	—
32. Women	—	—	8:2	—
33. Demoniac	—	—	11:14	—
34. Woman	—	—	13:10-13	—
35. Man	—	—	14:1-4	—
36. Ten lepers	—	—	17:11-21	—
37. Man's ear	—	—	22:50-51	—
38. Man's son	—	—	—	4:46-54
39. Lame man	—	—	—	5:1-9
40. Blind man	—	—	—	9:1-7
41. Lazarus	—	—	—	11:1-45
42. Many more	—	—	—	20:30-31; 21:25

The Healing Ministry of God Through Men

	Matthew	Mark	Luke	John
1. Disciples	10:1-15	3:15; 6:7-13	9:1-6	—
2. Unknown men	—	9:38-40	9:49-50	—
3. Seventy	—	—	10:1-20	—

The following overview gives a detailed picture of what Christ's healing ministry would have looked like to us had we lived during His time. This will offer tremendous insight to our discussion later on when we ask, "Does the pattern of alleged healings today look anything like those done by our Lord?" You can decide for yourself from this inductive study of the Gospels.

Reasons for Healing

Various reasons existed for Christ's healing ministry, all of which contributed to the authentication of the person of Jesus as the true Messiah. Christ never performed healing miracles merely for their physical benefit, as we can see from these New Testament passages. Healing miracles were—

• Matthew 8:17	A preview fulfillment of the messianic prophecy in Isaiah 53:4.
• Matthew 9:6	To let people know that Christ had the authority to forgive sins (*see also* Mark 2:10; Luke 5:24).
• Matthew 11:2-19	To authenticate the messianic ministry for John the Baptist, who was in prison (cf. Isaiah 35; *see also* Luke 7:18-23).
• Matthew 12:15-21	A preview fulfillment of the messianic prophecy in Isaiah 42:1-4.
• John 9:3	To let people see the works of God on display in Christ.
• John 11:4	For the glory of God through Christ.
• John 20:30-31	To call people to believe that Jesus is the Christ.
• Acts 2:22	God's authentication of Christ.

Characteristics of Christ's Healings

Healing Had Purpose

Although Jesus did many miracles, He did not perform them indiscriminately. He did not always heal everyone who needed healing (John 5:3-5), nor did He perform signs on request (Matthew 12:38-40), nor did He use His powers to avoid the cross (Matthew 26:52-53). Our Lord's miracles always accomplished the purposes documented above.

Healing Was Immediate

With three exceptions, all of Christ's healings were instantaneous (Matthew 8:22-26; Luke 17:11-19; John 9:1-7). No recuperative period was needed; the afflicted were immediately returned to complete health. There were no relapses or misunderstandings about being healed: "In order that you may know that the Son of Man has authority on earth to forgive sins—then He said to the paralytic—'Rise, take up your bed, and go home'" (Matthew 9:6-7).

Also, the three delays in healing involved *minutes* only, and the men involved were *totally* healed. For example, in Mark chapter 8 a blind man was brought to Jesus:

> After spitting on his eyes, and laying His hands upon him, [Jesus] asked him, "Do you see anything?" And he looked up and said, "I see men, for I am seeing them like trees, walking about." Then again He laid His hands upon his eyes; and he looked intently and was restored, and began to see everything clearly. And He sent him to his home saying, "Do not even enter the village" (verses 22-26).

Healings Were Abundant

Jesus' miracles were unlimited in number and scope. "The multitude marveled as they saw the dumb speaking, the crippled restored, and the lame walking, and the blind seeing; and they glorified the God of Israel" (Matthew 15:31). His miracles were never confined to special times or locations. Jesus healed in the course of His travels all over Israel. Out of the suffering masses, His attendants never selected only those few who would actually see Him; rather, He frequently healed all who came to Him.

Healing in Absentia

Healing did not require Jesus' physical presence. He merely

thought or spoke the word, and healing was accomplished. A centurion's slave (Matthew 8:5-13), a Canaanite's daughter (Matthew 15:21-28), and the son of an official in Capernaum (John 4:49-53) received their healings apart from Jesus' presence.

Healing Methods Varied

As is true of God's healings in the Old Testament, Jesus used a variety of healing methods in the New Testament. The power of God healed; nothing magical or cure-producing is connected to the method itself.

1. Christ touched (Matthew 8:15).

2. Christ spoke (John 5:8-9).

3. The afflicted touched Christ's cloak (Matthew 9:20-22).

4. Christ used spittle (Mark 8:22-26).

5. Christ plugged a man's ears with His fingers and placed spittle on his tongue (Mark 7:33-35).

6. Christ anointed with clay (John 9:6).

Jesus Approved of Doctors

Jesus recognized the normal means of physical healing—a doctor and medicine. Not once did He demean the medical profession. One day He announced, "It is not those who are healthy who need a physician, but those who are sick" (Matthew 9:12). He approvingly told of the Samaritan who used oil, wine, and bandages to help the abandoned Jew (Luke 10:30-37).

Healing for God's Glory

Although sickness can result directly from personal sin, as evidenced in the Old Testament, nowhere in the Gospel accounts is sickness attributed directly to personal sin. However, Scripture states twice that sickness occurred so that God could be glorified. For example, Martha and Mary approached Jesus one day and asked Him to heal their brother Lazarus. He responded, "This sickness is not unto death, but for the glory of God, that the Son of God may be glorified by it" (John 11:4).

Christ's Healing Ministry Was Unique

Scripture states emphatically that in previous history there had never been a healing ministry like Christ's: "As they were going out, behold, a dumb man, demon-possessed, was brought to Him. And after the demon was cast out, the dumb man spoke; and the multitudes marveled, saying, 'Nothing like this was ever seen in Israel' " (Matthew 9:32-33).

Jesus Shunned Acclaim

Jesus went out of His way to avoid public approval or reward for His healing miracles. In Luke 10:20 He told the disciples explicitly not to rejoice in the power they had been given but to rejoice in the fact that their names were recorded in heaven.

Christ never sought fame and fortune through healing. For a while He drew large crowds who heard His kingdom message, but later they crucified Him in spite of all the miracles.

Healings Were Undeniable

The spectator reaction to Christ's healings proved phenomenal. Everyone, including His enemies, stood amazed, astounded, and unable to deny or discredit the miracles.

In fact, one of the most incredible statements affirming Christ's ministry came from the unbelieving Pharisees and priests:

Therefore the chief priests and the Pharisees convened a council, and were saying, "What are we doing? For this man is performing many signs. If we let Him go on like this, all men will believe in Him, and the Romans will come and take away both our place and our nation" (John 11:47-48).

Reactions Were Widespread

Christ's healings brought widespread reaction. Mark 1:45 describes how the news of Christ's healing ministry spread to such an extent that He could no longer enter a city without being mobbed. Even though He remained in unpopulated areas, people came to Him from *everywhere*.

Christ's Healing Did Not Necessarily Save

Christ's miracles could not be denied (John 3:2), but they did not necessarily lead to faith. Consider the residents of Chorazin, Bethsaida, and Capernaum, for example:

> I say to you, it will be more tolerable in that day for Sodom than for that city. Woe to you, Chorazin! Woe to you, Bethsaida! For if the miracles had been performed in Tyre and Sidon which occurred in you, they would have repented long ago, sitting in sackcloth and ashes. But it will be more tolerable for Tyre and Sidon in the judgment than for you. And you, Capernaum, will not be exalted to heaven, will you? You will be brought down to Hades! (Luke 10:12-15).

Faith Was Not Necessary

An expression of a personal faith was *not* a necessary requirement for healing. Lazarus (John 11), Jairus' daughter (Matthew 9), and the widow's son (Luke 7) were all dead and incapable of displaying faith. Yet they arose from the dead.

Furthermore, wherever Jesus healed the multitudes it can be assumed that most, if not all, eventually rejected Christ and His gospel. In Luke 17, when Jesus healed ten lepers, only "one of them, when he saw that he had been healed, turned back, glorifying God with a loud voice, and he fell on his face at His feet, giving thanks to Him" (verses 15-16). Note Jesus' response:

> "Were there not ten cleansed? But the nine— where are they? Was no one found who turned back to give glory to God, except this foreigner?" And He said to him, "Rise, and go your way; your faith has made you well" (verses 17-19).

Another's Faith Honored

At times Christ healed when someone other than the one afflicted displayed his faith. Note especially Matthew 17:19-20; the disciples had been unable to cast out a demon and came to Jesus privately for further instruction. He informed them that they lacked faith. The parallel passage in Mark 9:28-29 adds that prayer would have been successful. Thus anyone who claims that a person can remain unhealed because of his or her own lack of faith needs to be corrected and warned. In this case the deficient faith belonged to the would-be healers.

Healings Were Not Prearranged

Jesus healed from the beginning of His ministry (Matthew 4:23-25) to the end (John 11:1-44). Often He initiated the interaction and approached the person, as He did the lame man at the pool of Bethesda (John 5:1-9). Furthermore, Jesus always healed during the normal course of His daily ministry. Two blind men who happened to be in the same vicinity as Jesus during His travels were healed when they asked Him for mercy (Matthew 9:27-29).

Healing for Satan-Caused Sickness

Not all sickness is directly caused by Satan or demons, but those who are possessed by demons are liable to have physical infirmities. Luke 13:10-17 provides a classic example, where a woman bound by Satan (possibly through a demon) was doubled over for 18 years.

Heavenly Healing Power

Because Christ had voluntarily abandoned the *independent* exercise of His divine attributes, His healing power came from God the Father; it was not self-generated:

- He cast out demons by the Spirit of God (Matthew 12:28).

- The power of the Lord was present for Him to perform healing (Luke 5:17).

- He cast out demons by the finger of God (Luke 11:20).

- "The Son can do nothing of Himself" (John 5:19).

- "Signs which God performed through Him" (Acts 2:22).

- Christ healed because God was with Him (Acts 10:38).

Healing by the Disciples

People other than Christ performed healings in the Gospel accounts. For example, Jesus Himself sent the disciples on their preaching and healing excursions (Matthew 10:1-15). Seventy others went out with a similar commission from the Lord to preach and heal (Luke 10:1-16).

A Final Word

The evidence is stunning. Christ's healings were—

- undeniable
- spectacular
- overwhelming
- abundant
- awesome
- instant
- authoritative
- without limitations
- total
- convincing

No one before or since has even fractionally approached the power of Jesus Christ to heal. He remains forever unique. No one could possibly claim to have a healing ministry like Christ's. However, God's healing power did not stop with His Son but continued on through the apostles. The Acts and New Testament epistles tell that story next.

7

The Apostolic Legacy

———◆———

The Lord Jesus Christ left His disciples with this expectation in the Upper Room: "Truly, truly, I say to you, he who believes in Me, the works that I do shall he do also" (John 14:12). He commissioned the twelve to preach the gospel accompanied by powerful works of God (Mark 16:14-18).

Jesus' word stood authoritative. Because He had promised, He would surely fulfill what He said. Just before Christ left the Mount of Olives, He told the disciples that they would shortly receive power (Acts 1:8).

The apostles had already seen God's healing power work through them before Christ died (Matthew 10:1-15; Luke 10:1-16). After Christ ascended to the right hand of God the Father, the apostles became His chief gospel-preaching representatives on earth and the ones through whom God worked miraculously (Acts 2:43).

And Jesus kept the promise He had made in John 14:12. Just as He Himself had been authenticated by miracles (Acts 2:22), so too were the apostles (Hebrews 2:1-4). The book of Acts and the New Testament letters prove this fact.

The Acts of the Apostles

Over the approximately 30-year span of Acts, only 16 incidents of healing are recorded. They follow the outward movement of the gospel from Jerusalem to Rome.

The Healing Ministry of God Directly

1. Acts 9:17-18—Paul healed by God (cf. Acts 22:12-13)

2. Acts 14:19-20—Paul healed by God

3. Acts 28:1-6—Paul protected by God

The Healing Ministry of God Through Men

1. Acts 2:43—Apostles performed signs and wonders

2. Acts 3:1-10—Peter healed a lame beggar

3. Acts 5:12-16—Apostles healed

4. Acts 6:8—Stephen healed

5. Acts 8:7—Philip healed (cf. 8:13)

6. Acts 9:32-35—Peter healed Aeneas

7. Acts 9:36-43—Peter resuscitated Dorcas

8. Acts 14:3—Paul and Barnabas performed signs and wonders (cf. 15:12)

9. Acts 14:8-18—Paul healed a lame man

10. Acts 19:11-12—Paul healed people at Ephesus

11. Acts 20:7-12—Paul resuscitated Eutychus

12. Acts 28:7-8—Paul healed Publius' father

13. Acts 28:9—Paul healed many at Malta

When God healed through men, the healings moved outward from Jerusalem to the ends of the earth in fulfillment of

Christ's commission to the disciples (Acts 1:8). Healings number 1 through 7 accompanied gospel preaching in Jerusalem, Judea, and Samaria (Acts 1–12). Only six healings (numbers 8 through 13) appear in all of Paul's journeys (Acts 13–28). Since there appears to be little repetition of the same scenario, Acts 4:29-30 would come the closest to establishing any pattern of healing ministry. There the apostles preached the Word while God did the healing.

As we did with Jesus in the Gospels, let us look at the major features of God's healings in the book of Acts. You can see for yourself what the Scriptures record and then compare that with what various people teach about healing (including this author). That way you will be a good "Berean" by searching the Scriptures to see if these things are so (Acts 17:11).

Healing Techniques Varied

As they did in the Old Testament and the Gospels, the healing techniques in the book of Acts were varied. Nonformula variety establishes the standard. Healing took place—

1. By command (Acts 3:6).
2. By being in the healer's shadow (Acts 5:15).
3. By touching a cloth from the healer's body (Acts 19:11-12).
4. By prayer and the laying on of hands (Acts 28:8-9).

Healing Was Immediate

In the book of Acts the afflicted people were immediately restored to full health. That is, the healings were instantaneous, with no recuperative period required. No one claimed their healing by faith, for they obviously had not received it yet if they were not healed on the spot.

> At Lystra there was sitting a certain man, without strength in his feet, lame from his

mother's womb, who had never walked. This man was listening to Paul as he spoke, who, when he had fixed his gaze upon him, and had seen that he had faith to be made well, said with a loud voice, "Stand upright on your feet." And he leaped up and began to walk (Acts 14:8-10).

Unbelievers Were Healed

As in Christ's ministry, saving faith in Jesus Christ was not a necessary requirement for healing.

The multitudes with one accord were giving attention to what was said by Philip, as they heard and saw the signs which he was performing. For in the case of many who had unclean spirits, they were coming out of them shouting with a loud voice; and many who had been paralyzed and lame were healed (Acts 8:6-7).

At the same time that unbelievers were being healed, saints such as Dorcas were ill (Acts 9:36-43).

Faith of the Afflicted Honored

At times the faith of the afflicted was praised. Peter delivered this commendation: "On the basis of faith in His name, it is the name of Jesus which has strengthened this man whom you see and know; and the faith which comes through Him has given him this perfect health in the presence of you all" (Acts 3:16).

Yet at other times a personal faith was not necessarily required of the afflicted: "Peter said to him, 'Aeneas, Jesus Christ heals you; arise, and make your bed.' And immediately he arose" (Acts 9:34).

Healings Were Undeniable

The healings done by the apostles were undeniable—even by the Jewish rulers and authorities that made up the Sanhedrin. Even the most vocal opponents of the gospel could not explain away the healings since they were so publicly spectacular.

> What shall we do with these men? For the fact that a noteworthy miracle has taken place through them is apparent to all who live in Jerusalem, and we cannot deny it. But in order that it may not spread any further among the people, let us warn them to speak no more to any man in this name (Acts 4:16-17).

Sin-Related Sickness

Sometimes God afflicted people because of personal sin. He afflicted Ananias and Sapphira after they lied to the Holy Spirit (Acts 5:5,10).

Paul (Acts 9:8), Herod Agrippa (Acts 12:23), and Elymas (Acts 13:4-12) all had the same kind of experience.

Life Restored

Two people were raised from the dead—Dorcas (Acts 9:36-43) and Eutychus (Acts 20:9-12). Add to these two the three Old Testament resuscitations plus the three in Christ's ministry, and only eight specifically named people were raised from the dead in all of Scripture. The only other mention of resuscitations is the onetime occurrence recorded by Matthew (27:51-53), when the veil in the temple was torn in two at Christ's death and many saints arose from the grave.

Healing in Absentia

God worked so powerfully through Paul that cloths touched by him could bring healing without his presence (Acts 19:11-12).

Nonapostolic Healing

Rarely did someone other than the twelve heal. The only possible exceptions involve Stephen (Acts 6:8), Philip (Acts 8:7), and Barnabas (Acts 14:3).

Sickness in the Epistles

While the Gospels indicate that the disciples would see God do great miracles through them, just the opposite proves true in the epistles. There is no biblical expectation that the postapostolic generations of Christians would experience or perform the healing miracles of either Christ or His apostles.

Purpose of Healing

God used signs, miracles, and wonders to authenticate the apostles and their ministry (Romans 15:18-19; 2 Corinthians 12:12; Hebrews 2:4). Whether the apostles themselves (or, on rare occasion, those they ministered with) did the signs, those signs were to attest the authority of the apostles as revealers of truth (*see* Acts 2:42-43).

If nonapostolic Christians through the centuries were supposed to perform such deeds, then they could not have served as the signs of apostleship (*see* 2 Corinthians 12:12). The signs by the apostles attested that their words had equal authority with those of Jesus Himself, for He had chosen them as His spokesmen (*see* Matthew 10:11-15,20,40; 1 Corinthians 14:37). True signs could be counterfeited, but they would not fool God (Matthew 7:21-23). The church received continual warnings to be alert, to be on guard, and to be discerning (Acts 20:17-32; 2 Corinthians 11:13-15).

The Decline of Healing

In the epistles, Paul's frequency of healing declined with the passing of time.

1. Galatians 4:13-14—Paul was ill.

2. 2 Corinthians 12:7-10—Paul was possibly afflicted.

3. Philippians 2:25-30—Epaphroditus was ill.

4. 1 Timothy 5:23—Timothy was ill.

5. 2 Timothy 4:20—Trophimus was ill.

Medicine Approved

Paul recognized and recommended medicine. He suggested wine to settle Timothy's stomach (1 Timothy 5:23).

Sin-Related Sickness

James 5:14-20 outlines the biblical response for severe or untimely physical infirmities that could have their source in God's chastisement for personal sin. This passage is so important that we will discuss it fully in a later chapter. In the meantime, please observe that this passage says nothing about healing which in any way resembles healing through the apostles.

The Disappearance of Healing

Healings became significantly less noticeable with the passing of time in the apostolic era. Paul mentions nothing about future healing ministry in his last three epistles—1 and 2 Timothy and Titus. In his other letters, Paul also mentions nothing about current healing except to the Corinthians (1 Corinthians 12:9,28,30). Neither 1 or 2 Peter say anything about healing, although Peter does alert his readers to the possibility of suffering (1 Peter 4:19). Nor does John mention healing in his three epistles. Interestingly, not one of the nonapostolic epistles—Hebrews, James, and Jude—instruct the saints about future miraculous healing ministries.

Specific instructions from Christ for the church say absolutely nothing about physical healing either (Revelation chapters 2 and 3). In fact just the opposite happens: Jesus prepares the church at Smyrna for suffering and death (2:10), warns the church at Thyatira of God's impending judgment involving sickness and death because of immorality and idolatry

(2:22-23), and rebukes the Laodiceans for boasting in their physical health to the exclusion of spiritual well-being (3:17-18).

A Biblical Summary of Healing

The biblical evidence can be summarized this way: Healing is *noticeable* in the Old Testament (over a span of 2000 years), *overwhelming* in the Gospels (about three years), *occasional* in Acts (about 30 years), and *negligible* in the epistles (about 40 years). As the apostolic age ended, miraculous healing by direct human intervention ceased. And the healings reported by early church historians do not compare to the biblical record as to the miraculous quality of instant, total, and undeniable healing.

Why So Much Confusion?[1]

One of today's great threats to a correct interpretation of the Bible is assuming that any specific historical experience in Scripture is a valid, general expectation for today. This line of thinking, which I call "generalizing," normally rests on such passages as Malachi 3:6, "For I, the LORD, do not change," or Hebrews 13:8, "Jesus Christ is the same yesterday and today, yes and forever."

Generalizing

This danger was emphasized to me recently when I visited the UCLA campus as one of three panelists discussing the charismatic movement. Each participant had been asked to "present his viewpoint and show his biblical support."

The first person said he believed that charismatic phenomena should be considered normative today because they were normative in the apostolic church. He showed from the early chapters of Acts that charismatic experiences were not unusual.

A different approach marked the next panelist. He reasoned that if God had done something in the past, then we should not deny that He could do it today. However, he did admit that tongues and other such experiences were not for everyone today.

In both instances, the other panelists based their thinking on the idea that if God has done something in the past we can automatically expect that He will do it again.

When my time came, I discussed several biblical truths. First, God's ability to do something is not the real issue. God is able to do *all* things at *all* times in *any* way He chooses.

Second, I showed that it is wrong to reason that because God has done a certain thing in the past He will automatically do it for you or others today. Don't let anyone send you on a guilt trip by convincing you that a failure to claim healing for today is to deny God or to make God less than God. Unless we can show by the authority of Scripture that it is *God's will to do something*, then to say He will do it and demand that He perform is to sinfully presume on God.

Third, I mentioned that God has always warned about the counterfeit—false prophets (Deuteronomy 13:1-5; 18:14-22), false apostles (2 Corinthians 12:12), and even false believers (Matthew 7:13-23). Jesus warned that neither exclamations such as "Lord, Lord" nor experiences like miracles or exorcisms necessarily distinguish between the true and false (Matthew 7:21-23). *To generalize is to open the gate of error and deception.*

If we were to apply generalization to *all* biblical experiences, we would come to some rather obvious wrong conclusions. For example, because a few people were raised from the dead in the past, we would believe that God raises people today. Because God supernaturally supplied food to the Jews in the wilderness (Exodus 16:1-21) and prevented their clothes and shoes from wearing out during their four-decade journey (Deuteronomy 29:5), we would expect God to feed and clothe us that way today.

We are not expecting to be taken up to the third heaven as Paul was (2 Corinthians 12:1-10). Nor do we believe that

leprosy patients who dip seven times in a river will be cured
(2 Kings 5:1-14).

Experientializing

Another obstacle to good Bible interpretation is what I call
"experientializing." This line of reasoning says that if I have
an experience that is portrayed somewhere in Scripture, then
it must be from God. This person uses experience to validate
Scripture rather than vice versa.

First we need to go to the Bible and ask if the experience
could possibly be from God. Remember that in the Corinthian
church there were some who claimed their tongues-speaking
was from God, yet Paul said, "No one speaking by the Spirit of
God says, 'Jesus is accursed' " (1 Corinthians 12:3). In other
words, God's Spirit could not be the source of their tongues-
speaking because of what they were saying about Jesus.

If an experience *could* come from God, then it needs to be
tested by Scripture and other godly people. Jesus taught that
fruit would be the test (Matthew 7:20). Paul said that prophets
were to be tested by prophets (1 Corinthians 14:29) and that
all things were to be tested to see whether they are good or
evil (1 Thessalonians 5:21-22). John also warned about false
prophets and commanded believers to test them and see if they
were from God (1 John 4:1).

If we are careful to use Scripture to evaluate experience
rather than read experience back into the Bible, we will help
end today's confusion on the issue of healing.

8

Is There Healing in the Atonement?

W hile I browsed through some commentaries at my favorite bookstore in Columbus, Ohio, a dear lady whom I had recently visited and prayed for in the hospital entered and walked toward me. Greeting her, I remarked how well she looked.

She responded, "By His stripes I have been healed. Praise God there is healing in Christ's atonement."

Immediately I decided that the bookstore was no place for a theology discussion. I didn't want to dampen her joy, nor did I want to rob her of her confidence that somehow God had been involved in her physical restoration. However, her understanding of Isaiah 53:5 and 1 Peter 2:24 did not accurately describe what she had experienced.

I wondered where she had learned those proof texts. Perhaps she had read or listened to a faith healer's explanation of Isaiah 53. A friend or neighbor may have told her about those verses, and perhaps you have wondered about them too.

Is there healing in the atonement? If there is, what kind? How much? When do we get it? Let's find out.

The Atonement

Isaiah 53 serves as the heart of healing theology.[1] The "Magna Carta" of God's healing promises focuses on Christ's sacrificial death at Calvary. The atonement appears first in Leviticus as a part of the Mosaic sacrificial system. On one appointed day of the year, Israel's high priest entered the Holy of Holies, approached the Ark of the Covenant, and sprinkled blood to atone for the sins of Israel.

Aaron, the brother of Moses, became the first high priest. Leviticus 16:3 tells us that Aaron entered the Holy Place with a bull for an offering. Now was that a sin or a sick offering? Unquestionably, it was a sin offering. Aaron offered a bull for a sin offering—first for himself and then his household (verses 5-6; cf. verses 11,16,21,34).

Moses instituted the Day of Atonement by the authority of God around 1440 B.C. Hundreds of years later (about 700 B.C.), Isaiah wrote about a coming Servant who would be "the atonement." The atonement ritual that Moses established was later fulfilled by Jesus Christ when He died for our sins—not our sicknesses.

By studying the book of Hebrews (the "Leviticus" of the New Testament), you can appreciate the unity of Scripture. When the final atonement occurred, Christ served as both the high priest and the sacrifice (Hebrews 9:11-12). Jesus Christ as God incarnate became the Lamb slain for the sins of the world.

Hebrews 10 contains several passages that relate to the atonement's fulfillment in Jesus Christ.

> Then He said, "Behold, I have come to do Thy will." He takes away the first in order to establish the second. By this will we have been sanctified through the offering of the body of Jesus Christ once for all (Hebrews 10:9-10).

Year after year the high priest had to first make atonement for himself and his family and then for the nation. But Christ had to offer Himself as a sacrifice only once (Hebrews 10:12,14). That is what Isaiah 53 anticipated.

Both Leviticus and Hebrews demonstrate that in God's mind the atonement dealt primarily with sin, not sickness. It had everything to do with our sin problem and the redemption needed to remove sin so that we might stand eternally before a holy God. Christ's atonement paid the due penalty for sin, which involved God's wrath being poured out upon Jesus Christ. Clearly the major emphasis of Isaiah 53 centers on spiritual salvation.[2]

The Text of Isaiah 53

Isaiah 53:4-6 raises the question, What, if anything, does the prophet promise about physical restoration?

The Hebrew words translated "griefs" and "sorrows" in Isaiah 53:4 can legitimately refer to either physical or mental pain *and* spiritual problems. Those who say that the language refers *only* to physical problems should more accurately say that the words *may* refer to physical problems.

Fortunately, words are always used in a context and with an intended meaning by the author. Normally, the surrounding context indicates what the author meant by the words he used.

Note that the word "iniquity" is used four times in Isaiah 53 and identifies the passage's major emphasis. In 53:5, Christ was crushed for our iniquities. According to 53:6, the Lord "has caused the iniquity of us all to fall on Him." He will bear our iniquities (53:11), and He Himself bore the sins of many (53:12; cf. Hebrews 9:28). *The primary thrust of Isaiah 53 is on the spiritual and the eternal effects of sin,* not on its physical and immediate effects upon the body.

In Isaiah 53:4 we read that He "bore" our griefs and "carried" our sorrows. Isaiah used these same verbs in verses 11 and 12. As we compare verses 3 and 4 with verses 11 and 12, we see that the primary emphasis again relates to salvation.

Making the Meaning Clear

Now let us consider some additional Scriptures that affirm what we have just discovered about Isaiah 53.

First, our present body is corruptible; that is, it will degenerate until we will die. The physical will ultimately be separated from the spiritual (James 2:26). But the good news for all believers is that one day we will put on the incorruptible—a form that will remain constant, pure, and without sin for all eternity (Romans 8:23; 1 Corinthians 15:50-54).

Second, Christ died for our *sins*. The gospel is immediately good news about our sin problem, but not so with our physical problems. You can read about that in Matthew 1:2, John 1:29, 1 Corinthians 15:1-3, and other passages.

Next, Christ was *made* sin and not sickness. Second Corinthians 5 talks about His ministry of reconciliation (*see* verses 18-21).

Fourth, Christ *forgave* our sins, not our sicknesses. John says: "I am writing to you . . . because your sins are forgiven you for His name's sake" (1 John 2:12).

Fifth, Christ *gave* Himself for our sins and not for our sicknesses (Galatians 1:3-4).

Next, the Bible teaches that if a person is truly saved, he cannot lose his salvation (John 5:24; 10:28-29; Philippians 1:6; Jude 24). Now let's carry this thought to its logical conclusion: If physical healing shares in the atonement, as does spiritual healing (redemption), we should not lose our physical health and thus should never die.

But is that what really happens? No, Scripture says we all must die (Hebrews 9:27). We could look at such godly examples as Abraham, Isaac, Daniel, Paul, and Timothy to show that God's greatest saints endured sicknesses and also eventually died. Therefore we can biblically conclude that while there is a related aspect of physical healing in the atonement, it won't be applied until *after* death and the redemption of our bodies by resurrection (Romans 8:23).

Seventh, as true believers we are assured of our salvation but have no guarantee of our physical life or our health. James

4:13-14 tells us we have no certainty that any of us will even be here tomorrow. But there is every assurance that if we place our faith in Jesus Christ, we will be His sons and daughters forever (Ephesians 1:5).

Next, if healing is in the atonement and if it applies physically today, those who ask by faith for physical healing and are not healed have no logical right to be assured of their salvation. In contrast, God says that if we are saved, we have every right to believe in our salvation. So if physical healing were in the atonement and if we ask to be healed and are not, not only do we lose our assurance of the physical, but we should also lose our assurance of the spiritual. Fortunately, such an unbiblical conclusion can be reached only if we have first taken a wrong approach to what the atonement is really all about—the forgiveness of our sins.

Ninth, assuming that physical healing in the atonement were to be applied today, eternal life must also be applied today with the acquisition of immortal bodies.

But death remains our great nemesis and stumbling block to that proposed truth. We are all going to die (Hebrews 9:27). Death will not be abolished in human experience until the eternal state begins. Therefore whatever physical benefits are supposed to be found in the atonement would not be experienced fully until we are in the presence of God.

Consider this as well: If Christ paid the penalty for our sin and we are still sinning, what ought to be the parallel experience in the physical realm? Total health or impaired health? Just as we have impaired spiritual health, so also will we continue to have impaired physical health until the experience of sin is removed. That won't happen until death or until the Lord comes.

In reality, Christ paid the penalty for sin but He did not remove sin from the life of the believer. Christ cared for the *cause* of sickness: *sin,* which is the cause of sickness in its moral sense. But He did not remove sickness from the life experience of believers because He did not free them from besetting sin.

Finally, if it is true that Isaiah 53 addresses sin and not sickness, then the New Testament will verify that fact. The Scriptures are marvelously unified and will not contradict themselves.

As expected, Isaiah 53 has its New Testament counterpart. Philip encountered the Ethiopian eunuch reading Isaiah 53 (Acts 8:28,32-33). When the eunuch asked Philip for an explanation, "Philip preached Jesus to him" (Acts 8:35). Apparently the eunuch invited Christ to be his personal Savior and Lord, because he next asked about baptism. The point we should note is this: Both Philip and the eunuch understood Isaiah 53 to be dealing with *sin,* not sickness.

Matthew on Isaiah 53

Matthew chapters 8 and 9 record the most concentrated period of healing in the Gospel record. And in Matthew 8:14-17 we find a reference back to Isaiah 53:4—a reference that some people might use to support the claim that physical healing is a part of the atonement:

> When Jesus had come to Peter's home, He saw his mother-in-law lying sick in bed with a fever. And He touched her hand, and the fever left her; and she arose, and waited on Him. And when evening had come, they brought to Him many who were demon-possessed; and He cast out the spirits with a word, and healed all who were ill in order that what was spoken through Isaiah the prophet might be fulfilled, saying, "He Himself took our infirmities, and carried away our diseases."

While at first it may appear that Matthew 8:14-17 affirms the idea that the atonement includes physical healing, a closer look at the text reveals what our Lord was actually trying to teach.

The Greek words translated "took" and "carried" in Matthew 8:17 are different from the corresponding Greek words that are used in the Septuagint, which is the Greek translation of Isaiah 53. Good reasons account for the change.

The words in Matthew 8 mean "to take away from," not "to bear." (Remember that the words used in Isaiah 53:4 mean "to sacrificially bear"; hence the idea that "He took our sins upon Him.") Matthew is saying that Christ "took away" people's sicknesses. Christ did not "bear" in a substitutionary sense the sickness of Peter's mother-in-law. He didn't say, "Move the fever from her into Me." He just touched her and it was gone. Neither did He bear the afflictions of those who were ill nor the spirits of those who were possessed (Matthew 8:16). Later He would bear sin on Calvary, but at this point in Matthew 8 He had only taken away sicknesses.

This next thought is important: What Christ did at Calvary occurred several years after His healing ministry at Capernaum as reported in Matthew 8. There is absolutely no effectual relationship between what Christ did in Capernaum and His atonement on the cross at Calvary. Rather, Matthew employed a normal illustrative use of the Old Testament. He found a point of continuity—a point of identity between Isaiah 53 and Christ's healing ministry in Capernaum.

Here is another way to look at it: Matthew 8 is to Isaiah 53 as Matthew 17 (the transfiguration of Christ) is to Revelation 19. It is merely a preview, just as Matthew 8 is a preview of the coming eternal kingdom that will be free of sin and sickness. One scholar writes:

> Indeed, as I have argued elsewhere, Matthew 8:16-17 explicitly connects Jesus' miracles of healing and exorcism with the atonement that had not yet taken place. They serve as foretastes of and are predicated on the cross-work that is their foundation and justification.[3]

To suggest that there is now no sickness because Christ cared for physical affliction at Calvary is like suggesting that there is now no sin because Christ bore our sins at Calvary. As long as sin exists (which it does), the moral basis for sickness will continue.

Peter on Isaiah 53

Did Christ die for our sins or for our sicknesses? Some teach that 1 Peter 2:24, which says, "By His wounds you were healed," is an affirmation that Christ took care of physical sickness on the cross. But the context of the passage demands that we understand that Christ died for our sins.

A question often asked is, What does the word "wound" mean, or the phrase "by His stripes"? The word translated "scourging" in the NASB, "stripes" in the KJV, and "wounds" in the NIV is best translated from the Hebrew text in Isaiah 53:5 as "wounds from physical abuse." That is exactly how Peter understood Isaiah.

In context, Peter is not speaking primarily of the scourging that Christ received in a preparatory way at the hands of the soldiers, but rather the totality of excruciating torment He endured at Calvary (Psalm 22:14-17). The beatings and afflictions that He suffered before He was nailed to the cross were nothing in comparison to the agony He suffered at Calvary itself when He bore the sins of the world. First Peter 2:21-24 deals with our spiritual healing and Christ's payment for sin, not with our sicknesses.

Summing It Up

Isaiah 53 refers to the atonement and its redemptive value, not its therapeutic effect in a physical sense. Four lines of evidence support this conclusion:

1. The idea of atonement in Leviticus and Hebrews clearly applies to salvation.

2. The context of Isaiah 53 focuses primarily on the atonement's provision for sin.

3. The theological context of Christ's death and salvation centers on sin.

4. Matthew, Peter, and the Ethiopian eunuch understood Isaiah 53 in reference to sin.

All the scriptural evidence affirms that Isaiah 53 deals with the spiritual being of man. Its major emphasis is on sin, not sickness. It focuses on the moral cause of sickness, which is sin, and not on the immediate removal of one of sin's results—sickness.

Recall the question which we asked at the beginning: "Is there healing in the atonement?" My answer is "Yes!" but with this explanation: There is healing "through" the atonement or "as a result of" the atonement, but it is never promised to believers for the present.[4] When sin is ultimately removed, physical healing for believers will be in full—but only in the future, when our bodies have been redeemed by the power of God (Romans 8:23; Revelation 21:4).

> Therefore, that the healing is in the Atonement should not be preached on the basis of Matthew 8:16-17 unless it is endorsed by Scripture statement elsewhere. But it is not taught elsewhere, and it certainly cannot be safely adduced solely from Matthew 8:16-17. No, healing for our mortal bodies is not in the atonement. This conclusion is supported at once by the fact that forgiveness of sins and cleansing from guilt are offered through the cross freely and certainly and at the present moment to all who sincerely "believe" whereas healing for all our infirmities and sicknesses is not offered freely and certainly at present to all who believe. Not one of those who have believed for forgiveness and cleansing has ever been denied, but thousands and thousands who have believed for physical healing have been denied. That cannot be gainsaid—for a very pertinent reason. Permitted sin in the present is never a part of God's plan or purpose for us, but permitted sickness often is, as we learn both from Scripture and from Christian testimony. . . . Both Scripture and experience, then, say no; bodily healing is not in the atonement.[5]

By 1) looking at the language used, 2) understanding the context in which the above passages are found, 3) seeing the complementary passages in Leviticus and Hebrews, and 4) realizing what was involved in the atonement, we can conclude that the atonement dealt with sin and the need to satisfy the righteous wrath of a just and holy God. Not until death removes sin from our personal existence will you and I have any hope of guaranteed physical well-being.[6] When the resurrection adds the full fruit of redemption to the present firstfruits (Romans 8:23), we will know the fullness of physical healing provided through the atonement.

J.I. Packer eloquently captures the intent of Isaiah 53 with this insightful summary.

> Again it is true: salvation embraces both body and soul. And there is indeed, as some put it, healing for the body in the Atonement. But, we must observe that perfect physical health is promised, not for this life, but for heaven, as part of the resurrection glory that awaits us in the day when Christ "will change our lowly body to be like his glorious body, by the power which enables him even to subject all things to himself." Full bodily well-being is set forth as a future blessing of salvation rather than a present one. What God has promised, and when he will give it, are separate questions.[7]

9

Is James 5 for Me?

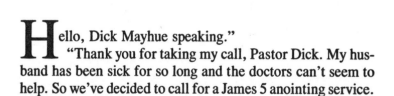

"Hello, Dick Mayhue speaking."

"Thank you for taking my call, Pastor Dick. My husband has been sick for so long and the doctors can't seem to help. So we've decided to call for a James 5 anointing service. Will you and the elders come?"

"I'm thrilled that you want to depend on God for this important issue. Have you carefully read James 5:13-20 and do you understand what it teaches?"

"Not exactly, but it's in the Bible, and it seems like our last hope. Won't you and some of the elders please come?"

Such a telephone conversation is not unusual. Real issues of life and death, quality of living, and peace of mind are at stake. Emotions run so high with this kind of call that a lengthy theology lesson at the moment would be inappropriate. This is a time for compassion, love, and caring. However, the best way to prepare for this situation is to provide right teaching about James 5 before the crisis call hits.

Our Challenge

A casual reading of James 5 can raise more questions than

it answers. Our challenge is to properly interpret this passage and then apply it in practical terms.[1] To be successful, we will have to carefully examine every bit of the text. Here are some legitimate questions that James 5 raises: Is the passage limited to the first century or is it applicable today? Does it apply to all humanity or just Christians? Does it extend to all Christians or just some? Is its purpose to prepare people to die or to restore people to quality living? Does it refer to physical, emotional, or spiritual problems? Are the problems in James 5 severe or ordinary? Is the practice to be done in a public service or a private one? Does the intent involve medicinal or symbolic anointing? Is the healing miraculous or providential? Is the promise absolute or conditional?

The Key

Generally speaking, a picture is worth a thousand words. That is why James wisely used 30 percent of the text to illustrate his point (37 out of 130 words). Elijah and Israel (5:17-18) portray a parallel to the truth which James teaches in 5:14-16 and then preaches in 5:19-20. If we understand the illustration first, then we will have the key to unlocking the practical riches of James 5:13-20. Fortunately, the illustration is exceptionally clear.

The prophet Elijah lived a righteous life. He was a man with a nature *(pathos)* like ours, and his prayers accomplished much. Because of sin in Israel, Elijah announced that rain would be withheld (1 Kings 17:1). For 3½ years the land suffered drought (James 5:17).

This is not unexpected if we understand the Old Testament context. God had promised disease on the land (including drought) if Israel forsook her covenant with Him (Deuteronomy 28:23-24; 29:22-27). Later Solomon prayed with this in mind:

> When the heavens are shut up and there is no
> rain, because they have sinned against Thee, and

> they pray toward this place and confess Thy
> name and turn from their sin when Thou dost
> afflict them, then hear Thou in heaven and for-
> give the sin of Thy servants and of Thy people
> Israel, indeed, teach them the good way in which
> they should walk. And send rain on Thy land,
> which Thou hast given Thy people for an inheri-
> tance (1 Kings 8:35-36; cf. 2 Chronicles 6:26-27).

After King Ahab's day, Israel experienced God's curse on several more occasions (Jeremiah 14:1-9; Amos 1:2; Haggai 1:9-11). God chastised the nation physically because of pro-longed patterns of unrepentant sin.

God told Solomon how the curse could be reversed: "If I shut up the heavens so that there is no rain . . . and My people who are called by My name humble themselves and pray, and seek My face and turn from their wicked ways, then I will hear from heaven, will forgive their sin, and will heal their land" (2 Chronicles 7:13-14).

James uses this exact experience of Israel as an illustration of what he is teaching on a personal level in James 5:14-15. King Ahab had sinned grievously without precedent (1 Kings 16:30,33). So God chastised the king and his kingdom with drought (1 Kings 17:1,7; 18:5). Not until after Elijah con-fronted the false prophets of Baal and Asherah did the people repent—even to the point of slaying the idolatrous priests (1 Kings 18:37,39-40). When the people turned back to God, the need for physical chastisement of the land no longer exis-ted, so Elijah prayed and it rained (1 Kings 18:42,45). God healed the land according to His promise to Solomon.

Now that we understand James' illustration, let's go back to James 5:13-20 as a whole and see what we can learn.

The Situation

James writes in 5:13, "Is anyone among you suffering? Let him pray. Is any among you cheerful? Let him sing praises."

The word for "suffering" in verse 13 should not be confused with the word for "sick" in verse 14 (although sickness could be a part of the suffering). "Suffering" is a general word that may involve either mental or emotional affliction or a combination of both. In context, it looks back to James 5:10, where the noun form refers to the prophets who suffered (cf. 2 Timothy 2:3,9). James writes, in effect, "If you have a problem in your life because of circumstantial suffering, look to God in prayer. If everything is going well and you are cheerful, look to God with praise."

Then James shifts to a new emphasis with "sickness" in 5:14. The word for "sick" involves the Greek word *astheneia* (literally, "without strength"), which has the basic meaning of being weak either emotionally, spiritually, or physically.[2] Only context can give the author's intended meaning, but what is important to note here is that the word means "to be weak." However, the term does not indicate the severity of the weakness.

Let's look ahead now at verse 15: "The prayer offered in faith will restore the one who is sick." The word "sick" is not the same Greek word as that used in verse 14—*astheneia* is used in verse 14 and *kamnō* is used in verse 15. It is the comparative use of those two words that helps us to identify the severity of the weakness.

Kamnō in its most general sense means "fatigue," or something that is worn out or weary. It described documents that have become threadbare by frequent use.

From a broad survey of Greek usage, we learn that *kamnō* frequently meant severely sick in the physical realm; that is, sick to the point that death is imminent. It was also used to describe those who were dead. Thus *kamnō* gives us the added dimension to understand that James is talking about a very serious problem, not just an ordinary occurrence. James 5 does not describe some generic ritual that Christians should engage in every time they encounter illness of any sort. That would trivialize what God intended to be sacred.

Some have suggested that James 5:14-15 does not deal with the physical at all, but rather with emotional or spiritual distress.[3] However, when you consider 1) the very normal use of *astheneia* in the Gospels and Acts, 2) the fact that *kamnō* refers to serious physical illness, and 3) the illustration of Elijah in James 5:17-18 (which unquestionably establishes the problem as physical chastisement), then the suggestion that James 5 doesn't deal with the physical is less than compelling. Undoubtedly the author's word choices in James 5:14-15 combined with the illustration in James 5:17-18 led the KJV, NASB, and NIV translation scholars to unanimously use "sick" in both 5:14 and 5:15 to translate both *astheneia* and *kamnō*. Bible commentator Doug Moo writes:

> James' language makes it impossible to eliminate the physical dimension. First, while *astheneō* can denote spiritual weakness, this meaning is usually made clear by a qualifier (cf. Romans 14:2, 'in faith'; 1 Corinthians 8:7, 'in conscience') or the context. Moreover, in the material that is most relevant to James, the Gospels, *astheneō* almost always refers to illness. The same is true for *kamnō*. And *iaomai*, when not used in an Old Testament quotation, always refers in the New Testament to physical healing. Beyond this, it is significant that the only other mention of 'anointing with oil' in the New Testament comes in a description of physical healing (Mark 6:13).[4]

The Process of Healing

It is clear from James' frequent use of "brethren," a common New Testament term for Christians, that he is writing to believers. James also writes of his readers' faith in Jesus Christ (2:1). So we know that James 5 applies to Christians today, and is not limited to the Jewish church of the first century only.[5]

The Call

James says to the one who is physically sick in a severe way, "Let him call for the elders" (5:14). "Call" *(proskaleō)* means to summons or to call to one's side. The sick one is to ask the elders to come to him; he is not (most likely prevented by physical infirmity) to go to them. Therefore, anointing services that are held in the front of the church—the kind to which the church invites the sick—are foreign to the language and meaning of James 5. In fact, James 5 does not support the idea of any public meeting for healing.

> The rite is prescribed only for members of the church; no public invitation is given indiscriminately to the sick and afflicted of the world.[6]

Who are the elders? They were the men whom God appointed to oversee the church. The qualifications for eldership are found in 1 Timothy 3:1-7 and Titus 1:6-9. Three words in the New Testament describe the office, with each describing a different aspect of it. "Overseer" refers to the basic function of leading; "elder" indicates the maturity of one's life; and "pastor" implies the role of daily activities. These are righteous men of prayer and spiritual leaders like Elijah.

The sick Christian is to call for the elders to come to him. The arriving men will first anoint with oil and then pray over the person. Unmistakably, confession of sin plays prominently in the process. James 5:15-16 strongly implies that an unconfessed pattern of sin in the life of a believer is responsible for the weakened physical condition. And in the immediate context, James focuses directly or indirectly on sin in each verse of James 5:15-20.[7]

Notice also that the sick believer calls for the elders, not someone with "gifts of healings" (1 Corinthians 12:9,28,30). A careful reading of the text on "gifts of healing" does not relate to or limit its distribution to elders. Therefore we can conclude that there is no explicit nor implicit relationship between James 5 and the "gifts of healings" in 1 Corinthians 12.[8]

When sin is the problem, sickness can follow from guilt over a sin (as with David in Psalm 32) or directly from the sin itself. In 1 Corinthians 11 Paul said that some of the Corinthians were weak and sick and some of them even slept (were dead) because they made an abomination of the bread and the cup. There is even sin unto death (1 John 5:16). James focuses on spiritual problems that lead to God-imposed physical infirmities.

The Anointing

The question has often been raised as to whether the anointing is medicinal or symbolic.[9] In the first century, oil was used in a medicinal sense; the ancients believed that oil had a healing effect on people. The Samaritan picked up the man who had been mugged and poured oil and wine on his wounds (Luke 10:34). The apostles anointed people and healed them (Mark 6:13; cf. Isaiah 1:6).

The expected word for symbolic anointing, *chriō*, is not used here. The word in our text, *aleiphō*, is normally used in extrabiblical Greek literature to speak of anointing with oil for medicinal purposes. But three times in the Greek Old Testament (the Septuagint translation—Genesis 31:13; Exodus 40:13; and Numbers 3:3) the Greek verb that was used translated the Hebrew word where symbolic or ceremonial anointing was meant. Therefore, whether the anointing in James 5 is used in a medicinal or symbolic sense must be determined by the context, not by linguistics alone.

Let us ask this question: "If the oil were understood in a medicinal sense, how would it cure cancer, tuberculosis, arteriosclerosis, or a myriad of other diseases?" Actually, we know that oil provides no medicinal aid for any of these problems. If it did, then there would be no need for the elders' prayer and the Lord's power. Further, the view that oil represents medical care does not take into account the remainder of James 5.

Both the well-known use of the term "anoint" and common sense point to a *symbolic* use of the oil. But if the oil is symbolic, what does it represent? In light of the context of physical weakness and the symbolic use of *aleiphō* in James 5:14, the most normal sense from a well-known Old Testament usage would be to picture what is promised in the passage—physical well-being (cf. Psalm 23:5; 133:2). Oil symbolized health and well-being, which is what James promised would be forthcoming (5:15). So the elders picture the outcome of physical well-being by symbolically anointing the repentant Christian with oil "in the name of the Lord" (James 5:14). It is by the Lord's authority ("in the name of the Lord") that they act.

The Prayer

After the anointing comes prayer: "Let them pray over him" (5:14). Who does the praying? The elders. A "prayer offered in faith will restore the one who is sick" (verse 15). So whose prayer and whose faith is it? It is the elders' prayer and faith. The faith of the sick person actually has little, if anything, to do with the restoration (cf. Matthew 8:10,13; Mark 2:5).[10] He has already expressed his faith by calling the elders. This truth once and for all exposes the error that says if a person has enough faith he will be healed, or that if a person is not healed at a healing service, it was because of his lack of faith.[11] These common assertions do not square with James 5. The effective prayer of righteous elders, like Elijah, accomplishes much on behalf of the sick one.

The End Result

"The prayer offered in faith will restore the one who is sick, and the Lord will raise him up, and if he has committed sins, they will be forgiven him" (5:15).[12] The link between the physical and the spiritual could not be clearer!

Note that the instrument for raising up the sick person is not *his* prayer but that of the *elders*. The power that raises him up is not the elders' power; it is the Lord's intervention. Healing through the channel of human healers is absolutely foreign to James 5. This passage superbly illustrates 1 John 5:14-15, where God promises to answer prayer that corresponds to His will (see note #13 on page 276 for further discussion).

This becomes the point of James 5:13-20: A believer has wandered off into sin and has remained in sin. God has chastised him by bringing sickness into his life to bring him back to Himself. When the believer recognizes that God has brought an untimely and severe illness to incapacitate him, he is to call for the elders of the church. The elders are then to come. He is to confess his sin, and they are to anoint him with oil and pray over him. If sin is the cause of the sickness, then God will raise him up.

The healing is never said to be instant or miraculous, but it will be complete. Because sin is cared for through confession, there will be no further need for chastisement. So God takes away the chastisement and the believer is restored to physical health.[14] This is the absolute promise of James 5:15 in context and in harmony with the point of the Elijah illustration in James 5:17-18. When the condition of physical chastisement for unrepentant sin is dealt with according to James 5, the repentant Christian will be healed because there is no longer a need for physical chastisement. We might consider this the ultimate form of a divinely imposed church discipline which ends with restoration (cf. Matthew 18:15-20).

The Bigger Picture

James 5 indicates to us that some people in the church were experiencing God's chastisement for unchecked sin, just like in Corinth (1 Corinthians 11:30). The assembly to which James wrote had problems with their perseverance, faith, anger, good deeds, favoritism, conversation, jealousy, selfish ambition, worldliness, self-centeredness, and oaths. James said they were to confess their sins one to another (cause) so that they could be healed (effect) (5:16). The Greek word *iaomai*, translated here "healed," can be used in a physical sense (Matthew 8:8; Acts 3:11) or a spiritual one (Hebrews 12:13; 1 Peter 2:24). However, the predominant use (at least 24 of 28 appearances) in the New Testament involves physical restoration. Not being foreign to the context here, and being the majority usage, physical healing explains the text best.

James also seems to suggest a broader practice in 5:16 (one another) than he does in 5:14-15, which is limited to the elders. For lesser spiritual problems or less established patterns of sin this was, most likely, how they were to keep a short account with God and prevent deterioration into a life-threatening situation that demanded the restoring process of 5:14-15.[15] James speaks more of *prevention* than correction, as indicated by the subjunctive mood (mood of probability) of the verb *iaomai* ("to heal").

Those who use James 5 to advocate a restoration of physical healing ministries to the church miss the whole point. James emphasizes dealing with sin, not securing physical healing. What the church needs today is a renewed emphasis on confessing and dealing with sin.

The Exhortation

James 5:19-20 amplifies the previous verses on healing. Verses 19 and 20 say in effect, "My brothers, if any believer among you strays from the truth and another believer turns him back so that he returns to the straight and narrow, let him know that he who turns a sinning Christian from the error of his way will save his soul from physical death and will restore him from the consequences of a multitude of sins."

Yet doesn't the saved person already have his soul redeemed? Once again a look at the Greek language helps. The text here literally reads "will save his soul." The word for "soul" is frequently used to describe the person—the whole human being. Physical restoration, not redemptive salvation, fits best here. The NIV translation accurately catches James' thrust: "will save him from death." It is not unlike Ezekiel's exhortation in Ezekiel 18:24-29. The use of *sōzō* ("to save") in both James 5:15 and 5:20 strongly suggests that James 5:19-20 summarizes what James has just written in 5:14-18.

The redeemed sinner will be saved from the physical death which can come through God's chastising discipline. James writes in the spirit of Matthew 18:15-20 and Galatians 6:1, with the goal of restoration in view.

We can draw at least three conclusions from James 5:19-20:

1. God asks believers to be responsible for restoring straying brothers and sisters in the faith.

2. To continue in unchecked sin can result in death because the believer has disqualified himself from representing God or accomplishing His work.

3. Restoration is possible even if the sins are frequent and serious; confrontation will cover a multitude of sins. We cannot sin so badly that God cannot forgive us, but for God to forgive us we need to turn from our sin back to God.

A Practical Example

The biblical conclusions we have discovered about James 5 invalidate most of what contemporary healing ministries teach. Usually James 5 is used as a proof text to find New Testament support for all sorts of healing ministries. To avoid these kinds of errors, here is a clear example of what a James 5:14-15 experience might be like.

> The person who was seriously ill was a believer who happened to be the wife of a medical doctor. She suffered from terrible, almost-unbearable pain all across her back. Physicians could not find the cause. Several

competent orthopedic specialists worked together on her case, all to no avail. . . .

Her incredible pain had led the physicians to begin intense medication that could become habit-forming, and her husband was very concerned about that, naturally, as she was. Finally they hospitalized the woman.

Because we were longtime friends, she contacted me and asked, "I wonder . . . if you could get together a group of the elders from the church and if several of you could come and pray." I responded, "Certainly we'll come." And we went, about six or seven of us.

We walked into her hospital room on a Sunday night following the evening service. She was in such pain she could hardly talk. "I don't know what I'm going to do," she said. "I'm getting desperate. . . . What can we do? What can we do?" I replied, "We can do what God instructed us to do . . . pray. We will pray that if it is His sovereign will, He will save you, restore you, raise you up!"

We closed the door, turned the lights down, and several of us dropped to our knees and began to pray. I finished my prayer by pleading with God to bring relief and, if it were His will, to bring full restoration. As another man began to pray, the woman reached down and touched me on the shoulder. She was pushing on me, as if she wanted to say something. I reached over to the man who was praying and took him by the knee and held tightly, as if to say, "Wait a minute." He stopped. Spontaneously she said, "Excuse me for interrupting, but the pain is all gone." And she began to weep. Several of us wept as well. We were so grateful to God at that moment.

"I must tell all of you something," the woman said, and she sat up in bed—something she had not been able to do for days. Actually I think she could have gotten up and walked out of the hospital, stepped into her car, and driven home that night. The pain was completely gone.

She said, "I need to tell you something about my life." Quietly, yet without hesitation, she began to unfold a story of sin that had been a part of her lifestyle. It is not necessary that I go into the details . . . only to say that she had been living a life of deception before us as well as before her family. But there had been something compelling about our prayer and the sincerity of our faith gathered around her that brought her to such a burning awareness of her sin she couldn't even let us finish. God heard her prayer of confession and desire for repentance.[16]

What Now?

If James 5 does not apply to your own physical situation, what should you do? How can you biblically face sickness whose cause is not a pattern of sin and whose source is not the chastising hand of God?

Very simply, look to the Lord in prayer. Invite your pastor, your family, and your Christian friends to pray that God's will be done and that God's glory be manifested through you. Prayer always remains in season.

Also, as you move on in this book, you will want to pay special attention to the chapter "On My Back by Divine Design." There you will discover the spiritual benefits of what most of us would consider a severe setback. You will find that suffering, from God's perspective, can become a major spiritual advancement.

10

Demons and Sickness

Many Christian leaders these days affirm the reality of demons and the possibility of demonic residency within a person. Consider one such testimony:

> One evening I was called to the church, and found one of our elders contending with a demon-possessed girl. The demons used her mouth to speak, but the voices coming out of her mouth were not her own. Amazing things were going on in that room. She had flipped over a desk and was smashing other things in the room.
>
> When I walked into the room, she suddenly sat on a chair, gave me a frenzied look, and in a voice not her own said, "Get him out! Get him out!" I was glad that the demons knew whose side I was on. At first we didn't know what to do. We tried to speak to the demons. We commanded them to tell us their names, and we ordered them in Jesus' name to go to the pit. We spent two hours trying to send those demons out of her.
>
> When we finally stopped trying to talk to the demons

and dealt directly with that young woman, we began to make some headway.

We presented the Gospel to her, explaining that she needed to confess and forsake her sins. She prayed with a repentant heart, confessed her sin, and found true deliverance in salvation. By doing so, she shod her feet with "the Gospel of peace." She left that night standing firm. The demons were gone and have never troubled her since.[1]

Key Questions

The last decade in America has spawned many new books on spiritual warfare, with the greatest emphasis on demon residency and expulsion. Surprisingly, the books have been rather evenly distributed between charismatic/Third Wave authors[2] and noncharismatics.[3]

You might be asking, "Why are demons all of a sudden getting so much attention?" Are all the new materials biblically correct, or are they just the musings of uninformed people who see a demon behind every bush and under every rock? Has demon activity accelerated in America? How can I know which concepts are biblically accurate and which aren't?

This subject deserves a full-length book,[4] but we will summarize it in this chapter. Let me begin by making some general observations in order to avoid being misunderstood or misrepresented.

1. I believe in the historical reality of Satan and demons, both in the past and in the present, as verified in the Bible.

2. I believe the Bible admonishes us to expect Satan and demons to operate now much as they did in both Old and New Testament times.

3. I believe we are currently seeing an increase of demonic activity in the United States.

4. I believe the Bible teaches that, in living out our Christian life, we will experience real spiritual battle with Satan and his army of demons.

5. I believe that Scripture alone, independent of personal experience or clinical data, will truthfully determine the reality of demonic experiences and provide understanding of our encounters with Satan and demons.

The Battlefield

In Scripture, Satan and demons prominently involve themselves with spiritual darkness (Ephesians 6:12), deception (2 Corinthians 11:13-15), and death (John 8:44). They thrive in these kinds of environments. I believe our nation has rapidly accelerated toward these conditions over the last ten years, as witnessed by increases in false religion and idolatry, sexual immorality and perversions, drug use, occultic activity, interest in Satanism, godlessness, shamelessness over sin, lawlessness, devaluation of human life, and societal attempts to suppress biblical truth.

Not only has our nation created a setting where Satan and demons thrive, but the Christian community has also unwittingly set itself up for great deception. In the church, this normally finds two extremes—overemphasis or underemphasis on the spirit world.

Much of the Christian community today pays too little attention to scriptural teachings and warnings about Satan and demons. Because demonic activity in American has been relatively quiet in the past, they reason it should remain that way in the future. For some Christians, an ignorance of Scripture combined with an attitude of materialism produces an unhealthy indifference to the invisible war with darkness. For others, an unrealistic attitude of spiritual invincibility dominates. This leaves many Christians greatly vulnerable and unprepared for spiritual warfare.

In contrast, a growing segment of evangelical Christianity has not only recognized the need to be alert, but has made spiritual warfare a top priority, even to the extreme. Much of the overemphasis we see today comes as a reaction to being raised in a tradition that underemphasized Satan and demons. The conclusions of these believers come as much from clinical and counseling reports and personal experience as from Scripture.[5] The Christian imagination has also been fueled by contemporary Christian fiction that exceeds and at times distorts what Scripture teaches on Satan and demons.[6] J.I. Packer observes, "With the fading of interest in supernatural holiness, interest has grown in supernatural healing and in the supernatural powers of evil with which Christians must battle."[7]

Certainly not all of these factors are true of every Christian who embraces spiritual warfare. I do believe, though, that this general profile fairly and accurately portrays both the secular and evangelical community in America during the 1990's.

The Biblical Record

God's special revelation in the Bible gives the only reliable information and understanding about Satan and demons. You might be surprised how little is said about demons in Scripture outside the Gospels. The following biblical summaries focus on clear, historical accounts of human involvement with demons.

I start here so that everyone begins with the biblical record. Whatever conclusions we reach must come from this Scriptural database. Listed here are the uncontested, historical accounts and reports of personal encounters with demons in Scripture.

Old Testament

1. Saul	1 Samuel 16:14-23
2. Saul	1 Samuel 18:10
3. Saul	1 Samuel 19:9
4. Prophets of Ahab	1 Kings 22:22-23[8]

Jesus in the Gospels[9]

	Matthew	Mark	Luke	John
1. Multitudes	4:24	1:39	—	—
2. Multitudes	8:16	1:29-34	4:38-41	—
3. Gadarene man	8:28-34	5:1-20	8:26-40	—
4. Dumb man	9:32-34	—	—	—
5. Blind/dumb man	12:22	—	—	—
6. Gentile girl	15:21-28	7:24-30	—	—
7. Epileptic	17:14-21	9:14-29	9:37-43	—
8. Man	—	1:23-28	4:33-37	—
9. Multitudes	—	3:11	—	—
10. Mary Magdalene	—	16:9	8:2	—
11. Multitudes	—	—	6:18	—
12. Multitudes	—	—	7:21	—
13. Man	—	—	11:14	—
14. Woman	—	—	13:10-17	—
15. Multitudes	—	—	13:32	—
16. Judas[10]	—	—	—	13:27

Others in the Gospels

	Matthew	Mark	Luke	John
1. The twelve	10:1,8	6:7,13	9:1	—
2. The twelve	—	3:15	—	—
3. Unknown disciples	—	9:38	9:49	—
4. The twelve	—	16:17	—	—
5. The seventy	—	—	10:17-20	—

Acts[11]

1. Multitudes	5:16
2. Multitudes	8:7
3. Paul and slave girl	16:16-18
4. Paul and multitudes	19:12
5. Sons of Sceva	19:13-17

Indwelling Demons?

There can be no question that demons do at times reside within human beings. Otherwise there would be no need to cast them out.[12] Scripture also affirms that when demons indwell human beings, they frequently debilitate the human host. Epilepsy (Matthew 17:14-18), blindness (Matthew 12:22), deafness (Mark 9:25), and the inability to speak (Matthew 9:32-33) have occurred as a result of demonic residency. When the demon is evicted the physical problem also departs and the person is healed.

The question that many people are asking today is, "Can true Christians be indwelt by demons who account for an illness which would be cured by exorcism?" Let's search for our answer with a careful study of Scripture rather than experience.

Are there any clear biblical examples of true believers being indwelt by demons in the Scriptures? A survey of the biblical data quickly eliminates all but two of the possibilities—Saul in the Old Testament and the woman bent double in Luke 13:10-17.[13] In every other case, demons have indwelt unbelievers only.

Saul

First, let's look at Saul. Was he a true believer? For the sake of this discussion, let's assume that he truly trusted God for salvation. As evidence, note the eight times Saul received the accolade "the LORD's anointed" (1 Samuel 24:6,10; 26:9, 11,16,23; 2 Samuel 1:14,16). Also, Samuel told Saul that in death the two of them would be together (1 Samuel 28:19).

Since Saul at least appears to be a believer, we can ask, "Was he indwelt by demons that needed to be cast out?" The following language describes Saul's encounters with the "evil spirit":

- "terrorized him"—1 Samuel 16:14-15
- "on you"—1 Samuel 16:16

- "came to Saul"—1 Samuel 16:23
- "upon Saul"—1 Samuel 18:10
- "on Saul"—1 Samuel 19:9

None of these phrases suggests that the evil spirit existed *within* Saul. In every instance the text speaks about *external* torment. So we can safely conclude that while Saul might have been a believer, he is not an example of a believer who had a demon within. Be aware, however, that Saul presents an extreme example and certainly provides no basis for developing or generalizing a Christian's experience with demons.

The Woman in Luke

Let's turn next to the woman bent double in Luke 13:10-17. No one can question the fact that she suffered physical distress for 18 years because of a spirit (verse 11) identified as Satan (verse 16). But was she a believer? Those who say yes do so because Christ refers to her as "a daughter of Abraham" (verse 16). They suggest a parallel with Zaccheus, who, upon becoming a believer, was called "a son of Abraham" by Jesus. But a close look at Luke 19:9 paints a different picture:

> Jesus said to him, "Today salvation has come to this house, because he, too, is a son of Abraham.

Salvation came *because* Zaccheus was a "son of Abraham" and *because* "the Son of Man has come to seek and to save that which was lost" (Luke 19:10). Jesus came to save His people (the Jews) from their sins (Matthew 1:21). Zaccheus didn't become "a son of Abraham" as a result of salvation in the sense of Galatians 3:7, which says that "it is those who are of faith who are sons of Abraham. Rather, he was a Jew—also known as a "son of Abraham"[14]—and because Jesus came to save His people, He drew Zaccheus to saving belief. Zaccheus had always been "a son of Abraham"; only later did he believe in the Lord Jesus Christ for salvation.

Likewise, the woman in Luke 13, a daughter of Abraham, was an unbeliever who had been bound by a physical infirmity from Satan and demons. She received release from her torment through the ministry of Jesus. She experienced resident evil not as a believer, but as an unbeliever.

There is not one clear instance in Scripture where a true believer had resident demons that needed to be expelled.

A New Testament Overview

The New Testament epistles never warn believers about the possibility of demon inhabitation, even though Satan and demons are discussed rather frequently. Nor do the New Testament epistles ever instruct believers about how to cast out demons from either a believer or an unbeliever.

It is biblically inconceivable that a true believer could be indwelt by demons when the Bible presents no clear historical example and when no warnings or instructions are given for such a serious spiritual experience.

At least five other biblical factors affirm this conclusion:

1. The thrust of 2 Corinthians 6:14-18 precludes the Holy Spirit and unclean spirits cohabitating in true believers—even temporarily.

2. Salvation, as described in Colossians 1:13, speaks of true "deliverance" from Satan and transference to the kingdom of Christ.

3. The following passages, combined together, make a powerful statement that precludes demonic indwelling of Christians:

   • Romans 8:37-39—We overwhelmingly conquer through Christ.

   • 1 Corinthians 15:57—God gives us victory through our Lord Jesus Christ.

   • 2 Corinthians 2:14—God always leads us in His triumph in Christ.

- 1 John 2:13-14—We have overcome the evil one.

- 1 John 4:4—The greater power resides in us.

4. The sealing ministry of the Holy Spirit protects the Christian against demon invasion (2 Corinthians 1:21-22; Ephesians 4:30).

5. The promise of 1 John 5:18 makes the idea of demon invasion an unbiblical concept and an impossibility for a true believer.[15]

> We know that no one who is born of God sins; but He who was born of God keeps him and the evil one does not touch him.

Now let's come back to the question, "Can true believers be indwelt by demons with a need for these demons to be evicted?" After a complete study of the appropriate Scriptures, the answer is "No!"[16] Therefore Christians cannot be sick because of indwelling demons. The Bible concludes that the deliverance of a Christian from indwelling demons is an oxymoron.

For all the other issues that could be discussed in the demonic realm, I must defer for the sake of space to other books which have more broadly discussed the subject.[17] But now let us answer one remaining question.

Can Demons Heal?

Can demons heal like Jesus or the apostles?

As I mentioned in chapter 4, "Understanding Reported Healings," I do not believe that Satan or demons possess creative power and can miraculously heal as God heals.[18] However, when demons depart from unbelievers (of their own volition), there could be a departure of the illness also. This would give the appearance of the miraculous.

It seems that a negative answer to the question "Can demons heal?" was a self-evident truth to the first-century Palestinians. Jesus had been accused of having a demon on at least six occasions: 1) Matthew 9:32-34; 2) Matthew 12:22-29; Mark 3:30; 3) Luke 11:14-26; 4) John 7:20; 5) John 8:48-49,52; and 6) John 10:20-21. Those who best knew the fruit of Christ's ministry responded to this charge, "A demon cannot open the eyes of the blind, can he?" (John 10:21). Biblically speaking, demons can possibly give the convincing appearance of healing, but they cannot miraculously heal in reality.

The Bottom Line

The Bible stands supreme as the unique source of divine revelation to tell us about the spiritual world of Satan and demons. Clinical and counseling experiences will never be equal to Scripture and should never be used to draw conclusions which are not first clearly taught in the Word of God.

The Bible convincingly teaches that true believers cannot be inhabited by Satan or demons. However, they can be tormented and harassed externally, even to a severe degree. Should demons actually be found to indwell a person, this would be evidence that he or she lacks genuine salvation, no matter how strongly that person or a counselor or a pastor or a demon argues otherwise. If we encounter a truly demonized person, then we must recognize the strength of the enemy, appeal to God in prayer, and use the power of Scripture—especially the gospel—to deal with the situation.

11

Answers to "What About . . . ?" Questions

◆

Debbie Stone urgently asked me to meet her in the Grace Community Church patio. I have never forgotten that day. She had just returned home from the hospital and her distress sounded obvious over the phone.

No one ever accused Debbie of being ordinary. Shortly after being born out of wedlock, this infant Jewess contracted polio. In her early life she was shuttled from one foster home to another. Debbie never took a step in her whole life; rather, she always sat in a wheelchair or lay in a bed. Having later come to believe in Jesus Christ as her Savior and Lord, Debbie reflected the joy of the Lord as an adult.

However, when I walked out on the patio, her laughing had been replaced with weeping. After regaining her composure, Debbie agonizingly told me about her latest hospitalization. Apparently some well-meaning (but terribly misguided) Christians had stopped to talk with her and tell her that she could be healed completely if only she had enough faith. They visited her on several occasions to deliver this supposed "good news."

In the midst of a discouraging trial, Debbie began to doubt all that she had been taught from Scripture and wondered,

"Just maybe, just maybe, if I believe hard enough, God will heal me and I will be free to walk and enjoy life like everyone else without the millstones of a wheelchair and occasional time in an iron lung."

When she tried to believe as hard as possible but nothing happened, Debbie began to doubt. She wondered if the problem was not having enough faith on her part. Or maybe God didn't love her anymore. Could it be that God couldn't give everyone the same kind of attention, so she was neglected? Or if God wasn't omnipotent like the Bible teaches, then this would also explain why she still had great physical disabilities. Why hadn't she been healed? Was God out on a break or gone on vacation? Why?

Now you understand the reason Debbie returned home distraught. She cried out, "Dick, please tell me that what I've learned from the Bible about God and sickness is still true! I've lost my assurance in God's love and power."

After we prayed, we opened up God's Word and read some great passages about God's power, including Isaiah 40–48 and Romans 8. We reveled together in thinking about God's love— love so great that while we were yet sinners, Christ died for us (Romans 5:8). Soon Debbie's lovely smile returned and she remembered, "I know what we have read is true. God loves me and one day will call me home to be with Him forever, to enjoy His glory and to experience perfect health."

As I write this remembrance, Debbie presently lives out both of her former hopes without any of the physical infirmities that both you and I now endure. Debbie is now living at home, in heaven, with Christ.

Cutting It Straight

This chapter is for all the Debbies in the world; it's about good theology. But it's about more than just presenting sound doctrine; it's about understanding God, His promises, this life, and what the future holds. It's about living hope.

As Debbie found out, nothing can be quite so cruel as being given hope for physical healing if the Scriptures do not really provide that hope. So it is imperative for us to correctly interpret Scripture in order to avoid creating the damaging despair that people like Debbie experience.

Several frequently misinterpreted texts *supposedly* offer the promise of physical healing. The erroneous hope of physical healing today for everyone who believes comes from these interpretive errors. Let's take some time to understand these passages correctly and spare our friends the agony of false hope, and even unintended abuse.

Exodus 15:26 (Exodus 23:25; Deuteronomy 7:15)

> If you will give earnest heed to the voice of the LORD your God, and do what is right in His sight, and give ear to His commandments, and keep all His statutes, I will put none of the diseases on you which I have put on the Egyptians; for I, the LORD, am your healer.

Many people claim this passage as a promise for healing today. But is it?

After Moses led the children of Israel out of Egypt and across the Red Sea, they went into the wilderness of Shur. For three days they suffered without liquid. Finally they found water, but it was bitter and they grumbled at Moses. He prayed to God and then took a tree that the Lord showed him and threw it into the water, and the water became sweet.

In Exodus 15:26 God strongly exhorted the Jews to do what was right and to obey all His commandments. If they did, God would not afflict them as He did the Egyptians. The Jews had a visual aid to emphasize the scope of the Lord's statement: The agonizing look on Pharaoh's face in response to the plagues testified of God's power to afflict.

The theological basis for this exhortation centers on the fact that God takes ultimate responsibility for all healings regardless of the disease, the cure, or the spiritual state of the person cured. God says in Deuteronomy 32:39, "See now that

I, I am He, and there is no god besides Me; it is I who put to death and give life. I have wounded, and it is I who heal; and there is no one who can deliver from My hand." To reassure the Jews, God added in Exodus 15:26, "I, the LORD, am your healer."

By following the historic exodus of the Jewish nation further, we come to Deuteronomy 28, which broadly explains the subsequent history of Israel in the Old Testament. In Deuteronomy 28, God promised Israel that if she disobeyed Him she could expect pestilence and disease (among other things), just as she had seen 40 years earlier in Egypt (verses 21-22, 27,35,59-61).

Years later Israel continually disobeyed, and God finally judged her. Examples of the fulfilled judgment promised in Deuteronomy 28 include Jeremiah 14:12; 21:6; Ezekiel 5:12; 6:11; and Amos 4:9-10. Israel sinned; God judged. Psalm 106 also provides an excellent panoramic view of Israel's sin from God's viewpoint during that period.

Two matters need clarification: First, Exodus 15:26 makes a conditional promise to a specific group of people (Israel). Second, the promise is temporal in nature. It is conditioned not upon God's ability to heal, but upon Israel's obedience. Because of Israel's disobedience, God carried out His conditional promise primarily in judgment, not healing.

Furthermore, although Israel did enjoy God's blessing with regard to health, that blessing did not preclude the use of health-related care or doctors. God appointed Levitical priests to serve as health officers (Leviticus 13). The sanitation laws of the Levitical code provided means to health that were not even practiced by the Western world until the last two centuries.

We today do not expect any of the judgments promised to Israel (Deuteronomy 28:15-68). Likewise, we are not experiencing any of the blessings that were enjoyed during Israel's 40-year wilderness sojourn (such as the daily rations of manna and quail in Exodus 16:1-21 or the clothes and shoes that never wore out, as mentioned in Deuteronomy 29:5).

The conditional promise to Israel in Exodus 15:26 does not apply to believers today. God has been, is, and always will be capable of healing any disease at any time, but only according to His revealed will in Scripture. Exodus 15:26 is simply not a promise to be claimed by Christians today.

Psalm 103:1-3

> Bless the LORD, O my soul;
> And all that is within me,
>   bless His holy name.
> Bless the LORD, O my soul,
> And forget none of His benefits;
> Who pardons all your iniquities,
> Who heals all your diseases.

Psalm 103 opens with a five-verse monologue by David, in which he recalls to his own soul the blessings which the Lord has bestowed on him. It is a beautiful combination of both spiritual and material blessings.

The Hebrew word for "diseases" in verse 3 appears five times in the Old Testament and always refers to physical disease. In typical Hebrew poetic parallelism, David eloquently contrasts God's spiritual blessing of pardoning iniquities with God's material blessing of physical healing. David restates here what Moses wrote in Deuteronomy 32:39—that the Lord is ultimately responsible for all healings.

Anyone who recovers from a physical affliction, believer or unbeliever, can thank God for the recovery. Many doctors will admit that even after the best medical technology has been applied to the problem, it is really God who heals. David merely rejoiced in that eternal truth.

So far as biblical history records, David never suffered from an incurable disease. He had always recovered from sickness, and in each instance he gave God the glory.

David's life clearly demonstrates that sin can be responsible for physical ailments. Psalm 32:3-4; 38:3; and 41:4 all refer to physical symptoms that stemmed from a spiritual malady. David, who was a man after God's heart, knew how to recognize sin, but he was not always careful to avoid it. The guilt of David's conscience produced negative physical effects. As he anguished over his sin, his body wasted away (Psalm 32:3-4), but his confession and repentance brought both spiritual and physical relief (verses 5-7). In David's case, his guilt stemmed primarily from a spiritual rather than a physiological problem, yet he experienced definite physical effects.

We should not take David's statement in Psalm 103:3 to mean that God heals all disease. God is capable of such healing, but He does not always choose to do so. David was simply rehearsing for himself the fact that God had healed all of his prior illnesses.

Psalm 103:3 also does not deny, preclude, or prohibit the use of means to attain health. In fact, David's comments complement the truth that whatever means are used, God should be given the glory.

Therefore, what was true of David's life in terms of physical relief is not necessarily true (nor is it a promise of such) in any other believer's life. David himself was subject to death, slept with his fathers, and was buried in the city of David (1 Kings 2:1,10; Acts 2:29; 13:36).

Isaiah 35:4-5

> Say to those with anxious heart,
> "Take courage, fear not.
> Behold, your God will come with vengeance;
> The recompense of God will come,
> But He will save you."
> Then the eyes of the blind will be opened,
> And the ears of the deaf will be unstopped.

A quick reading of Isaiah 35 tells us that the prophet was writing about a spectacular time in the future of Israel. When is that time? Both Matthew 11:2-6 and Luke 7:18-23 record the fact that Jesus referred to Isaiah 35 when He verified His messianic authority by curing many diseases and afflictions as well as granting sight to many people who were blind (Luke 7:21). He told John the Baptist's disciples to return to John and report what they had seen. Christ knew that when John heard the report, he would know without doubt that Jesus was the Messiah.

The earthly ministry of Christ did not begin to realize most of the promises in Isaiah 35. What Christ did during His ministry with regard to healing was only a preview of what is yet to come during His thousand-year reign on earth (Revelation 19:1–20:15).

At the end of the millennial period, Christ will deliver up the kingdom to God the Father (1 Corinthians 15:24). But He must reign until He has put all His enemies under His feet, and the last enemy to be abolished is death (verses 25-26).

When death has been abolished, it will signal the end of sin. No longer will there be a basis for sickness. Even the millennial healing ministry of the Messiah will no longer be needed. Revelation 21:4 says that death, mourning, crying, and pain will have passed away. Revelation 22:3 reveals the reason: The curse in Genesis 3:8-22 will exist no more; it will have been removed.

Isaiah 35:4-5, then, refers primarily to future millennial conditions. Christ's healing ministry in the Gospels, and specifically for the disciples of John, previewed things to come and authenticated Jesus as Messiah. Isaiah 35 has little bearing on our understanding of God's work of healing today other than to encourage the earnest believer through the knowledge of his future eternal relationship with God, when there will be no sin and thus no sickness.

Mark 16:9-20

After He had risen early on the first day of the week, He first appeared to Mary Magdalene, from whom He had cast out seven demons. She went and reported to those who had been with Him, while they were mourning and weeping. And when they heard that He was alive, and had been seen by her, they refused to believe it. And after that, He appeared in a different form to two of them, while they were walking along on their way to the country. And they went away and reported it to the others, but they did not believe them either. And afterward He appeared to the eleven themselves as they were reclining at the table; and He reproached them for their unbelief and hardness of heart, because they had not believed those who had seen Him after He had risen. And He said to them, "Go into all the world and preach the gospel to all creation. He who has believed and has been baptized shall be saved; but he who has disbelieved shall be condemned. And these signs will accompany those who have believed: in My name they will cast out demons, they will speak with new tongues, they will pick up serpents, and if they drink any deadly poison, it shall not hurt them; they will lay hands on the sick, and they will recover." So then, when the Lord Jesus had spoken to them, He was received up into heaven, and sat down at the right hand of God. And they went out and preached everywhere, while the Lord worked with them, and confirmed the word by the signs that followed.

The concluding verses of Mark's Gospel remain one of the most controversial textual problems in the New Testament. But this Great Commission passage deserves the extra effort needed to understand it. Three textual possibilities exist:

1. Mark 16:1-8—normal ending
2. Mark 16:1-20—longer ending
3. Mark 16:1-8—with a special addition

Mark 16:9-20 does not appear in the oldest existing Greek manuscripts (Codex Sinaiticus [about A.D. 340] and Codex

Vaticanus [about A.D. 325-50]) or in a number of other important early New Testament manuscript witnesses. Many scholars believe that "on the basis of good external evidence and strong internal considerations it appears that the earliest ascertainable forms of the Gospel of Mark ended with 16:8."[1]

On the other hand, conclusive evidence that verses 9-20 are *not* genuine does not exist either. In fact, later manuscript evidence that is considered reliable argues in favor of their authority. However, the evidence is not conclusive enough either way to dogmatically assume a correct solution. Even if Mark did not record verses 9-20, it does seem to be a genuine primitive addition. In such a case, it would be just as real as Joshua's concluding summary of Moses' death in Deuteronomy 34:1-12.

Assuming the longer ending to be authentic for this discussion, let us make several observations about it.

1. Jesus was addressing the disciples and referring to those immediate converts who would believe the apostles' preaching (verse 20).

2. The sole purpose of the "signs" focused on confirming the word preached (verse 20).

3. Scripture gives not the slightest hint that those phenomena (the signs) would continue beyond the ministry of the apostles.

4. Either all the signs are present today or none of them remain currently active. Nowhere in the church today do all of those signs authenticate a salvation experience in a new convert (verse 17) and thus confirm the truth of the word preached (verse 20).

5. The apostles experienced the fulfillment of verses 17 and 18 among their converts, as explained in verse 20.

We lack sufficient proof to conclusively substantiate any one of the three possible endings of Mark 16, but our brief investigation of verses 9-20 indicates that if the longer option contains the true words of Christ, He limited its fulfillment to the time of the apostles and their immediate converts.

But regardless of one's conclusions, we need to exercise caution. Because of the uncertain textual evidence, Mark 16:9-20 should not be used as the primary biblical support for any theological position. A.T. Robertson has wisely advised against a dogmatic use of these verses:

> The great doubt concerning the genuineness of these verses (fairly conclusive proof against them, in my opinion) renders it unwise to take these verses as the foundation for doctrine or practices unless supported by other genuine portions of the New Testament.[2]

Some people have recently reasoned that since we should obey all that Christ commanded in the Great Commission of Matthew 28:18-20, and since Mark 16:9-20 expresses the Great Commission, then all believers throughout time should obey the Great Commission commandments of Mark 16.[3]

But there is a mistake in their logic. They equate the *churchwide mandate* of Matthew 28 with Christ's *specific instruction* to the disciples in Mark 16, then try to make their healing conclusion before even proving their initial argument. (They also treat the text lightly, with little exegetical precision.)[4] But the disciples' mandate is not necessarily the church's mandate.

We have already seen that the textual evidence for Mark 16:9-20 is uncertain at best, and that a fair interpretation of the text really does limit it to the time of the disciples. Therefore we conclude that "the church has no specific ongoing mandate from Jesus to heal that is recorded in authentic Scripture."[5]

John 14:12

> Truly, truly, I say to you, he who believes in Me, the works that I do shall he do also; and

greater works than these shall he do, because I go
to the Father.

Christ addressed the eleven disciples (Judas had already
departed) and told them that the disciples present, who were
believing in Him, would do the same works as He had done (*see*
Acts 2:22 and Hebrews 2:4) and even greater works; that is, not
only would they do sign miracles, but also greater works
through those sign miracles.

Our earlier inductive study of Acts and the epistles revealed that the disciples did not do *greater* sign miracles than
Christ either in quantity or quality. In fact, they were *fewer*
in quantity, not more. Also, they did not perform creation
miracles (bread, fish, wine) or miracles of nature (calming
storms, maneuvering fish).

J. Sidlow Baxter takes the logic one step beyond the disciples. He wisely notes that no Christian today performs
miracles of creation or nature either.

If we take His words, "the works that I do
shall he do also," and insist on applying them
today, we ought to be turning water into wine,
walking on the sea, causing fish swarms, feeding
multitudes with miraculously multiplying vic-
tuals, and fishing up coins to pay dues. We are
inconsistent if we claim only the *healing* miracles
while admitting that the others obviously do *not*
apply today.[6]

How do we know whether the believing ones of John 14:12
refers to the immediately present disciples or all believers? To
answer that key question, note first that Christ was addressing
only the eleven. We are faced with the options of limiting the
passage to the immediate hearers only or concluding that it
applies equally to all believers in the church age.

It seems obvious that Christ was addressing the disciples
because He used the personal pronoun "you" throughout the

passage. It is unwarranted to assume that Christ switched from addressing the disciples in John 14:10-11 to focusing on all believers in 14:12 and then reverted back to the disciples in 14:13. Just as we would not understand Christ's commission to the twelve in Luke 9 to apply to all believers, neither is such an understanding demanded or even necessary in John 14:12. Christ's charge to the disciples should not automatically be assigned to all believers throughout the ages unless specifically indicated by the text. Nothing here points beyond the disciples.

Why did Jesus say the disciples would be able to do greater works? Christ explained, "I go to the Father." Now if those greater works were merely physical miracles, Christ would not need to go to the Father, because the Father was already doing such miracles through Him on earth. Christ went to the Father to serve as our priestly intercessor before the throne of God (1 Timothy 2:5) and so that the Holy Spirit would come (John 16:7-11). The book of Hebrews explains Christ's work in the presence of the Father (Hebrews 1:3; 4:14-16; 7:23-28; 9:11-28). John 3:1-21 expands on the greater works that the Holy Spirit would do through the disciples in relation to the spiritual miracle of salvation.

John 5:20-21 strongly verifies this conclusion. Verse 20 refers to "works" and "greater works than these." Verse 21, parallel with verse 20, explains that the "works" were physical miracles (resurrection, only to die physically again), but that the "greater works" were spiritual miracles (eternal life).

Along the same line, when the seventy returned in Luke 10:20, Jesus told them not to rejoice in physical miracles but rather in their own salvation: "Nevertheless do not rejoice in this, that the spirits are subject to you, but rejoice that your names are recorded in heaven." *Salvation,* not physical miracles, stands out as preeminent.

John 14:12 does not promise that Christians today will do the same physical miracles or even greater physical miracles than Christ did. However, it does teach that the introduction of one person to salvation in the Lord Jesus Christ is greater than any physical miracle Christ ever did. There will be more joy in heaven over one sinner who repents than over 99 righteous persons who need no repentance (Luke 15:7,10). Samuel Storms concluded:

> When Jesus says that His going to the Father will lead to "greater works" on the part of His followers, He indicates that a new day in the history of redemption is about to dawn.[7]

Romans 8:11

> If the Spirit of Him who raised Jesus from the dead dwells in you, He who raised Christ Jesus from the dead will also give life to your mortal bodies through His Spirit who indwells you.

J. Sidlow Baxter understands this passage to promise the renewal of physical life after salvation but before death.[8] He reasons that Paul switched from the normal Greek verb for resurrection, with reference to Christ, to *another* expression in regard to believers. The change of verbs, he concludes, means that Paul in Romans 8:11 promises believers some sort of physical restoration after their salvation.

Two observations from the biblical text strongly point in the direction that Paul in Romans 8:11 reasons like this: "Just as the Spirit raised Christ from the dead, He will do likewise with believers." First, note the word "also." This strongly suggests that whatever the Spirit did for Christ, He would do as well for believers. Second, the alternate verb *(zopoieō)* appears elsewhere in the New Testament within the context of resurrection (John 5:21; Romans 4:17; 1 Corinthians 15:22; 1 Peter 3:18).

So Romans 8:11 does not refer to the improvement of a Christian's physical life before death. Rather, it promises restoration of life after death by resurrection.

1 Corinthians 12:9,28,30

> To another faith by the same Spirit, and to another gifts of healing by the one Spirit. . . . And God has appointed in the church, first apostles, second prophets, third teachers, then miracles, then gifts of healings, helps, administrations, various kinds of tongues. . . . All do not have gifts of healings, do they? All do not speak with tongues, do they? All do not interpret, do they?

"Gifts of healings" is the most enigmatic phrase that deals with healing in the entire Bible. Why? Because that phrase is mentioned only three times in the New Testament, and all three instances appear in 1 Corinthians 12. The verses provide no further explanation of what the manifestation involved. Nor does the gift appear in other New Testament gift lists. So there is very little biblical evidence to draw from.[9]

However, several biblical observations may help. First, both words in the term are plural—"gifts of healings." The plural surely does not require that the gift will be manifest on more than one occasion by the same person, for that would mean "word of wisdom" in 1 Corninthians 12:8 was a one-time occurrence only.

The parallel plurals "effectings of miracles," "distin-guishings of spirits," and "kinds of tongues" could very well indicate that the manifestation was temporary (one-time only) and had to be renewed by God at His will.[10] For instance, Paul healed multitudes (Acts 19:11-12) but couldn't heal himself (Galatians 4:13), Epaphroditus (Philippians 2:25-30), or Tro-phimus (2 Timothy 4:20). That would also explain why Paul did not direct Timothy (1 Timothy 5:23) to a person with this gift. Someone who had exercised it on one occasion would have no reason to suspect that it would be manifested again. James 5 can be similarly understood; this early epistle (about A.D. 50) exhorted sick individuals to call for the elders rather than for a person who manifested "gifts of healings."

Other than their association with the apostles, the "gifts of healings" appear rarely. Only Philip is mentioned specifically (Acts 8:6-7). Stephen (Acts 6:8) and Barnabas (Acts 14:3) might also have exercised this sign gift. That would explain why Barnabas, who may have healed others with Paul in Iconium (Acts 14:3), did not heal Paul himself when he was nearly stoned to death in Lystra (Acts 14:19-20).

The "gifts of healings" seems to be a sign that was given to authenticate the apostles (Hebrews 2:4). Therefore it is not surprising to discover its absence from the gifts list of Romans 12, which was written later than 1 Corinthians. Once the apostles were authenticated and the early church established, the apostolic signs gradually disappeared, for they had served their God-intended purpose.

Neither are we surprised to see the total absence of sign gifts from the pastoral epistles written by Paul to Timothy and Titus. If those gifts were to be perpetuated, certainly Paul would have mentioned it, especially since Timothy suffered from stomach problems and other frequent afflictions (1 Timothy 5:23).

If God intended "gifts of healings" to function as something other than a miraculous sign gift, we would expect to see it manifested in the lives of Paul's numerous associates. But there is not the slightest hint of its appearance after A.D. 59. An argument from silence alone is not conclusive, but it is one more piece of evidence that needs to be seriously considered because it is consistent with the other indications mentioned above.

Most likely, "gifts of healings" involved a temporary sign gift which was used by God to authenticate the apostles, was evidenced sparingly apart from Peter and Paul, was bestowed on a one-time basis only, and was to be renewed by God's sovereign will. Therefore the "gifts of healings" in 1 Corinthians 12:9,28,30 would not be intended by God to be seen today.

I want to add that the temporary nature of the "gifts of healings" does not mean that God is not healing today.

Because the sparse number of healings in the Old Testament and the innumerable healings of Christ did not depend on the "gifts of healings," neither would divine healing be dependent on that sign gift today.

Because the term "gifts of healings" and its context remain so ambiguous, a person should not build a theological superstructure on this paper-thin foundation. Those who develop their healing theology for the church today on this passage do so by reading their conclusions into the text rather than by finding any clear direction from other New Testament letters.

First Corinthians 12 appears to be a haven of rescue for healing advocates who understand how perilous their case would be if it rested on the healing pattern of Christ and the apostles. J. Sidlow Baxter correctly concludes that the healing miracles of neither Christ nor the apostles continued past the apostolic age.

> Neither from our Lord's miracle healings nor from those of the apostles can we safely deduce that such are meant to continue today, nor should we presume so. If such healings were divinely intended to continue in the same way today, then all who come for healing today would be healed without exception, as was the case in the days of our Lord and the apostles. But thousands who come for healing today are not healed. Therefore, by that simple, practical text we know that healings today are not on the same basis as in those days of long ago.[11]

However, Baxter then turns to the New Testament epistles and develops the idea—primarily from Romans 8:11, 1 Corinthians 12, and James 5:13-16—that bodily healing has been promised by Scripture for today.[12] He does it, however, with this honest caveat:

> Those seem to be all there is in the Epistles by way of clear promise or statement concerning divine healing

or renewal of the human body in this present age. What is the first thought which leaps to mind? Is it not the *very small space* given to physical healing? In a way, it seems disappointingly small. Let it tell us the comparatively small importance which *God* puts upon it. Let it indicate its comparatively minor place over against the major emphases of the New Testament letters to Christian believers.[13]

Jack Deere also looks to 1 Corinthians 12 as a major biblical text to explain healing for today.[14] He reasons that since 1) the apostles were the most gifted of all people in the church, 2) spiritual gifts range in strength and intensity, and 3) miraculous gifts were not limited to the apostles but distributed throughout the church, then 1) there is a distinction between signs/wonders and "gifts of healings," and 2) it is wrong to insist that apostolic miracles set the standard by which to measure today's healings. He concludes 1) that healings today will not be as spectacular as Paul's or Peter's, 2) that healings might not be as abundant as in the apostolic era, and 3) that this allows for some failure in attempted healings.

My response would be that Dr. Deere has developed a theory more from what Scripture *doesn't* say than what it *clearly* says. His theory fails, in my opinion, for several reasons.

1. The phrase "gifts of healings" is so ambiguous in its contexts that no one can really know for sure what it means. Certainly something as important as a theology of physical healing should not be built on such a shallow foundation.

2. His theory does not explain the decline in quality and quantity of even the apostolic healings as the apostolic age drew to a conclusion.

3. His theory does not adequately account for "gifts of healings" appearing only in the 1 Corinthians 12 gift list.

4. His theory does not anticipate the total lack of instruction in the epistles on the matter of healing (with the exception of what is found in James 5). I have suggested in a previous chapter that James 5 and 1 Corinthians 12 are not connected.

5. His theory assumes throughout that if Scripture does not prohibit healing or does not speak directly about the cessation of apostolic healing, then implicitly the Scriptures teach healing for today.[15]

6. Dr. Deere seems to contradict his own theory when he writes, "I believe that God is doing New Testament-quality miracles in the church today, and I believe He has done them throughout the history of the church.[16] The only quality of miracles we know of from Acts are those done by the apostles. Yet Dr. Deere elsewhere theorized that the miracles of the church were substandard compared to those of the apostles. Both cannot be true.

2 Corinthians 12:7-10

Because of the surpassing greatness of the revelations, for this reason, to keep me from exalting myself, there was given me a thorn in the flesh, a messenger of Satan to buffet me—to keep me from exalting myself! Concerning this I entreated the Lord three times that it might depart from me. And He has said to me, "My grace is sufficient for you, for power is perfected in weakness." Most gladly, therefore, I will rather boast about my weaknesses, that the power of Christ may dwell in me. Therefore I am well content with weaknesses, with insults, with distresses, with persecutions, with difficulties, for Christ's sake; for when I am weak, then I am strong.

Paul lets the cat out of the bag in verse 7 when he describes the "two-sided coin" experience that resulted from his adventure in the third heaven, which up to this time he had chosen not to reveal: God would use Satan's messenger to keep Paul from pride. On the other hand, the devil would work to deflate Paul's faith with his sharpened thorn.

What is the thorn? This figure of speech appears four times in the Old Testament (Numbers 33:55; Joshua 23:13; Ezekiel 28:24; Hosea 2:6). Three times it refers to people, and once to life circumstances. However, interpreters most commonly identify Paul's thorn in 2 Corinthians 12 as a physical problem, since it is "in the flesh." Malaria, epilepsy, headaches, or eye problems have all been suggested.

Following the Old Testament usage, there are several strong possibilities. As in Hosea 2:6, Paul's thorn could have been the adverse circumstances he experienced while serving the Lord (2 Corinthians 11:23-28). Or we could identify Paul's thorn in the flesh as people who are a thorn in the side or a pain in the neck.

Alexander the coppersmith (2 Timothy 4:14), Hymenaeus with Philetus (2 Timothy 2:17-18), Elymas (called by Paul a "son of the devil" in Acts 13:10), and false apostles (2 Corinthians 11:13-15) all qualify. Let me suggest even another possibility—the Corinthians themselves. It is fascinating to note that Paul is coming to the Corinthians for the *third time* (2 Corinthians 13:1). He might have prayed on the occasion of each visit, "Lord, please spare me the pain."

On the other hand, since "thorn" is used figuratively in 2 Corinthians 12, immediate context more than broad usage should determine the reality behind the figure of speech. Paul did suffer with eye problems (Galatians 4:13-15), and he certainly sustained physical infirmities from numerous lashings, beatings, and stonings (2 Corinthians 11:23-27). A good case could be made for either physical problems or problems from persecution.

Earlier Paul had written, "We have this treasure in earthen vessels, that the surpassing greatness of the power may be of

God and not from ourselves" (2 Corinthians 4:7). For most people, the affliction, perplexities, persecutions, and beatings Paul experienced would be enough to finish them off for good. But because of God's power graciously perfected in Paul's weakness, Paul became a divinely enabled survivor who was not crushed, did not despair, and was neither forsaken nor destroyed.

Whether the suffering was in his body through sickness or in his person through persecution, several features in 2 Corinthians 12 stand out.[17]

1. The suffering was sovereignly given by God (verse 7).

2. Frequent prayers offered in faith did not remove the suffering (verses 8-9).

3. God intended the suffering for Paul's spiritual good (verses 9-10).

Whatever is true of suffering in general would also be true of sickness as a particular category of suffering. Therefore these three lessons from 2 Corinthians 12:7-10 apply regardless of one's exact interpretation of Paul's "thorn in the flesh." In many ways, Paul's experience generally parallels Job's experiences, with the exception that Job eventually regained his health. Whether Paul shed his thorn eventually we do not know.

Galatians 3:5

> Does He then, who provides you with the Spirit and works miracles among you, do it by the works of the Law, or by hearing with faith?

Jack Deere cites this passage on at least seven occasions as proving "that miracles were common among the Galatian churches."[18] Galatians 3:5 can reasonably be interpreted in three different ways, no one of which stands conclusive. The three possibilities include:

1. God worked miracles through Paul.
2. God worked miracles through the Galatians.
3. God worked the miracle of salvation in the Galatians.[19]

Space does not permit a lengthy treatment here. However, let me say that a passage as inconclusive as Galatians 3:5 should never be used so centrally in developing one's theology—especially to the degree that it is used frequently as a proof text for a never-proven conclusion.

Hebrews 13:8

> Jesus Christ is the same yesterday and today,
> yes and forever.

Those who look for promises of healing often turn to this truth. They reason that because God healed in the past and never changes, then He also must heal in the same way today.

Several errors produce that kind of thinking. Biblically, we know that God will not heal forever. One day sin will be conquered and sickness will no longer exist; God's healing will not be needed. Just as it is not true to say that if God healed in the past then He must heal forever, so also it is not necessarily true to say that if He healed in the past then He heals today.

Within its context, Hebrews 13:8 is speaking specifically about God's unchanging nature (Malachi 3:6; Hebrews 1:12), not the varying *manifestation* of His nature. For example, Ananias and Sapphira offended God's holiness by lying and thus evoked His righteous wrath and died as a result (Acts 5:1-11). God's holiness and righteousness never change, but He does not always strike each liar dead as soon as the untrue words are spoken.

And what about Paul's unique visit to the third heaven (2 Corinthians 12:1-10)? Although God is still omnipotent, Christians today should not expect a similar trip.

God's goodness supplied the Jews supernaturally with food and clothing during their 40-year wilderness sojourn

(Exodus 16:1-21; Deuteronomy 29:5). Christians should not expect that kind of supply today, but God's goodness remains the same and will be forever.

Hebrews 13:8 speaks of Christ's *person,* not His *purposes.* We must distinguish between *who God is*—His character, which never changes—and *what God does* in carrying out His personal will for individual believers. If we fail to make these distinctions we can misinterpret Scripture. Even worse, we can misunderstand God and misappropriate His promises.

Hebrews 13:8 generalizes the specific Old Testament illustration used as a promise in Hebrews 13:5-6—that God is forever present with believers. Take a look back at Acts 12, where James and Peter depended on God for protection. We know that James was put to death but Peter was miraculously released. For reasons unknown to us, God's unchanging nature was manifested in two entirely different ways within the same situation.

Here is a modern-day parallel to James and Peter:

> In the June 1980 issue of *Our Daily Bread*, I told how a Christian providentially escaped death. An unexpected delay in New York kept him from catching Flight 191 in Chicago, which crashed with all 254 aboard. That article brought this note from a reader: "I just had to let you know about one of God's great saints who ran to make Flight 191—and made it!" His name was Edward E. Elliott, beloved pastor of the Garden Grove Orthodox Presbyterian Church in California. His plane from Pennsylvania was late, and a friend who had accompanied him to Chicago said he last saw him "dashing forward" in the terminal to make his connection.[20]

Hebrews 13:8 was equally true for both men. But one died, while the other was spared. With regard for the physical, Hebrews 13:8 does not necessarily promise believers that God will heal them today as He healed others in the past. His ability to heal has never changed, but His will is yet to be revealed on an individual basis.

3 John 2[21]

> Beloved, I pray that in all respects you may prosper and be in good health, just as your soul prospers.

At first glance someone might think that 3 John 2 has some relationship to healing. But a second reading points in another direction. This passage represents a normal salutation in a first-century letter. The writer wishes Gaius the best in the interest of getting the gospel out—both for life in general and in his physical well-being under extreme conditions and hardships.

Look at the text again and note the point of reference. John wishes Gaius good health in proportion to his spiritual well-being—that is, "just as your soul prospers." Third John 2 means nothing more than what it says: John wishes Gaius the best in every dimension of his life. Third John 2 does not even hint of a healing promise.

12

What About Miracles?

A recent publication contained this remarkable comment. What is your reaction to it?

> If you take a new convert, who prior to his conversion knew nothing about the history of Christianity or the New Testament, and you lock him in a room with a Bible for a week, he will come out believing that he is a member of a body that is passionately in love with the Lord Jesus Christ and a body that consistently experiences miracles and works miracles. It would take a clever theologian with no experience of the miraculous to convince this young convert differently.[1]

At first glance and without much thought, we might agree. But look at the statement again. For me, this quickly becomes an agree/disagree situation.

I agree that a new convert who is totally ignorant of history, who has no experience interpreting the Bible, and who has no study tools might conclude that the church today experiences miracles like the first-century church.

But I totally disagree, and I suspect you do, too, that the new convert would be correct. Since when do we ask a new convert with nothing but a Bible for the correct theological expression of a subject so complex as miracles? Further, why would the theologian have to be "experienced" in the miraculous to be credible if we believe that the Scriptures are sufficient to articulate clear doctrine (2 Timothy 3:16-17)?

This raises an even bigger question: Why do trained theologians, who do have a knowledge of history and who do have the capabilities to use good Bible-study tools, come up with the same immature conclusion as a new believer who knows nothing? Could it be that they have used a combination of experience and a predetermined theology to override otherwise reasonable conclusions?

A Biblical Definition

The Bible defines a miracle using various words that describe the "effect spectrum" of a miracle.

In the Old Testament

Four different Hebrew words describe the various shades of a miracle.

1. *Pele'* has the basic idea of "wonder" (Exodus 15:11; Psalm 77:11).

2. *'Ot* indicates a "sign" that establishes a certainty that was not previously present (Exodus 4:8-9; Numbers 14:22; Deuteronomy 4:34).

3. *Gebudāh* means "strength" or "might" (Psalm 145:4, 11-12; 150:2).

4. *Mopēt* basically means "wonder," sign," or "portent." It is used frequently in conjunction with *'ot*, as in Deuteronomy 4:34; 6:22; and Nehemiah 9:10.

In the New Testament

The New Testament uses four Greek words which correspond exactly to the Old Testament Hebrew terms.

1. *Teras* ("wonder") describes the miracle that startles or imposes. Its extraordinary character indicates the marvel or wonder that is inspired by the miracle. *Teras* does not occur alone in the New Testament and forms the Greek counterpart to *mopēt* and *pele'* (*see* Deuteronomy 4:34, Septuagint). Christ illustrates the usage in Acts 2:22, and the apostles in Hebrews 2:4.

2. *Semeion* ("sign") leads a person to something beyond the miracle. It is valuable not for what it is, but rather for what it points toward. It is the Greek counterpart of *'ot* (*see* Numbers 14:22, Septuagint).

3. *Dunamis* ("power" or "miracle") pictures the power behind the act and points to a new and higher power. It corresponds to *gebudāh*, the Hebrew equivalent (*see* Psalm 144:4, Septuagint).

4. *Ergon* ("work") is used by Jesus in the Gospels to describe distinctive works that no one else did (*see* John 15:24).

These various elements constitute a biblical miracle. By integrating each descriptive part, a miracle from God may be defined as—

An observable phenomenon delivered powerfully by God directly or through an authorized agent (*dunamis*), whose extraordinary character captures the immediate attention of the viewer (*teras*), points to something beyond the phenomenon (*semeion*), and is a distinctive work whose source can be attributed to no one else but God (*ergon*).

That's a heavy definition. Boiled down to its core meaning, a miracle could be described as "God calling time-out on natural laws and personally reaching into life to rearrange people and their circumstances according to His will."

Let me outline the terms which seem to best describe the various works of God. By using these definitions, some semantic confusion can be avoided.

I. God's originating works of creation

II. God's continuing works of providence[2]

    A. Supernatural/miraculous/immediate
       1. Without human agency
       2. With human agency

    B. Natural/nonmiraculous/mediate
       1. Explicable/known laws
       2. Inexplicable/unknown laws

All of the above works involve God's divine participation at some level. With regard to healing, any physical recovery can be called "divine healing," but not all healing can be termed "miraculous."

Dr. C. Everett Koop explains this distinction from his renowned medical perspective.

> I don't know how many operations I actually performed in my surgical career. I know I performed 17,000 of one particular type, 7,000 of another. . . . Patients were coming to me from all over the world. And one of the things that endeared me to the parents of my patients was the way my incisions healed.
>
> These "invisible" scars became my trademark. But was I a *healer?* . . .
>
> I was the one who put the edges together, but it was God who coagulated the serum. It was God who sent the fibroblasts out across the skin edges. It was God who

had the fibroblasts make collagen, and there were probably about fifty other complicated processes involved about which you and I will never know. But did God come down and instruct the fibroblasts to behave that way?

In a sense, He did. But He did it through His *natural laws*, just the way He makes the grass grow, the rain fall, the earth quake. The question, then, is not, Does God heal? Of course He heals! We are concerned with this question: Granted that God heals, is it *normally according to natural laws* or an *interruption* of those laws (i.e., a miracle)?[3]

Why Involve People?

Three New Testament statements speak directly about divinely initiated miracles done through people.

First, consider Peter's inspired commentary on the purpose of Jesus' miracles in Acts 2:22: "Men of Israel, listen to these words: Jesus the Nazarene, a man attested to you by God with miracles and wonders and signs which God performed through Him in your midst, just as you yourselves know."

Christ's works were displayed for the purpose of certifying His claims to deity and messiahship. The miracles of our Lord did not by themselves prove His deity, just as the apostolic miracles did not prove that the apostles were deity. Rather, the miracles attested undeniably to the truth of Christ's claim to be the God-Man (John 11:47-48). They distinguished Christ, who had impeccable miraculous credentials, as the true Messiah in contrast to all of the false christs throughout history.[4]

Next, 2 Corinthians 12:12 contains Paul's direct statement about miracles in relationship to the apostles. He notes emphatically that the marks (*semeia*) of an apostle were signs, wonders, and miracles. God used those supernatural phenomena to authenticate the apostolic messenger and thus validate His message (Acts 2:43; 5:12). Much the same method was used by God to authenticate the Old Testament prophet—1) by fulfilling the prophets' message, and 2) through miracles (*see* Deuteronomy 13:1-5; 18:21-22). Miracles distinguished between true and false prophets and apostles.[5]

Third, one of the proofs used by the author of Hebrews involves the salvation message being authenticated by God through miracles. Hebrews 2:3-4 states that God bore witness to true salvation through the apostles by miracles.

These passages from Acts, 2 Corinthians, and Hebrews teach that God's primary purpose for the miracles He worked through men was *to authenticate His messengers as bearing a true revelation from God.*

There are many illustrations of this major purpose in the Old Testament. In Exodus chapters 3 and 4, God finally convinced Moses that he should represent Him in Egypt. To every one of Moses' objections God responded with a supernatural sign that would authenticate Moses' commission. In Exodus 4:30-31 the signs were performed, and the Jews believed. After one sign and three plagues, the magicians of Pharaoh believed (Exodus 8:18-19). After ten plagues and the Red Sea incident, Pharaoh believed (Exodus 14:26-30), and the Jews' faith was rekindled (Exodus 14:31).

After feeding Elijah with her last morsels, the widow of Zarephath saw her food supernaturally replenished (1 Kings 17:8-16). At the death of her son she doubted (verses 17-18), but when her son was supernaturally brought back to life, she believed (verse 24). Elijah had been attested as authentic by a miracle from God. This happened again on Mount Carmel, at the command of Elijah, when fire came from heaven and made believers of the people in the midst of rampant unbelief and gross idolatry (1 Kings 18:30-40). Naaman was convinced of Elisha's credibility after being healed of leprosy (2 Kings 5:14-15).[6] Nebuchadnezzar knew Daniel's reliability after he correctly reviewed and interpreted the king's dream (Daniel 2:46).

Clearly God used miracles through men to authenticate His messenger. The miracles were never used merely for display, for frivolity, or to exalt the messenger.

History of People and Miracles

A review of biblical history reveals three major time periods during which God performed miracles through men. (Miracles through men did occur in other eras, but only rarely by comparison.) These three major periods are:

- Moses and Joshua, ca. 1450-1390 B.C.
- Elijah and Elisha, ca. 860-800 B.C.
- Christ and His apostles, ca. A.D. 30–60.

But even in those periods, miracles were not the norm for all of God's servants. Speaking of John the Baptist, our Lord said, "I say to you, among those born of women, there is no one greater than John" (Luke 7:28). Yet John writes of the Baptizer, "While John performed no sign, yet everything John said about this man [Christ] was true" (John 10:41). (Later John's message was vindicated by Christ's miracles.) So the stature of a man of God was not primarily evidenced by sign miracles, but rather by the truthfulness of his message.

Reports of miracles are not limited to biblical history or even Christianity. In fact, if the mere number of alleged miracles were used to measure the authenticity of a religion, true Christianity would be eclipsed by false religion.

The fact that alleged miracles happen outside the Christian faith should cause Christians to be wary of those who claim to do the miraculous. Mormons, Christian Scientists, most Eastern religions, and pagan spiritists all claim miracles. They even claim that the miracles have been verified by competent witnesses.

The history of alleged miracles within the sphere of Christianity since A.D. 100 is abundant in the area of healing. Benjamin Warfield, a noted theologian, observes:

> There is little or no evidence at all for miracle-working during the first fifty years of the postapostolic church; it is slight and unimportant for the next fifty

years; it grows more abundant during the next century (the third); and it becomes abundant and precise only in the fourth century, to increase still further in the fifth and beyond. Thus, if the evidence is worth anything at all, instead of a regularly progressing decrease, there was a steadily growing increase of miracle-working from the beginning on.[7]

However, do the character and quality of postapostolic miracles match those recorded in Scripture? Philip Schaff, the eminent church historian who believes that miracles extended beyond the apostolic age, offers these weighty considerations against the majority of those miracles.

- They are of a much lower moral tone and far exceed biblical miracles in outward pomp.

- They do not serve to confirm the Christian faith in general.

- The further they are removed from the apostolic age, the more numerous they are.

- The church fathers did not truthfully report all there was to know about the alleged miracles.

- The church fathers admitted there were extensive frauds.

- The Nicene miracles met with doubt and contradiction among contemporaries.

- The church fathers contradicted themselves by teaching that miracles no longer took place and then reporting the occurrence of actual miracles.[8]

We need to heed history's warning regardless of our position on miracles done through human agents. Satan will do all he can to mislead and deceive Christians along the dead-end path of alleged miracles (2 Corinthians 11:13-15). Those on the path will one day approach Jesus with claims of their miracles in His name, but to them He will respond, "I never knew you; depart from Me" (Matthew 7:23).

Are Miracles for Today?

Have miracles through men really continued beyond the apostolic age? Earlier we saw from Scripture that miracles served to authenticate the messenger of God and ultimately God's message. However, when the book of Revelation was recorded by John, the canon of the New Testament and the total revelation of Scripture from God was completed. After A.D. 95, God had no revealed reason to perform miracles through men to authenticate His message; the canon closed with the completion of Revelation. Therefore, God's will to work miralces through men ceased.

> These gifts were not the possession of the primitive Christian as such, nor for that matter of the apostolic church or the Apostolic Age for themselves; they were distinctively the authentication of the apostles. They were part of the credentials of the apostles as the authoritative agents of God in founding the church. Their function confined them to distinctively the apostolic church, and they necessarily passed away with it.[9]

There is no one clear biblical statement that specifies whether miracles through men ceased with the apostles or continued on, but if we consult the whole counsel of God, we will find the answer. Here are some New Testament indicators that the age of miracles through men indeed ceased with the apostolic age.

Acts 2:22, 2 Corinthians 12:12, and Hebrews 2:4 indicate that sign miracles were for the purpose of authenticating the messenger of God. With the completion of the canon, those signs no longer served their God-intended purpose.

Just as there were miracles of benefit in the New Testament era, there were also miracles of judgment. Yet no one today would want to claim that God is dealing with liars as He did with Ananias and Sapphira (Acts 5:1-11). Neither would any would-be healer claim that God is supernaturally inflicting grave physical maladies through human agency, such as the blindness inflicted upon Elymas by Paul (Acts 13:8-11). But it is inconsistent to deny miracles of judgment yet promote miracles of benefit; that is not the biblical pattern. Either both or neither are present. That neither type of miracle is being done through men at the present can be supported biblically and historically.

Following the historical progress of the apostles who wrote about miraculous gifts, miracles diminished in scope as time moved onward. In 1 Corinthians (A.D. 55), Romans (A.D. 51), and Acts 19:11-12 (A.D. 52) we read of extraordinary miracles that were taking place. Later epistles indicate that those phenomena were waning. Paul did not heal Epaphroditus (Philippians 2:27, A.D. 60). Trophimus was left sick by Paul at Miletus (2 Timothy 4:20, A.D. 64). Paul prescribed wine for Timothy's stomach ailment (1 Timothy 5:23, A.D. 62-63) instead of recommending that Timothy submit himself to someone who could heal. Paul himself had severe health problems (Galatians 4:13 and possibly 2 Corinthians 12:7) that he could not cure by miraculous means.[10]

James, writing around A.D. 50, exhorted believers who were seriously ill to call for the elders to anoint them and pray over them rather than to call for someone who had the ability to heal.

In the seven letters to the seven churches (Revelation 2:1–3:22, A.D. 95) no mention is made of miraculous sign gifts.

The Scriptures teach that miracles through human agents served a very specific purpose. That purpose focused on authenticating the prophets and apostles of God as certified messengers with a sure word from heaven. When the canon of Scripture closed with John's Revelation, there no longer existed a divine reason for performing miracles through men. Therefore, such kinds of miracles ceased according to the Scriptures.

Points to Remember

Miracles, according to the biblical definition, preclude the necessity of secondary means and are not limited by the laws of nature. They involve God's supernatural intervention. Jesus' miracles were never limited; they were never doubted; they were performed in public; they were abundant and instant. Anything that would claim the title "miracle" today should also possess those qualities. Unfortunately, the contemporary church tends to trivialize the idea of miracles by labeling anything out of the ordinary as "miraculous."

Also, miracles do not automatically produce spirituality in those who witness them. The Israelites, set free from Egypt by miracles, very quickly degenerated into idol worshipers (Exodus 32) even though the marvelous miracles of God were fresh in their minds. Elijah performed spectacular miracles from God, yet the believing remnant of Israel became so small (7000 people) that Elijah thought he was fighting the battle alone (1 Kings 19). After Jesus fed the 5000 and spoke of the miracle's significance, many of His disciples withdrew and would no longer walk with Him (John 6:66).

Just the opposite seems to happen today. While first-century witnesses to Christ's authentic miracles walked away from them and from Him, twentieth-century Christians seem to be curiously drawn to experiences that are not even worthy to be compared with Christ's miracles.

13

God Heals Today!

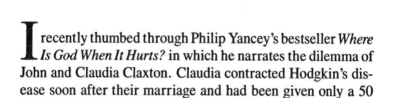

I recently thumbed through Philip Yancey's bestseller *Where Is God When It Hurts?* in which he narrates the dilemma of John and Claudia Claxton. Claudia contracted Hodgkin's disease soon after their marriage and had been given only a 50 percent chance to live.

Many of Claudia's friends stopped by the hospital to encourage her. Yancey shares an account of one such visit.

> Another lady had dropped by who had faithfully watched Oral Roberts, Kathryn Kuhlman, and "The 700 Club" over the years. She told Claudia that healing was the only escape. "Sickness is never God's will," she insisted. "The Bible says as much. The devil is at work, and God will wait until you can muster up enough faith to believe that you'll be healed. Remember, Claudia, faith can move mountains, and that includes Hodgkin's disease. Truly believe that you'll be healed and God will answer your prayers."[1]

Claudia tried to build up her courage and muster up her faith. But she grew weary in the process, and concluded that she would never have enough faith. She struggled with the question we want to answer right now: Does God heal today?

A Brainteaser

Answer this tantalizing question: Is there anything that God cannot do? Think about it! Jeremiah asserts of God, "Nothing is too difficult for Thee" (Jeremiah 32:17).

So perhaps our answer should be *no*. But then, what about these verses? Read Titus 1:2: "God . . . cannot lie," or 2 Timothy 2:13: "He [God] cannot deny himself."

What about Genesis 9:11? God can't flood the earth again. And James 1:13? God cannot be tempted. How can we resolve these apparent contradictions? The issue actually involves God's *nature and will* rather than His infinite power.

God cannot lie because that would contradict His true nature. He cannot be tempted because that would contradict His infallible Word. He cannot deny Himself because that would contradict His eternal existence. He cannot flood the world again because that would contradict His revealed promise.

Crucial Questions

Our brainteaser points out that God cannot and will not act contrary to His divine nature or revealed will. In those areas He is self-limited.

Now let's consider these questions:

- Can God heal?

- Can God heal miraculously?

- Can God heal miraculously through men?

The answer to all three of those questions is an overwhelming *yes*.

These next three questions are not so easily answered:

- Will God heal?

- Will God heal miraculously?

- Will God heal miraculously through men?

The answers to these questions do not involve God's *ability* but rather His *revealed practice*. Our answers will be formed not by God's unlimited capacity to work but by His conformity to His own will. At times God chooses to not do something that He has the power to do.

God's Perspective on the Physical

We need to consider God's view of the physical side of life, especially three distinct dimensions, if we are to find adequate answers to the above questions. When we see God's view of the physical from the vantage of the metaphysical, the moral, and the material dimensions, we will begin to understand why God has acted the way He has in history.

The Metaphysical Dimension. God's sovereign involvement in our physical being comes first.

> The LORD said to him, "Who has made man's mouth? Or who makes him dumb or deaf, or seeing or blind? Is it not I, the LORD? (Exodus 4:11).

> See now that I, I am He, and there is no god besides Me; it is I who put to death and give life. I have wounded, and it is I who heal; and there is no one who can deliver from My hand (Deuteronomy 32:39).

> The One forming light and creating darkness, causing well-being and creating calamity; I am the LORD who does all these (Isaiah 45:7).

What do those Scriptures teach? That God is ultimately the first cause of all life, all death, all sickness, and all health. He shoulders that responsibility. Many doctors acknowledge that. In difficult cases we often hear them say, "I have done my best. Now it is in God's hands."

Whenever I have taught on this topic over the years, I have presented some simple but thought-provoking questions to my audiences:

- Have you ever been sick?
- Did you recover from your illness?
- Have you been divinely healed?

If you have ever been sick, and if you have recovered, then you have in one sense been divinely healed. To not acknowledge this fact ignores God's everyday, providential involvement in our life. Don't ever let anyone rob you of the joy that comes from knowing that God was involved in your physical well-being. God's divine involvement in your recovery from sickness must not be denied or minimized. The cooperation of your bodily processes and medical treatment demonstrates God's creative and providential genius.

The Moral Dimension. Sin entered the human race as a result of Adam and Eve's fall from sinlessness (Genesis 3:1-19). Sin will continue as an inherent trait of everyone in the human race until God removes the curse (Revelation 22:3).

> Therefore, just as through one man sin entered into the world, and death through sin, and so death spread to all men, because all sinned (Romans 5:12).

> When lust has conceived, it gives birth to sin; and when sin is accomplished, it brings forth death (James 1:15).

After the fall of Adam and Eve, God expressed His love toward mankind through Christ. By God's mercy sinners did not receive the death they deserved. To satisfy God's justice, Christ took upon Himself the penalty for our sins. Through God's grace we received what we do not deserve—eternal life in Jesus Christ.

But God's love does not negate the *consequences* of sin, two of which are sickness and death. Sin explains the moral basis for all sickness: As long as sin exists in the world, so will sickness.

The Material Dimension. Do you have one or more of the following problems?

Baldness	Wrinkles
Dandruff	False teeth
Nearsightedness	Fatigue
Sagging muscles	Gray hair

Many more evidences (such as accidents, germs, and genetic defects) testify to sin's physical effects on our lives. The universal evidence causes us to conclude that sin has afflicted everyone. Because all have sinned, all will die (Psalm 103:10; Ecclesiastes 7:20).

> It is appointed for men to die once, and after this comes judgment (Hebrews 9:27).

It is simply not true that God wills every Christian to be perfectly healthy. We saw earlier that Old and New Testament saints were sick and that God at times even afflicts people with illness and death.

Unless we see God as metaphysically sovereign and sin as the moral cause of sickness, we will not fully understand the decaying world around us. When God *does* heal, He does so because of His grace, not because of our goodness.

What About Today?

Let's come back to our three questions about God's will in regard to physical health. Will God heal today? Yes! We know that He will because of His promise revealed in James 5:15: "The prayer offered in faith will restore the one who is sick, and the Lord will raise him up, and if he has committed sins, they will be forgiven him."

Will God heal miraculously these days? Yes! That does not violate His nature or His will.

Will God heal miraculously through men these days? No! Such an approach does not serve God's revealed purposes as presented in Acts 2:22 and Hebrews 2:1-4.

Going back to Claudia Claxton, whom we met at the beginning of this chapter: Did God allow her to die in the midst of her misery? He could have, but He didn't. Instead, He chose to make her the object of divine healing. After receiving a series of cobalt treatments, her cancer was in remission.[2] God healed providentially through medical technology.

How Much Focus on Healing?

Although Reuben Archer Torrey ministered in an earlier era, his thoughts are perfectly applicable to our day, so I have included his thoughts here.

> The main question is: Does God heal in answer to prayer today? Does He really heal people who are beyond the skill of the physician and beyond all human help? Does He work miracles today? To all these questions I unhesitatingly reply, He does. Not only does the Bible teach it, but experience demonstrates it. . . .
>
> Why, then, do I not go into the business of healing the sick? I am confident that I could soon draw tens of thousands to hear me, in the hope of obtaining physical health or of seeing some new wonder. Why do I not do it? Two reasons: First, it is not Scriptural, and that of itself would be decisive; Secondly, I have far more important business to do. I would rather be used to save one lost soul than to heal a thousand sick bodies.[3]

Authentic Healings

James Randi has listed the criteria which his rational mind demands in order to validate a genuine healing miracle of God. They include:

1. The disease must not be normally self-terminating.

2. The recovery must be complete.

3. The recovery must take place in the absence of any medical treatment that might normally be expected to affect the disease.

4. There must be adequate medical opinion that the disease was present before the application of whatever means were used to bring about the miracle.

5. There must be adequate medical opinion that the disease is not present after the application of whatever means were used to bring about the miracle.[4]

Randi might be surprised, but the Bible sets an even higher standard for miraculous healing.

1. The healing must be instantaneous.

2. The healing must be of a disease that neither the medical community nor the human body can heal, such as AIDS—either instantly or absolutely.

3. The healing must be total.

4. The healing must be completely convincing, even to skeptics.

5. The healing must be done in public with no elaborate services involved.

6. The healing must be of an organic disease.

These criteria marked God's healing power through Christ and the apostles.

Because fraud and deception run rampant in our day, we need to ask hard questions of those who claim to heal. No one does it better than John MacArthur.

> Since no Charismatic healer (or personality who is letting the Holy Spirit do it) can come up with consistently verified cases of healing organic disease instantly, totally, by word or touch...
>
> Since no Charismatic healer heals everybody (hundreds go away from their services as sick or as crippled as when they came)...
>
> Since no Charismatic healer raises the dead...
>
> Since the Bible is complete and revelation has ceased and no more miracle signs are needed...
>
> Since the Word of God needs no confirmation outside of itself and is sufficient to show the way of salvation to man...
>
> Since Charismatic "healings" are based on questionable theology of the atonement and salvation...
>
> Since Charismatic writers and teachers appear to disallow God His own purpose in having some people stay sick...
>
> Since Charismatic healers seem to need their own closed environment...
>
> Since the evidence they bring forth to prove these healings is often weak, unsupported, and overexaggerated...
>
> Since Charismatics are not known for going into hospitals to heal (where there is plenty of faith on the part of many)...
>
> Since they cannot heal all who come to them...
>
> Since many instances of healings by Charismatics can be explained in many ways other than God's unquestioned supernatural intervention...
>
> Since Charismatics get sick and die like everyone else...
>
> Since all this confusion and contradiction surrounds

what "is happening," let me ask the return question, "How do *you* explain it?" Certainly not as the biblical gift of healing![5]

What About Organic Disease?

Organic disease looms as the Achilles' heel of all who claim that God heals today through men in the same way that He healed through the prophets, Christ, and the apostles. Most, if not all, of the diseases Jesus healed fell into the organic category. Therefore, if God is healing through men now as He did in the past, then we would expect to see the same quality and quantity of organic diseases healed today. However, at best we see some functional problems relieved and occasionally healed, but no real organic healing.

What are organic and functional diseases? Dr. William Nolen defines a functional disease as one that causes the dysfunction of an organ.[6] The organ itself is sound, but for some reason it does not work properly. In contrast, an organic disease involves damage or disease to an organ—such as a diseased heart, broken bones, amputated limbs, or congenital deformities.[7]

Dr. Nolen adds two notes in his description of these types of diseases. First, some organic diseases, such as a cold or a minor sprain, are self-limiting in that the body has the capacity to be restored without other help.[8] Second, some diseases have both functional and organic characteristics.[9] In this case it is possible to heal the functional aspect and bring great relief, yet leave the organic side unrestored.

When Jesus healed, He healed organic diseases. He healed blindness, an amputated ear, and congenital defects. John Wimber, a contemporary healing advocate, honestly notes that not once does Scripture mention a functional disease healed by Jesus.[10] But, having acknowledged this, Wimber still doesn't seem to get the point that the healings he and every other healer are involved with don't begin to match those of Jesus.

In a Nutshell

The thrust of our discussion together is not to determine whether God can or cannot heal. He can and He does!

Our examination of the Scriptures has demonstrated that there is no biblical basis for a ministry of miraculous healing *directly through a human healer* today. That ceased with the apostolic age. Alleged contemporary faith-healing ministries fall embarrassingly short of the biblical pattern in time, scope, and intensity.

On the other hand, God does at times act in such a way that the only adequate explanation for physical healing is direct intervention on His part. Healing by God's direct intervention is not always instantaneous nor always complete. Our Lord's unmistakable touch is not brought about by any demand, gimmick, method, or plea from a would-be healer. It is God's response to the earnest prayer of a believer that heals a child of the King for our Lord's glory.

Part 4

A Christian's Response to Sickness

14

What About Faith, Prayer, and Doctors?

O ne Monday morning I received a call at my church office from a woman who joyfully reported, "I've just tossed my prescriptions in the trash and claimed my healing by faith!"

I congratulated that dear woman for wanting to place her faith in God, then lovingly urged her to retrieve the medicine and to continue following the doctor's orders. We then discussed the right relationship between faith, prayer, and doctors.

During that conversation, my Monday-morning caller raised some questions that I want to share with you in the next few pages. Let's begin by examining faith.

What Is Faith?

We find faith's *definition* in Hebrews 11:1: "Faith is the assurance of things hoped for, the conviction of things not seen." The fourth-century church father Augustine put it simply: "What is faith, unless it is to believe what you cannot see?"

According to Romans 10:17, faith is *derived* from God's Word. It starts with Scripture, which has the capacity to generate faith in the redeemed listener.

Faith also has its *demand*—to believe that God is, and to believe that He is a rewarder of those who seek Him (Hebrews 11:6). Without faith it is impossible to please God.

Paul highlights faith's *design* in 2 Corinthians 5:7: "We walk by faith, not by sight." When the lights are out and the fog has rolled in, we are to navigate through life on instrument control. The Bible is our compass, and we are to follow it, by faith, wherever it guides us.

Hebrews 4:2 presents the *dynamic* of faith. The Word of God must not only be heard but also united with faith for it to be profitable.

The *duty* of faith is to live by it. "For in it the righteousness of God is revealed from faith to faith; as it is written, 'But the righteous man shall live by faith'" (Romans 1:17). Faith should distinguish our lives.

Simply put, faith willingly takes the hand of God's Word and allows it to lead us through life—the dark and complicated or the simple and easy. Faith takes God at His Word and quietly obeys. To do less is to be of little faith. To go beyond is presumptuous at best and blasphemous at worst.

How Is Faith Measured?

Is faith measured by the yard or the meter? By the gallon or the liter? Though that might sound absurd, it is important to know how God measures faith. When someone says, "Lord, give me more faith," how much is more? How much faith is enough?

The Scriptures never give a unit of measurement for faith. Rather, faith is merely described. In Matthew 8:10, notice how our Lord commends a centurion's faith: "When Jesus heard this, He marveled, and said to those who were following, 'Truly I say to you, I have not found such great faith with anyone in Israel.'" Jesus described the man's faith as "great."

He had the same reaction to the Canaanite woman in Matthew 15:28: "O woman, your faith is great."

How then did Christ rebuke faithlessness? He most often responded, "O men of little faith" (Matthew 6:30; *see also* 8:26; 14:31; 16:8). In Matthew 17:19-20 the disciples had been unsuccessful in their attempt to exorcise a demon, so they asked Jesus the reason. He rebuked them for the "littleness of [their] faith" and went on to say, "If you have faith as a mustard seed . . . nothing shall be impossible to you."

What did Christ mean? Simply that it is not the size of faith that is crucial (the mustard seed was the smallest garden-variety seed in Palestine [Matthew 13:32]), but rather where and under what conditions the seed is planted. If God is the sole object of our faith, then all things are possible to us because all things are possible for God, in whom faith's seed is planted (Matthew 17:20; Mark 9:23; Luke 18:27). *God's will,* however, is the controlling factor of what He will do for us and through us.

The only requirements for our faith are 1) that it not depend on sight (2 Corinthians 5:7); 2) that it be without doubting (James 1:5-8); 3) that it believes God can do all things (Matthew 19:26); and 4) that it be satisfied to let God's will prevail (1 John 5:14).

On occasion, personal faith was not even necessary for healing. Lazarus, Jairus' daughter, and the widow's son were incapable of displaying faith, yet they were raised from the dead.

At times Christ healed when faith was displayed by someone other than the afflicted person. So those who claim that a person remains unhealed due to his own lack of faith have missed God's mark of truth. Occasionally Jesus would commend the faith of the afflicted, but almost never was faith a prominent or necessary feature of Christ's healing ministry.

The book of Acts and all of the epistles correspond to the Gospels' record in that faith was not required for healing. Note James 5:15, where the faith of the elders is demanded, not the faith of the afflicted.

At times in Acts, the faith of the afflicted was commended, as in the Gospels (Acts 3:16; 14:8-10). But more often a personal faith was not required of the afflicted. Also, faith is not mentioned as a requirement for healing in the Old Testament. Naaman, the reluctant Syrian, serves as a classic example (2 Kings 5:1-14).

Now consider this related question: How much faith is required for a person to be saved? If the sick person will exercise the same faith that he had for salvation and trust God to work according to His will regardless of the outcome, then he will be a person of faith.

It is not *the amount of faith* but rather *the Person in whom that faith fully rests* that defines "great faith." Nowhere in the Scriptures do we find anyone admonished to measure his faith. That would be impossible. A person either believes or does not believe. There is no middle road. We must believe that God does all things well—for our good and, more importantly, for His glory.

Since prayer represents the natural response of faith in our heavenly Father, let's now turn our attention to prayer.

How Should I Pray?

Prayer follows a basic pattern.[1] First there is *admission*—"I can't do it myself."

> Abide in Me, and I in you. As the branch cannot bear fruit of itself, unless it abides in the vine, so neither can you, unless you abide in Me. I am the vine, you are the branches; he who abides in Me, and I in him, he bears much fruit; for apart from Me you can do nothing (John 15:4-5).

Fruitful prayer always begins by acknowledging that apart from Jesus Christ we are, in God's mind, helpless creatures.

The sooner we acknowledge that humbling truth, the sooner we will know God's intentions for us.

Next comes *submission*. We are to submit our desires before our sovereign Savior.

When Jesus taught the disciples to pray He said, "Thy will be done, on earth as it is in heaven" (Matthew 6:10). When He agonized in Gethsemane's garden His words were, "Yet not as I will, but as Thou wilt" (Matthew 26:39). Our prayers should be like the Savior's: "Lord, let my will always be brought into submission to Yours."

That leads to the third stage—*transmission*. Jesus modeled the pattern when He prayed, "Our Father who art in heaven" (Matthew 6:9). Because we often do not know how to pray, God's Spirit intercepts our petition and intercedes on our behalf (Romans 8:26). We can know with confidence that God is able to do "exceeding abundantly beyond all that we ask" (Ephesians 3:20).

Meditate on this aspect of God's omnipotent nature: We can pray as high or as far as our human capacities allow us, and still we will not have begun to equal the power of God. That is our heavenly hope when we send our deepest needs before the gracious throne of our Father (Hebrews 4:16).

The fourth step is often the hardest—waiting on God. The *intermission* period, from the time we ask until the time God answers, can sometimes seem like forever. From time to time we want to scream out, "Lord, please hurry; I can't wait any longer!" Yet the parable about the unrighteous judge and the needy widow (Luke 18:1-8) shows us that we should continue to pray and not lose heart if God's answer is not immediate.

Finally comes God's response. I believe God always answers prayer. He can do it either through *permission* or *revision*. That is, He can respond "Yes" or "Another way."

At times He *delivers* as we pray. For example, Peter was miraculously freed from his Roman chains and guards while the Jerusalem church prayed (Acts 12:5-17). At other times God *detours*, such as He did with Christ. Instead of allowing Christ to ascend to heaven before Calvary, He waited until after His Son's work on the cross (Mark 14:36). Christ ultimately reached His destination, but by an alternative time route.

God also *delays*. Zacharias and Elizabeth had prayed for a son over the decades of their married life, but not until they were beyond childbearing age did God answer (Luke 1:13).

God also can say, "No."

> If I regard wickedness in my heart, the Lord will not hear (Psalm 66:18).

> When you spread out your hands in prayer, I will hide My eyes from you; yes, even though you multiply prayers, I will not listen. Your hands are covered with blood (Isaiah 1:15).

Scripture tells us that "we do not know how to pray as we should" (Romans 8:26). God knows what is best, and sometimes that includes a negative response. So do not be discouraged or give up when God denies your petition. God does, at times, say no to an obedient, submissive Christian simply because the prayer request is not within His will (*see* 1 John 5:14-15).

The next time you pray for healing (or anything else, for that matter), I encourage you to follow these biblically outlined steps.

Biblical Prayers of Faith

The psalmists frequently appealed to God for relief, restoration, and healing. Often they prayed to be removed from the stress of living righteously among unrighteous people from whom they faced opposition and persecution. And they always recognized the possible direct or indirect consequence of their own sins.

These petitions for help are filled with sincerity, faith, and hope. They don't resemble any kind of "formula prayers," nor do they presume on God. Rather, they exemplify the kind of prayer that a spiritual child should pour out to the heavenly Father in times of distress. They focus more on the spiritual side of restoration than the physical (Psalm 147:3; *see also* Psalm 6:1-3; 31:9-10; 38:3-4,21-22; 41:1-4).

Keys to Fruitful Prayer

Someone once remarked, "When you get caught on water in the middle of a raging storm, row for shore as though your safety depended on you, while praying all along as though it all depended on God." Here's the point: Life always involves the unexplainable combination of God's sovereignty and man's responsibility. Of the two, God will always be the determining factor.

The same is true of prayer. God knows our needs ahead of time (Matthew 6:8). He is able to provide "exceeding abundantly beyond all that we ask or think" (Ephesians 3:20). But Christians are still commanded by Scripture to pray—without ceasing (1 Thessalonians 5:17).

These next thoughts on prayer relate specifically to our responsibility in prayer. They focus primarily on who we are in the sight of God based on what we do in the presence of other people. Check yourself and see if you are praying as God would want you to.

1. Praying for the right reason—for God's pleasure.

What is the source of quarrels and conflicts among you? Is not the source your pleasures that wage war in your members? You lust and do not have; so you commit murder. And you are envious and cannot obtain; so you fight and quarrel. You do not have because you do not ask. You ask and do not receive, because you ask with wrong motives, so that you may spend it on your pleasures (James 4:1-3).

2. Praying in the right relationship—with love.

> You husbands likewise, live with your wives in an understanding way, as with a weaker vessel, since she is a woman; and grant her honor as a fellow heir of the grace of life, so that your prayers may not be hindered (1 Peter 3:7).

3. Praying with the right rest—in faith.

> If any of you lacks wisdom, let him ask of God, who gives to all men generously and without reproach, and it will be given to him. But let him ask in faith without any doubting, for the one who doubts is like the surf of the sea driven and tossed by the wind. For let not that man expect that he will receive anything from the Lord, being a double-minded man, unstable in all his ways (James 1:5-8).

4. Praying with the right responses—in obedience to God.

> Whatever we ask we receive from Him, because we keep His commandments and do the things that are pleasing in His sight (1 John 3:22).

5. Praying in the right realm—according to God's will.

> This is the confidence which we have before Him, that, if we ask anything according to His will, He hears us. And if we know that He hears us in whatever we ask, we know that we have the requests which we have asked from Him (1 John 5:14-15).

6. Praying with the right restraint—patiently at all times.

> Now He was telling them a parable to show that at all times they ought to pray and not to lose heart (Luke 18:1).

If we live out all of these principles in our prayers, we will be delighting ourselves in God. When we do that, He promises to give us the desires of our heart (Psalm 37:4).

But what if God does not answer immediately or in the way we requested? First, remember that God's delay is not necessarily God's denial. Second, it is possible that we have prayed outside God's will and that He sovereignly prevailed in the circumstances. But be assured that whatever God does will always be right (Psalms 19:8; 119:128).

What About Doctors and Medicine?

Some people claim that the medical profession and medicine are a contradiction to prayer and faith for a Christian. The mistaken notion of the woman who phoned me that Monday morning came from this kind of reasoning. John R. Rice made this keen observation.

> God can save a sinner without the use of any human aid, but certainly He does not usually do so. If God can use a man, with his consecrated wisdom and love and skill in winning a soul, why should He not use a doctor, a pharmacist, or a nurse with their consecrated skill in healing the sick?[2]

Those who would dissuade Christians from a supposed "faithless" use of medicine often appeal to one Old Testament passage. However, Asa (2 Chronicles 16:11-14) was rebuked not for merely going to a doctor, but because he disobeyed God by seeking a godless pagan physician rather than the divinely appointed Levitical priests (Leviticus 13). True to his previous pattern, Asa depended on man, not God, to deliver him.

As we have already noted, Paul told Timothy to take wine (1 Timothy 5:23). He traveled extensively with Luke, the beloved physician (Colossians 4:14). Jesus recognized doctors and medicine as legitimate agents (Matthew 9:12; Luke 10:30-37).

In fact, there is not one verse of Scripture that hints at the idea that believers should not use doctors and medicine.[3]

The strongest biblical evidence that God intended believers to use medical means resides in the health aspects of the Mosaic legislation. Consider these laws:

- sanitation (Exodus 29:14; Deuteronomy 23:12-14)

- sterilization (Leviticus 11:32,39-40; Numbers 19:11; 31:21-24)

- quarantine (Leviticus 13:1–14:57; Numbers 5:2-4)

- hygiene and diet (Leviticus 11:1-47)

Of those who condemn medicine, who would stop washing with soap, stop brushing his teeth, stop eating, or stop exercising? All of these contribute to good health. Loraine Boettner observes:

> We have no more reason to believe that our sicknesses and diseases will be cured without means than we have to believe that if we fail to plow and plant we will nevertheless be given food. . . . Surely faith-feeding is quite as rational as faith-healing. And if diseases are to be cured by faith, then why may not death, which is simply the result of disease or injury, also be eliminated in the same way?[4]

Medical practitioners, in their training, participate in the inexhaustible study of God's created processes. They make God's creative genius available for the physical healing of the human race through sound medical practice. Hospitals, the latest in medical technology, and sophisticated pharmaceuticals involve God's provision to restore a sick person to health.

However, where doctors and medicine can no longer help, faith and prayer continue. When we are sick, doctors work as though our health depended totally on them, while at the same time Christians pray with faith as though their recovery rested totally in the sovereign hands of God.

Trusting Divine Wisdom

Let's take one more look at health from a biblical perspective. God's wisdom in Proverbs provides us with the basics on both the preventive and the recuperative sides of health.

In general, the fear of God and obedience to the Word of God provide a setting where the best of health can be experienced.

> Do not be wise in your own eyes;
> Fear the LORD and turn away from evil.
> It will be healing to your body,
> And refreshment to your bones
> (Proverbs 3:7-8).

> My son, give attention to my words;
> Incline your ear to my sayings.
> Do not let them depart from your sight;
> Keep them in the midst of your heart.
> For they are life to those who find them,
> And health to all their whole body
> (Proverbs 4:20-22).

The book of Proverbs also looks at the emotional, volitional, and spiritual factors of health. These are not intended to be cure-alls; rather, they express truisms about health.

> Hope deferred makes the heart sick,
> But desire fulfilled is a tree of life
> (Proverbs 13:12).

> A tranquil heart is life to the body,
> But passion is rottenness to the bones
> (Proverbs 14:30; *see also* 15:13).

A soothing tongue is a tree of life,
But perversion in it crushes the spirit
(Proverbs 15:4; *see also* 16:24).

Bright eyes gladden the heart;
Good news puts fat on the bones
(Proverbs 15:30).

A joyful heart is good medicine,
But a broken spirit dries up the bones
(Proverbs 17:22; *see also* 18:14).

These wise thoughts, if taken seriously and lived out consistently, can have a major impact on our well-being. That way, God has the last word on health and healing.

15

Joni Eareckson Tada on Sickness

Most people in America know the story of Joni Eareckson Tada and have become acquainted with her through her books, paintings, music, and speaking. Twenty-five years ago, Joni, a young teenager, dove into shallow water and broke her neck. The accident left her a quadriplegic. Since then God has used her tremendously in ministry to the disabled.

But the vast majority of the public doesn't see the "day-by-day" Joni. Most people do not understand her struggle to do the ordinary things of life, such as bathing or eating. They only see her as a superstar.

I visited Joni at her modest Woodland Hills home overlooking the San Fernando Valley in Southern California. Joni was in bed because of pressure sores, but she very graciously welcomed me to spend an afternoon with her. I want to share our conversation with you.

DICK: Do you believe the faith-healing movement and its message are misleading?

JONI: I recently flew to a speaking engagement in Saint Louis, and during the flight I got into a conversation with a young stewardess who just had the love of Jesus written all over her face. She was one of the most bubbly, effervescent persons I've ever met. She was obviously a new Christian in love with the Lord. She told me, "Joni, I just could not serve a God who did not want everybody healed—a God whose will it was not to heal everybody."

My comment to her was, "Well, obviously, just from a casual observation of our world, we can see that it is not God's will that everyone be healed, because not everyone is healed. Man cannot resist God's will, and if it was God's purpose and design and will that all men be healed, nothing could stop that. We would see evidences of it in the world around us, but we don't. So it's clearly not God's will that everybody be healed."

Her next comment to me was something to the effect of, "Well, doesn't our faith have anything to do with it?" I guess that's one thing that would be good for us to discuss, because people, aside from having an incorrect view of God's kingdom and an incorrect hermeneutic, will tend to pull out certain portions of Scripture, little verses here and there that speak of faith, and base a whole theology around that faith.

I see faith as merely a vehicle through which God's grace works. Others, of the persuasion of that stewardess, perhaps see faith as the club that we hold over God's head, or the string we have to pull for God to work. In my view that does not seem to be faith; it seems to be presumption. It almost makes God a puppet.

DICK: Have you ever gone to a faith-healing service?

JONI: Frankly, I went to a couple of Kathryn Kuhlman's meetings. I think the idea is wrong in a very subtle way in that it fosters the mentality that the stewardess had—that God's purpose in redeeming mankind is primarily to make us happy, healthy, and our lives free from trouble. Pursuing those kinds of avenues of grasping at straws and pulling levers to manipulate God or twisting His arm or trimming Him down to our size—those are very desperate attempts to get our wants met and our prayers answered the way we think we ought to have them answered. His purpose in redeeming us is to conform us to Christ's image, and we often forget that.

DICK: When you went, did you get in the healing line?

JONI: Yes. As I recall, it was at the Hilton in Washington. It was packed, and I was way in the back. There were chairs all around and none of us could move. We were all wedged up against one another.

There were people with chairs, people with walkers, people with crutches, just like myself. You must understand, Dick, that I got to the point where I was inventing sins to confess. I wanted to make sure that everything was totally up-front with God. Way down deep I felt a little foolish being there, but I felt it was necessary for me to be foolish in front of God, in front of all those people. I thought it was necessary for me to prostrate myself and make myself totally and openly vulnerable, not only before Him but before those people. And I had others praying for me as I went to that meeting.

I had been anointed with oil already. Countless numbers of people had laid hands on me. I thought, *That's really good because that means all the proper stuff is being done.* All that stuff you think is supposed to happen—pastors laying hands on you, anointing with oil, prayers, and sins that I confessed. I did everything. And I went to Kathryn's meeting believing that God had been paving the way and preparing the scene and that I was going to be able to wheel right onto the platform and that would truly be it.

But nothing happened. I could not understand for the longest time why my hands and my legs were not getting the message my mind was telling them. I remember looking at my appendages as though they were separate from who I was and what I thought. My heart and mind said, "You're healed, body!"

I wanted to make sure that I believed with a capital *B*.

DICK: Had you been programmed by reading some of the faith-healing literature?

JONI: Yes. It was a matter of *my* faith—working that faith, getting it nice and exercised and in tip-top condition. I really believed! And yet my hands and feet did not respond to what I knew was true. Then I began to see that either God was playing some kind of monstrous, cruel joke on me, that I was the brunt of some divine comedy, or that my view of Scripture was wrong.

I could not believe that God was playing a joke on me. I had seen God work in other ways in my life and I believed the Scriptures. I just knew that this was not part of His nature and character; He is not the God of confusion or cruel tricks. So I resolved that the problem must be with me, but I knew it wasn't my faith, since I believed so much. I had called people and told them, "Watch for me on your doorstep tomorrow. I'm going to be bounding up your sidewalk, running." I really left myself open. I believed, so I knew that the fault could not lie with my faith. It had to lie with my wrong view of Scripture. That's when I began to look all the way back to the Garden of Eden, at the very root of suffering, disease, illness, injury, and death. I saw that sickness began with sin and, as I recounted in *A Step Further*, I very slowly and meticulously began to piece together God's redemptive flow of history throughout the Bible until I began to see it all fit together. When I got to the New Testament, I suddenly began to understand the miracles, the healing, and all the excitement when Jesus was down here on earth.

It made great sense that suffering was supposed to be part of the fabric and fiber of God's redeeming mankind. And even after salvation, suffering was supposed to fit into the fabric and fiber of the redemptive story. When Jesus came to deal with sin and sin's results, He put the process into motion and began to reverse the effects of sin and all of its results. But in doing so He was only laying the foundation. The world is still fallen; it still has people dying; it still has natural catastrophes and people getting sick, and will until He comes back.

It helped me so much to read through the Old Testament. As I read through all of those promises under the Old Covenant—

how the eyes of the blind were opened, the ears of the deaf were unstopped, and the anointed of the Lord obtained joy and gladness—I slowly began to see that when Jesus came, that was just the beginning. It really wasn't the entire picture. As we know, He's coming back, not as a humble servant but as reigning King. He will complete the kingdom and usher in all those glorious promises.

I guess that's why I don't mind being in a wheelchair and putting up with suffering. If it means more people being granted entrance to the kingdom of God, more folks being a part of His family, it all has meaning. To suffer without a reason is to suffer for nothing. That would be painful.

DICK: Let's come back to the stewardess. How did your conversation with her turn out?

JONI: The conversation I had with that stewardess was disturbing because it was truly, in capsule form, what is occurring in churches all over the country. When I got off the plane at the airport, I was greeted by my sponsors. They had brought with them a young woman who had broken her neck in an automobile accident a year before. She was a quadriplegic much like myself. She had come to the point where she could trust God with it and accept it.

But someone had told her that it was God's will for her to be healed. Well, she had believed and believed and worked hard and followed all those scriptural injunctions and had done everything that she thought was necessary—and yet she was not healed. That just catapulted her into depression; it was hurting her view of God.

In her thinking, He was becoming an ogre up there who was playing monstrous jokes on people down here. And then she was told, "Now wait a minute; your depression isn't showing a life of faith. And in fact, young woman, your depression is nothing more than sheer sin." Oh, it was cruel, awfully cruel!

Her comment to that person was, "Well, look at Joni. She loves the Lord and has a close walk with Christ, yet the Lord has not chosen to heal her."

She was told, "Well, Joni has resigned herself never to be healed. That's why Joni's not healed."

She was just so anxious to hear it from the horse's mouth. Did I ever get depressed? Did I believe it was God's will? Have I resigned myself to never being on my feet?

Fresh from that other conversation with the stewardess, my first statement to her was, "No, I have not resigned myself never to be healed." Some people on one end of the spectrum say that God never miraculously heals. They almost put God's actions in a box. But on the other end of the spectrum certain people say that God wants everybody healed. They too try to put God in a box. So I told her, "No, I have never resigned myself. I've opened all those doors. I've left them open. But it's God's responsibility; it's no longer mine. If I have a proper view of Scripture and a high view of God, then it's at His discretion."

But I do believe, as I told her, that healing is the exception to the rule—the rule being that God will not always miraculously heal in this day and age any more than He will miraculously raise people from the dead or walk on water. Those things just aren't occurring.

I told her that I often do get depressed. For instance, I'm in bed right now with a couple of stubborn little pressure sores. I've been down in bed for a number of months. It's been very discouraging and at times depressing. I've had people say that they're praying for my healing.

The young woman asked me with a curious look on her face, "Well, don't you think that's sin?"

I said, "If I allowed these emotions to alter my view of God, that would be sin. But it is not sin in that my view of God has not changed."

However, I am human. He knows my frame and remembers that I am but dust. He's made me a being with real tears. Emotionally, I'm not going to be real happy about lying in bed for three months, but that has not altered my view of God. The depression that I am experiencing is simply indigenous to what it means to be human. Some depression is just a part of what it means to face the everyday bumps and bruises of being human, whether you are a believer or an unbeliever. However, despair for the Christian is not necessary because we have hope—the hope of Christ setting up a new order of things.

DICK: That's a good distinction between *depression*, a part of our humanness, and *despair*, which should never be a part of our redemptive relationship with Christ.

JONI: It's so wonderful. I did despair when I was first injured—I just didn't know how to fit it all together. I had no idea that God was there; that He cared; that He was in control and that I didn't have to worry; that it was not an accident; that He had a planned purpose and had resurrection power to give me. I just didn't know all that. So in the early months of my disability, yes, I did despair. I thought there was no hope. But Christians should never have to despair, although they might get depressed.

DICK: Have you ever analyzed the stages of your thinking from the time you were a teen and first injured to the point where you are now? Have you noticed any marked stages that you've gone through?

JONI: Well, I think I followed the classic example of anybody who comes to the point of finally accepting his or her disabilities. There are five steps: the classic stages of shock, anger, denial, bargaining, and acceptance.

At first, yes—I was shocked and totally disbelieving. It's curious, Dick. I saw my body paralyzed, but it never clicked that this is the way it would always be. It wasn't that I refused to think about it; something simply was not connecting. It never clicked because it was all a shock. And then came anger: "God, how could You allow something like this to happen to me?"

Again, that's another matter that I have always been curious about—why we lay the blame on God. What is it about Him? It must be inherent in our rebellious natures that we should lay the blame on Him. We never really put the blame on man's initial rebellion; we throw the responsibility on God, not Satan. True to our human nature, such is the nature of the beast. It seems as if we can't accept responsibility for anything.

Then I went through denial: "This is not the way it should be. God, I just know that You're going to get me up on my feet." After that I went through the bargaining routine; then I finally came to the point where I accepted my disability. But it was not acceptance in the sense of hopeless resignation—"I guess this is the best that can be done with it, so I'll just accept it and go on"—a sense of self-pitying martyrdom. I'm talking about acceptance where you embrace what God has given you and take it with thanksgiving. I think that's genuine acceptance, and that only a Christian can express it.

I think many unbelievers accept suffering with a kind of a martyr complex or stoic resignation. Only Christians can embrace suffering with thanksgiving, knowing that they are receiving from the hand of God something that is not only for His glory but for their own good.

Back to my visit with the young quadriplegic. We chatted a bit about the kingdom of God. Whenever someone asks me about healing today, I'll first start talking about the kingdom and why Christ came and what those miracles were all about. I don't think you can give the answers to the questions until you give the framework, the structure in which you can couch your answers. We also talked about depression a bit more before I went to my hotel room.

The next morning I got up to speak at a ladies' luncheon. There were 1,000 women there, and I talked about the nature and character of God and our view of Him in the middle of our pain and problems. I prefaced my talk with the fact that I was depressed. And I was. This was about a week-and-a-half ago and, as I told you, I was really struggling with being in bed and feeling ugly and adding a few pounds, because when I get down, I eat.

I was describing this to the women because I wanted them

to understand that this was not some carefully constructed view of Scripture that I pieced together years ago.

After I spoke I went back to the hotel room to lie down, because I had to get off my bedsore. Then the phone rang. It was a woman who wanted to talk with me. I put the phone to my ear and she began by saying, "Joni, I have a word of knowledge for you from the Lord." She went on as people will often do when they say words of knowledge—"My daughter... "—as if God were actually speaking. She went on to say, "My daughter, your sin is keeping you from Me and healing. This depression that you have is blocking My fellowship with you."

I really had to bite my tongue at the end of her "word of knowledge." I simply said, "Thank you for calling and sharing your opinion." I afterward thought about how cruel and unfair that lady was. She used a convenient spiritual loophole to express her *opinion*. If you want to give me your opinion, call it your opinion. I didn't say that to her, but I was really boiling. Again, it goes right back to the stewardess and the girl in the wheelchair. When we trim God down to our size, somewhere along the line we've lost the high view of God that the men and women of the Bible had. We fit Him into our convenient box.

DICK: Oftentimes people look at you and imagine that you live a happy-go-lucky, normal life at home. How do you handle daily problems?

JONI: I suppose the problem that I can best talk about right now is this problem of having to be in bed with this bedsore, feeling that my world doesn't go beyond that back fence, sensing that my prayers don't go past the ceiling, or looking into a mirror—dirty hair and no makeup and sheets that smell of alcohol and antiseptic. To me it's a lesson in learning to effectively appropriate God's Word all over again.

I learned long ago that the key to going forward in my Christian walk is to systematically and intelligently approach God's Word, then break it down into some understandable portions speaking, let's say, of depression or trials or grace, and memorize them.

That still holds true today. I have to sidestep the feelings of my limitations, the sensations of my prayers bouncing off the ceiling, the impulses, the emotions, and the vacillation. I purpose in my mind, which I suppose is an act of faith, not to listen to my feelings, but instead to listen to the Word of God. So it's actually a volitional act; it's an intention of the will that I'm not going to let those feelings and emotions rip my faith apart and alter my view of God.

I'm going to accept them for what they are—emotions and feelings—and then continue on the straight line of listening to the Word of God. The Word of God tells me that all things fit together in a pattern for good. It doesn't say all things are good; it says all things *fit together* for good. I'm going to listen to the Word of God when it says to welcome trials as friends and to give thanks in everything. I think it's a systematic approach to His Word that makes the difference.

DICK: Don't people who are sick often ask and need to know why they are sick and what God's reasons are for their sickness?

JONI: Yes, or they ask, "Why am I not healed?" It's important to answer that question if we, the church, are going to minister to people with severe disabilities or spend time with them in discipleship or whatever.

Sometimes people will pray for healing for an aunt who is terminally ill or a husband who is dying of cancer. They claim that they just *know* God is going to raise up that individual. Then when that person dies, they rejoice because he or she has experienced what they call the epitome of real healing. That's clearly a loophole—a spiritual loophole—a very convenient out.

DICK: But there is an element of truth to it. That's what is so deceiving, isn't it?

JONI: Yes, because that is not what those people really mean. They are praying that this or that person be healed. In fact, they would not even want to think—for fear of showing lack of faith—that there might be a possibility that real healing means death.

DICK: In light of your experience and all the people you correspond with, what are the most important questions that really need to be answered for people who find themselves sick or suffering, or in circumstances that they will never be able to change?

JONI: I think the one that's hounding most people is, What responsibility does God have—how could God, a good God, allow suffering and evil in this world? And second, How much of my potential healing is up to me? Where does my faith fit into it? What is God's involvement?

We sort of covered the first; maybe we can talk a little bit more about the second. People have a tough time being convinced that when Jesus said, "Your faith has made you well," He was really talking about salvation in those particular portions of Scripture. I believe that He was; the healing was merely an evidence of being made well spiritually. But people still believe that it's a matter of exercising their faith. They still believe that those portions of Scripture, for instance, where Jesus says, "If you have faith the size of a grain of mustard seed, you say to this mountain, be moved, and it will move," place all the responsibility on them.

Sometimes I think God would read their heart intent; but then perhaps it is in the providence of God that they should be sorely mistaken so that they might be moved to take a closer look at Scripture.

Take, for example, that young stewardess. What will that dear girl do when her husband gets deathly ill? What will she do? My heart goes out to her in one sense. But yet, in another sense, I can see that God would want her to be sadly, sadly disappointed, so that as with me it would press her to go back to Scripture for a second, harder look. I feel for those folks. I can see myself, as I once was, in that position. I guess that makes it all the more imperative that people who are in a position of sharing God's truth should be accurate. It puts a great challenge before you.[1]

16

On My Back by Divine Design

❖

On November 19, 1966, Rabbi Harold Kushner received the news that his only son would suffer and die from a rare disease that strikes only one person out of 7 million people. The doctors diagnosed Aaron, only three years old, as having progeria—the rapid-aging disease.

On that day the rabbi looked heavenward and asked only one question: "If God exists and if He is even minimally fair, let alone loving and forgiving, how could He do this to me and to my innocent child?"

Eleven years later, in 1977, Aaron died at the age of 14. Then his father sought even harder for the answer to his question. When he thought he had found it, he published it in a book entitled *When Bad Things Happen to Good People*.[1]

Rabbi Kushner concluded that only one of three possible responses correctly answered his question of why all this had happened in his family: One, in this life, people get what they deserve from God. (That makes God nothing more than a cruel despot.) Two, perhaps God is cruel and allows people to get what they don't deserve. (That reduces our Lord to nothing more than a cosmic sadist.) Three, if the first two possibilities are not true, then God is not all-powerful and thus cannot prevent people from getting what they don't deserve. (This explanation makes God nothing more than a consecrated weakling.)

Many centuries ago a great man faced an even deeper crisis than Rabbi Kushner and his family. Job lost all his children and wealth in one catastrophic day, and close on the heels of that day he lost his physical health as well.

Undoubtedly Job asked hard questions like the ones asked by Rabbi Kushner or anyone else who faces unexplained physical trauma in his or her life or the lives of family and friends. Questions like, Does God ever use sickness for good? Is sickness always a result of personal sin? Is it God's will for me to be sick? Why?

Unlike Job's three supposed comforters—Bildad, Eliphaz, and Zophar (Job 2:11)—we need to look to God for the answers, and not to logic, philosophy, or human wisdom. You might be surprised by God's perspective on the spiritual benefits of sickness and suffering.

The Benefits of Suffering

Reveals God's Divine Character

Throughout the book of Job we get hints of the severity of Job's illness. He appeared so pitiful when his friends came to visit him that they didn't speak to him for one whole week (2:13). He groaned at the sight of food and cried tears like gushing torrents of water (3:24) because of his great pain. Worms and dirt infected his wounds; fluid ran out all over his body (7:5). Job hallucinated, in and out of complete consciousness, which might explain some of the comments he made later on (7:14). He was "decaying like a rotten thing" (13:28) and shriveling up (16:8); he suffered from halitosis (19:17) and unrelenting pain (30:17); his skin turned black and his fever raged (30:30); and he experienced dramatic weight loss (33:21). Such was Job, a righteous man who did no evil.

After the tragedies ended and with a four-chapter dialogue with God fresh in his mind (Job 38–41), Job uttered these words: "I have heard of Thee by the hearing of the ear; but now my eye sees Thee; therefore I retract, and I repent in dust and ashes" (Job 42:5-6). Job said, in effect, "I take back all the questions I asked and the foolish things I said. You have revealed Yourself, Lord, and now I can see who You are and understand the wonders of Your grace and the brightness of eternal hope."

Job's calamity provided an opportunity for God to emphasize His divine reality in ways that Job otherwise would not have contemplated. Those who spend their days looking heavenward frequently find that the Lord shows Himself in special ways that only the circumstances of sickness and suffering make possible.

Glorifies Christ

When Jesus heard that Lazarus lay seriously ill, He said, "This sickness is not unto death, but for the glory of God, that the Son of God may be glorified by it" (John 11:4).

If Lazarus had been healthy, the glory of God could not have been manifested through him. Those who suffer are candidates to be vessels through whom Jesus Christ might be exalted.

Ole Hallesby, the Norwegian theologian, offers this helpful thought:

> Do not forget . . . that prayer is ordained for the purpose of glorifying the name of God. Therefore, whether you pray for big things or for little things, say to God, "If it will glorify Thy name, then grant my prayer and help me. But if it will not glorify Thy name, then let me remain in my predicament. And give me the power to glorify Thy name in the situation in which I find myself."[2]

If this sounds unfair, remember that Christ first did Himself what He might be asking us to do. He suffered so that His heavenly Father might be glorified (Philippians 2:8-11).

Promotes Spiritual Maturity

Would you like to be mature, whole, and lacking nothing? Most Christians respond with an overwhelming *Yes!* While this is a worthy prospect, the result comes only by a process explained in James 1:2-4: Trials that test our faith produce patience; patience, when exercised, leads to the spiritual wholeness that Christians desire.

Sickness and suffering provide some of the many trials that God uses in this process.

Displays God's Workmanship

When confronted with a man who had been blind since birth, the disciples asked Jesus, "Rabbi, who sinned, this man or his parents, that he should be born blind?" (John 9:2). Jesus responded, "It was neither that this man sinned, nor his parents, but it was in order that the works of God might be displayed in him" (verse 3).

After Jesus gave sight to the man, the work of God was displayed in him everywhere he went. His testimony was dynamic and caused people to say, "Since the beginning of time it has never been heard that anyone opened the eyes of a person born blind. If this man were not from God, He could do nothing" (verses 32-33).

Fulfills God's Will

For a moment, consider the opinion of Benny Hinn.

> I believe it is not only God's will for you to be healed, but it is His will that you live in health until He calls you home. . . . I am not one who prays, "If it be your will, Lord, grant healing to this person."[3]

Now listen to God.

> It is better, if God should will it so, that you suffer for doing what is right rather than for doing what is wrong (1 Peter 3:17).

> Therefore, let those also who suffer according to the will of God entrust their souls to a faithful Creator in doing what is right (1 Peter 4:19).

Hinn not only contradicts God's wisdom with his unbiblical assertions, but he also refuses to follow the example of our Lord Jesus Christ, who prayed, "Father, if Thou art willing, remove this cup from Me; yet not My will but Thine be done (Luke 22:42).

Hinn also mocks the saints who were suffering while they lived and when they died. What about the martyrs in the book of Revelation? What about the apostle Paul? What about your loved ones who suffered before they died? What about the innumerable masses of Christians around the world who are not in good health?

Dr. C. Everett Koop, honored physician and former U.S. Surgeon General, comments on ignoring God's will in healing.

> When a faith healer commands God to perform a miracle, in the absence of a prayer that says "Thy will be done," it is, as far as I am concerned, the most rank form of arrogance.[4]

Submission to God's will on earth is received as the purest form of worship in heaven. In our physical weakness God can demonstrate His strength in mighty ways.

Secures Our Attention

Nebuchadnezzar needed the "wake-up call" of seven years of sickness to hear the message that God, not the King of

Babylon, ruled the universe (Daniel 4:30-37). Job needed postgraduate work through pain and sickness in order to understand God at a new level (Job 42:5-6).

C.S. Lewis, in his classic book *The Problem of Pain*, made this brilliant observation:

> [P]ain insists upon being attended to. God whispers to us in our pleasures, speaks in our conscience, but shouts in our pains: it is His megaphone to rouse a deaf world.[5]

When suffering strikes, it could be that God has an important message to send us that we could receive no other way than from the courier called pain.

Heightens Our Dependence

Suffering helps us to quickly realize our utter dependence upon God for everything. When Paul needed to be at his strongest because the challenges of ministry became so great, he found himself at a low point, humanly speaking. Whether the thorn that afflicted him represents suffering through sickness or by persecution, it nonetheless made Paul dependent on God rather than his own human resources (2 Corinthians 12:7-10).

Encourages Others

Consider this scriptural challenge:

> Therefore, since we have so great a cloud of witnesses surrounding us, let us also lay aside every encumbrance, and the sin which so easily entangles us, and let us run with endurance the race that is set before us (Hebrews 12:1).

The word "therefore" takes us back to Hebrews 11, where we find encouragement to be faithful now because of the faithfulness demonstrated by the saints—the great cloud of witnesses—who went before us. They were the ones who—

- from weakness were made strong
- were tortured
- experienced mockings and beatings
- endured chains and imprisonment
- died by the sword

Each succeeding generation of Christians has been greatly encouraged by men and women of God who valiantly stood firm in the faith.

Conforms Us to Christ

Paul's letter to the Philippians speaks of being conformed to Christ in humility and suffering, as well as in glory. He desired to know the fellowship of Christ's sufferings, being conformed to Christ's death (3:10). He also longed for the day when Christ would transform the body of his humble state "into conformity with the body of [Christ's] glory" (3:21).

Paul expressed this truth even more beautifully to the church at Rome:

> Whom He foreknew, He also predestined to become conformed to the image of His Son, that He might be the first-born among many brethren; and whom he predestined, these He also called; and whom He called, these He also justified; and whom He justified, these He also glorified (Romans 8:29-30).

Authenticates Our Faith

Peter stated a great truth which has encouraged suffering saints through the ages:

> In this you greatly rejoice, even though now for a little while, if necessary, you have been

distressed by various trials, that the proof of
your faith, being more precious than gold which
is perishable, even though tested by fire, may be
found to result in praise and glory and honor at
the revelation of Jesus Christ (1 Peter 1:6-7).

The heart of Peter's encouragement is simply this: "In this
you greatly rejoice . . . that the proof of your faith . . . even
though tested by fire, may be found to result in praise and
glory and honor at the revelation of Jesus Christ."

Our sufferings help to burn away the dross of our life and
authenticate our faith in the Lord Jesus Christ. We can have
both present joy and a living hope for the future not *in spite of*
our circumstances but *because of* them. Our dependence on
God in *all* our circumstances certifies the reality of our salvation.

This testimony shared by my mother bears witness to
Peter's teaching.

Both the pain of separation from a loved one
and physical suffering have been my experience.
My secret to enduring? "His grace is sufficient."
I often think of the Scripture "In everything give
thanks, for this is the will of God in Christ Jesus
concerning you" [1 Thessalonians 5:18 KJV]. My
husband used to quote this verse often. About 4¹/₂
years ago God saw fit to take him to be home in
heaven with his Lord. There was great pain in
separation through physical death. About 2¹/₂
years later I suffered a heavy stroke, paralyzing
my left side and leaving me practically helpless.
However, God in His loving-kindness and tender
mercies surrounded me with some of His people—
loving and caring—they take care of my every
need—physical, medical, emotional, and even
feed me spiritually. All of us have experienced
spiritual growth throughout all of this.[6]

Produces Endurance

Most of us have no trouble exulting in the hope of God's glory. But how many of us can with equal ease exult in our trials? Paul says that both exultations go together inseparably:

> Having been justified by faith, we have peace with God through our Lord Jesus Christ, through whom also we have obtained our introduction by faith into this grace in which we stand; and we exult in hope of the glory of God. And not only this, but we also exult in our tribulations, knowing that tribulation brings about perseverance; and perseverance, proven character; and proven character, hope; and hope does not disappoint, because the love of God has been poured out within our hearts through the Holy Spirit who was given to us (Romans 5:1-5).

God's love for us should never be doubted in the midst of trial because of the Holy Spirit, who comes as God's gift to us at salvation. The Holy Spirit makes it possible to have hope, which results from proven character, proven character from perseverance, and perseverance from trials. Thus we can exult in our trials because they produce endurance that leads to proven character that results in a hope which does not disappoint.

Subdues Self-Exaltation

Paul had been privileged to hear inexpressible words that were spoken in the third heaven. Because of the surpassing greatness of that experience, God allowed Satan to buffet Paul with a thorn in the flesh. The thorn's purpose was to keep Paul from exalting himself (2 Corinthians 12:1-7).

Paul's prayers for recovery were to no avail (2 Corinthians 12:8), so he finally rested in this wonderful thought:

[God] has said to me, "My grace is sufficient for you, for power is perfected in weakness." Most gladly, therefore, I will rather boast about my weaknesses, that the power of Christ may dwell in me (2 Corinthians 12:9).

So it is today: When suffering strikes, God's strength can be manifested through our weakness. In that way God gets all of the glory.

Chastens Sinning Saints

Does all sickness come as a result of sin? Yes and no. Yes, sickness comes as a physical by-product of our sin nature and a sinful world. But no, sickness does not necessarily come as a result of particular sinful deeds.

We can be encouraged to know that God does not usually punish our sin with sickness. The widow at Zarephath feared that her son had died because of her own iniquities (1 Kings 17:18). Jesus' disciples assumed that sin was the cause of a certain man's blindness (John 9:2). Bildad suggested that Job's trials came as a result of sin (Job 8:1-22). As a rule, however, God does not operate this way. There will be exceptions, such as those Corinthians who were chastened because they had desecrated the Lord's Supper (1 Corinthians 11:20-22,29-30). The punishment of Ananias and Sapphira for lying to the Holy Spirit is another example (Acts 5:1-11). And God offers the anointing service in James 5 for believers whose sin results in chastisement by sickness.

Provides Comfort

Have you ever noticed that people tend to listen to your advice more carefully if you have already been through a particular life experience yourself? That's just part of our human nature. Furthermore, Jesus knows our circumstances, for even He was tested: "We do not have a high priest who cannot sympathize with our weaknesses, but one who has been tempted in all things as we are, yet without sin" (Hebrews 4:15).

God can use your sicknesses and suffering to make you a vessel through whom He can comfort others. Your present trials will later become the platform from which you minister.

> Blessed be the God and Father of our Lord Jesus Christ, the Father of mercies and God of all comfort, who comforts us in all our affliction so that we may be able to comfort those who are in any affliction with the comfort with which we ourselves are comforted by God (2 Corinthians 1:3-4).

Accomplishes God's Unrevealed Purposes

After we exhaust all our answers or possibilities to explain suffering but our curiosity still is not satisfied, we appeal to these special Scriptures.

> It is the glory of God to conceal a matter, but the glory of kings is to search out a matter (Proverbs 25:2).

> The secret things belong to the LORD our God, but the things revealed belong to us and to our sons forever, that we may observe all the words of this law (Deuteronomy 29:29).

To admit that God acts in ways that exceed our reasoning and His written revelation does not beg the question. Scriptures such as these often serve as our last court of appeal. They should satisfy us just as much as the more specific answers. Isaiah anticipated our human dilemma by reminding us:

> "My thoughts are not your thoughts, neither are your ways My ways," declares the LORD. "For as the heavens are higher than the earth, so are My ways higher than your ways, and My thoughts than your thoughts" (Isaiah 55:8-9).

Years ago I attended a writing course in Chicago. An evangelist named Ben participated also. One morning between classes we were having coffee and discussing how Ben's life was different because he was blind. I do not remember all the conversation, but I did jot down one thought when someone asked Ben how he became blind. He unhesitatingly replied, "I am blind by God's design."

Ben embraced the divine perspective. He knew that anyone who experiences sickness or suffering does so "by God's design." But God may choose not to show us why until we reach glory.

A Biblical Prescription

When I first began to study the subject of healing I had never experienced a serious illness. I wrote on the subject of divine healing from the platform of Scripture and common sense. I had never personally had the opportunity to test the usefulness of my advice, although many people to whom I ministered had responded favorably.

Then an illness leveled me, physically and emotionally. I experienced terrible fear, a radical personality change, and at times uncontrollable crying—all for no apparent reason. For six agonizing months our family had no idea what caused those unexplainable phenomena. During that time I retreated over and over to the principles in this discussion even though, at the time, I believed there would be no recovery for me.

Eventually, after a five-hour glucose-tolerance test, a doctor diagnosed hypoglycemia as the source of my problem. Through exercise and a controlled diet, the Lord has very graciously restored my full health. But during those dark days my only sustaining help came from applying the truths I now share. I pray that these principles will help you as well.

We all search for one clear scripture that states, "When you are sick, this is what you should do." I certainly came up empty-handed when I looked for such a scripture. But God has provided us with a prescription that comes from various portions of His Word, and the combined wisdom of these truths will serve you well. Like a physician's consultation, this counsel needs to be taken in full.

First, acknowledge that God sovereignly rules life, and then personally rest in that unshakable truth. God controls our every moment, whether in sickness or health. "See now that I, I am He, and there is no god besides Me; it is I who put to death and give life. I have wounded, and it is I who heal; and there is no one who can deliver from My hand" (Deuteronomy 32:39).

Second, remind yourself of the biblical reasons for sickness. Think about those purposes which God can accomplish through your time of illness. Pray that God will use you in weakness to display His strength.

Third, it is extremely important to determine if your sickness is resulting from continued sin in your life. Is God using your illness as a chastisement? For most of us the answer will be no. But if your answer happens to be yes, confess your sin (1 John 1:9). It could be that the James 5 anointing service is for you. You will want to discuss that with your pastor.

Fourth, commit the entire matter to the Lord by faith. Pray for God's will to be done, seek His glory, and wait patiently for His response.

Fifth, seek the help of health-care professionals. Never disregard or ignore God's normal means of restoring health through medical experts. Do not presume upon God and wait too long or ignore your doctor altogether.

Sixth, recognize that it might not be God's will for you to fully recover. Many of God's great servants were sick—Isaac, Jacob, Moses, Job, Daniel, Paul, Epaphroditus, and Timothy. They all eventually died.

Seventh, thank God for the circumstances in which He has placed you, "always giving thanks for all things in the name of our Lord Jesus Christ to God, even the Father" (Ephesians 5:20). "In everything give thanks, for this is God's will for you in Christ Jesus" (1 Thessalonians 5:18). You are not thanking God that you hurt, but rather that He is who He is and that He will work His will through your circumstances.

Eighth, as you pray, ask God for the faith and patience to endure and the wisdom to understand why (James 1:2-5). He vowed that His grace would be sufficient (2 Corinthians 12:9). Claim that reassuring scriptural promise for yourself and rest in it.

Finally, pray that your circumstances would bring glory to God (1 Corinthians 10:31). Only when that becomes your constant preoccupation will you experience full victory in the midst of your circumstances and will Christ have preeminence in all of your life.

Prayer for Healing

Having accepted the biblical prescription, you might now be asking, "Is it right or wrong to pray for God's healing touch?" Let me assure you that there is absolutely nothing wrong with asking. Paul asked three times to be delivered (2 Corinthians 12:8). Jesus asked to be delivered (Matthew 26:39). However, we need to be willing to prayerfully receive God's answer regardless of what it is. We must submit our will to God's will.

The most appropriate words of wisdom I know of in this regard have been offered by Charles Wood. His wife fought several bouts with cancer. They had prayed often. He counsels, "In illness, I would pray for healing until God grants it or unless or until He makes it plain that it is not His will and gives peace about it."[7]

17

When Suffering Arrives

Tragedy often strikes swiftly and unexpectedly. For John and Patricia, their long-awaited family vacation in late July 1992 turned out to be anything but a holiday. One seemingly minor event while driving escalated into a life-threatening accident with heart-wrenching possibilities of disastrous proportions.

Many Christians recognize John MacArthur as an outstanding Bible expositor. He is heard daily on hundreds of "Grace to You" broadcasts around the world. He has pastored Grace Community Church in Sun Valley, California, since 1969. Dr. MacArthur additionally ministers as President of The Master's College and The Master's Seminary. People often ask about men with such unusual visibility and responsibility, "When hard times come, can they really live out their theology and preaching?"

God afforded the MacArthur family an uninvited opportunity to answer this question in a way they never had expected. Before we begin our conversation, let's ask John to frame this bittersweet picture of God's sovereign grace with the details about Patricia's near-fatal automobile accident.

How It Happened

"One afternoon while waiting for my son to join me at the golf course, I received a telephone call informing me that my wife, Patricia, and our youngest daughter, Melinda, had been involved in a serious automobile accident. Patricia had been gravely injured and was being airlifted to a hospital about an hour away from where I was. No other details were available. Inadvertently leaving my golf clubs on the practice tee, I immediately got into my car and headed for the hospital.

"That hour-long drive to the hospital will be forever etched in my memory. A thousand thoughts flooded my mind. I realized, of course, that I might never see Patricia alive again. I thought of the gaping hole that would exist in my life without her. I reflected on the essential part she has had in my life and ministry over the years. I wondered how I could ever manage without her. I remembered when we first met, how we grew to love each other, and hundreds of other little things about our life together. I would give anything to keep her, but I realized now that the choice was not mine to make.

"A supernatural peace flooded my soul. My grief, sorrow, uncertainty, and fears were all enveloped in that restful peace. I knew that Patricia and I were both in the Lord's hands, and under the circumstances that was the only place I could imagine any sort of safety. I did not know His design. I could not see His purposes. I could not understand what had happened or why. But I could rest in the knowledge that His plan for us was ultimately for our good and for His glory.

"When I arrived at the emergency room, I learned that Melinda had been badly bruised and cut but was not seriously injured. She was severely shaken but not in any danger.

"A doctor came out to explain Patricia's injuries to me. Her neck was broken. Two vertebrae were severely crushed. The damage had occurred above the crucial nerves in the spinal cord that control breathing. In most cases like hers, the victim dies immediately. But our Lord had providentially spared her.

"She had also sustained a severe blow to the head. The impact of the roof crushing down on her head as the car flipped was powerful enough to have killed her. They were giving her massive doses of a new drug designed to stop swelling in the brain. The surgeon was concerned that the head injury could yet prove fatal. He had used more than 40 sutures to close the wound in her scalp. Her jaw and several bones in her face were broken. She would not be out of danger for several days.

"Emergency room personnel were about to move Patricia to surgery, where doctors would attach a steel halo to her head by means of four bolts drilled directly into the skull. The device would suspend her head and stabilize her neck while the vertebrae healed. She would wear the halo for several months and after that undergo a grueling program of physical rehabilitation.

"In the next few days doctors discovered additional injuries. The right collarbone was broken. Worse, Patricia's right arm was paralyzed. She could move her fingers and grip things, but her arm hung limply and she had no sensation in it. Her left hand was broken and needed a cast. That meant that Patricia could not use either hand.

"This all has brought a wonderful opportunity for me to serve my wife. All our lives together she has cared for my needs, served the family, and ministered to us in a myriad of ways. Now it is my turn, and I have relished the opportunity. My love for her and my appreciation of all that she does has grown by magnitudes."[1]

The Outcome

As of this writing, 17 months have passed since the July accident. God has since poured out His great blessings on the MacArthur family and John's ministries. On the day after Christmas 1993 I sat down with John and Patricia to reflect on the accident and its outcome. You will be encouraged and strengthened by joining us for an inside update of how God glorified Himself through their tragedy.

DICK: How serious was the injury?

JOHN: The injury was serious enough to have taken Patricia's life. There's no question that most people who have had that same injury died.

DICK: Tell us about the initial prognosis by the doctors after she arrived at the hospital.

JOHN: Initially, she was alive and didn't have any apparent paralysis that they could identify. She had feeling in her legs and in her feet, but the right arm initially didn't function. They also told me, "We have to keep her head absolutely stable because any movement could cause the fragmented bones (she had what they call an explosion fracture where the bone just disintegrates) to impact the spinal cord and not only sever the spinal cord because of sharp fragments of bones but even bruise or injure the spinal cord." They were very concerned about keeping her absolutely stable until they could attach a steel halo and totally immobilize her head.

DICK: I can remember my brief visit with you both in the hospital, less than twenty-four hours after the accident. Patricia, were you fully conscious? Did you understand all that was going on in those first few days?

PATRICIA: I don't think so, Dick. People ask me what I first remembered after the accident and I just vaguely remember a few things here and there. It was two or three days after the accident before the heavy sedation began to wear off, so that I was aware of my situation and what was involved. I realized that God had been very gracious in sparing my life and allowing me to avoid paralysis, which every doctor thought I should have. Every time a new doctor would come in to see me, he would say, "Where's your paralysis?" I repeatedly said I didn't have any and they would always respond with, "You're lucky." About the third day I was fully aware of what had happened.

JOHN: Here's a footnote to that. Statistically, she is among the five percent of people who have survived that kind of injury. Ninety-five-plus percent die.

DICK: At this point are you saying her survival was a miracle? How would you describe this experience, both practically and theologically?

JOHN: A miracle is the intervention of God sovereignly and supernaturally to bypass nature and do something which cannot be explained in any other way; so by the technical definition of a miracle, it didn't appear to be a miracle. However, God could have miraculously intervened while she was tumbling around in the car and done something supernatural, even perhaps had an angel do something to keep her from leaning in a certain direction. God could have supernaturally intervened, but it seems better to see it as providential. God, with supernatural ability, controlled the road, the car, the flipping in the air, her position in the car, and every single thing that happened. This really falls under the particular definition of providence, where God orders a myriad of circumstances to effect His purpose rather than miraculously overruling nature. I've always thought that providence is a bigger miracle than a miracle itself because it would be easier to just overrule than to work with the infinite number of real-life contingencies.

DICK: I know that a lot of friends came to visit over the days and weeks after the accident. Did you have any friends like Job had?

PATRICIA: Not really. They didn't ever suggest anything in terms of God's chastisement. People were amazed and praising the Lord for His protection and His sovereign plan in my life.

DICK: I know that Joni Eareckson Tada stopped in to visit and you had a meaningful time. How do you remember that?

PATRICIA: She paid several visits, but the first one is the most memorable. I was immobile on my back, looking at the ceiling. She sang to me, "His Eye Is on the Sparrow." She also brought me a little ceramic sparrow that Ken had given her at a time when she was down, so it meant a lot to me. It was comforting to think about His eye being on the sparrow and knowing that if His eye is on the sparrow, how much more He cares for His ultimate creation. So it was a very special time. Joni had just recognized her twenty-fifth year of paralysis. Her dear husband Ken was also with her. Because my accident resulted only in a seemingly paralyzed arm—temporarily— Ken got down on his knees and took my arm in his hand and asked God to restore my one arm. Joni said, "Oh, Pat, I'm so glad you're not a quad." She knew how close I had come to being just that, and so her visit was very meaningful. I had a greater appreciation for all that she does and how she constantly glorifies the Lord in spite of her adversity.

DICK: Did you ever identify with Job in the midst of all of this? He was a righteous man whose life was going along well and all of a sudden the roof caved in.

JOHN: I have great confidence in God's sovereignty; but yes, the thought entered my mind. Here I am, in the middle of my ministry, very dependent on Patricia. When I first heard a garbled report of the accident, I assumed the worst. If you're driving on that particular highway, which I know very well, there is nothing in the middle; everybody's going 65; it's four lanes going right at each other and winding. All of a sudden, when you hear that your wife has been in a severe accident and she's being helicoptered to a trauma center—all you can imagine is that they just peeled the car off the front of a semi. Patricia is normally a very good driver and I just thought the worst. Of course, the first questions that entered my mind were, *How am I going to live my life? How am I going to all of a sudden step into all of her roles?* I kept thinking, *What will the children do? I can't meet their needs, the needs that only she can meet. What will the grandchildren do? What will our life as a family be like without her?* Patricia really is the glue. I'm sort of the foghorn, but she's the glue that holds everything in our family together. It was just one huge mystery, and I was very much aware of the fact that there is no one whom I had ever met who could replace her. There is no one who could step into her life to fulfill what she does. I didn't have a time when I didn't believe that God was in charge. I never thought, *God kind of goofed on this one.* That thought never entered my mind, but this one did: *What if she was gone, what in the world were we all going to do, and how would we put our lives back together?*

DICK: Do you ever wonder if Satan played a part in all this?

PATRICIA: I never did. I never had any question—I think my accident was a result of hitting the soft shoulder on the side of the road and overcorrecting. God took control, orchestrated the entire situation, and brought glory to Himself through it. I never thought th..t Satan had any influence in the accident in any way. There was no other party involved and it was a mistake that I had made. I can't explain to this day why or how it happened, but I believe God allowed it to happen for His purpose and His glory and my good. A lot of people benefited from it. We saw a worldwide prayer chain that resulted. God was very gracious in answering the prayers of many, many godly people.

JOHN: If a truck came across the highway and hit you, if a car hit you, if lightning hit you, if a telephone pole fell on top of you, then you might think that Satan had somehow intervened and thrown this horrible thing at you. But Patricia was so confident in her faith in the Lord and confident in her walk in the Lord that to believe that Satan made this happen would be to believe that Satan was operative in her life. Now, I don't know if Satan works with steering wheels and suspensions in cars or not. I do know he works in the hearts and minds of men. Whether he can intervene in the physical realm to that extent . . . I don't want to say he couldn't. I don't want to say the accident could not have been something that some demons were involved in. I don't know. We examined our hearts and she examined her heart many, many times over the issue of sin and giving place to Satan. If there is unconfessed sin in your life and there's something wrong in your life, then you give a place to Satan. Maybe there's a certain influence that he exerts there. But all the way along, we felt that there was nothing that wasn't being dealt with in terms of sin. So Satan wouldn't have had a special place where he was in control. But then, on the other hand, the supernatural is still mysterious to us and many, many people have said to me, "I think Satan was trying to strike a blow at your ministry." From my theological viewpoint, I'm not sure about that. Someday I will ask the Lord.

DICK: If Satan attempted to strike a blow at your ministry, how effective, if at all, has he been?

JOHN: He wasn't effective at all because God overruled. Either Satan was doing something and God overruled it, or God allowed the natural thing to happen within the framework of His will in order that He might demonstrate His power. The greatest reminder that came out of this was that God answers prayer. That's what Patricia has said over and over and over. I think that many people around the world—who tend to see me as strong and stable and not very emotional and maybe even not very human because I'm just this sort of "radio-preacher/teacher"—all of a sudden saw me as a very human person with all the same pains and problems and hurts and difficulties in life that they all have. The accident created a massive garrisoning of people around us to pray. God used that accident to increase our prayer group to the tens of thousands around the world. The effect of that has touched all of our ministries.

DICK: Speaking about prayer, Patricia, you have fully recovered in just a little over a year. Are there any residual problems?

PATRICIA: My arm is weak, but I have full use of it. My neck occasionally is tired. But that's to be expected. I'm almost one hundred percent. When the doctors examined my arm, they said, "If it does return from nerve damage, it could take up to a year and a half or more and never fully recover." It was less than a year after the accident that the use of my arm came back fully and the paralysis totally disappeared. I haven't been back to my neurologist in three or four months. Long after the accident, she still thought I would benefit from neck surgery. I asked for more time to let God work. She said, "Fine, that's your choice."

JOHN: Patricia demonstrated real faith in the Lord at that point because we were told that nerves are totally unpredictable. It was obvious that a major nerve had been devastated, but whether it was totally destroyed or not, they couldn't tell without some very exotic kinds of tests. They said it could return, or it could not return, or it could partially return. So at that point I have to believe that God really answered prayer. There has been a full and complete restoration. That nerve just completely rejuvenated itself. At this particular point it seems like God providentially intervened. There may have been something He did miraculous; we don't know. But certainly at this point we give Him the credit and the glory for what He did. Patricia kept saying, "No, I think I'm seeing this progress. It's not life-threatening. Let's give God time to demonstrate His power." He did!

DICK: Knowing that you were in an accident where you should have died, but not dying you should have been paralyzed, it's incredible that you're fully recovered. Looking back, how were you praying and how did God answer your prayers? Did you pray for complete recovery or did you just pray for the grace to endure it?

PATRICIA: Actually, I just believed that God is sovereign and He has a perfect plan for my life. I knew everybody else was praying. When my extremities went numb, I asked the Lord to restore me so that I wouldn't have to go through neck surgery. I had a little bit of a fear of neck surgery. I just prayed that the Lord would miraculously—whatever the cause—lay it aside and allow me to have full feeling restored in my limbs. I had three weeks from the time they took the halo off to go back and see my neurologist to schedule surgery. That's when I asked for more time because the feeling was beginning to come back. So I did pray that my hands and feet would be restored with feeling. But as I lay in bed, I told the Lord that if all I had to deal with after an accident like that was a paralyzed arm, I was willing to accept it as a reminder of His gracious kindness toward me in allowing me to escape paralysis.

I knew there were a lot of people praying and I've had so many expressions of love and reminders of prayer for me that it was a tremendous comfort. My situation and condition were taken to the throne of grace daily, so it was up to the Lord at that point.

DICK: John, you prayed for Patricia as her husband and then you prayed as her pastor. Did you pray the same in both roles?

JOHN: Absolutely! I prayed all the way to the hospital that the Lord would have spared her life. But I said, "I just want You to know that if You choose to take her life, I know she's with You, so I don't have that horrible fear of never seeing her again or of her being out of Your presence." I had the confidence that if the Lord had chosen to take her, she was in a better place and she was rejoicing in His presence. But I prayed the whole time that she might be alive, because I wanted to see her and talk to her. When I got to the hospital, she was still there and she was alive, and the doctors said that there appeared to be no paralysis, at least beyond the right arm. The spinal cord wasn't severed. Then it was just a matter of constantly praying daily that God would heal her. One day she said to me, "Specifically, I want you to pray that the Lord will give me back my right arm." This was after everything else started healing, and in time the Lord answered the prayer for her right arm. As I prayed, though, I said, "God, we want *Your* will." I had no hesitation about saying, "Lord, we want Your will to be done, but I'd like to ask You if Your will couldn't be full restoration, please."

DICK: Do you think the full recovery came about as a result of just medical science? Or medical science plus the ability of the body to recuperate? Or medical science plus the ability of the body to recuperate plus something that God did in addition, such as reaching in to cause the recovery to be quicker or more complete than would have been normal?

JOHN: Well, Dick, I wouldn't attribute it to medical science because basically they didn't do anything. There never was any surgery. All they did was immobilize her head; so it had to be a combination of things. It had to be the natural healing process because, given time, bone grows back. Given time, nerves can grow. Realize that Patricia had fractured her head, needing forty stitches to close the top of her head; she had fractured the orbital bones around the eye; and her jaw was broken. They wanted to do surgery on the jaw. We said, "Let's wait and see; let's give it some time." As time went on, they actually scheduled her for surgery. We said, "Wait a minute, there's not going to be any surgery." All of those bones around her eye healed and you can't tell any difference. The jaw, which was broken and separated, grew back together in a very normal fashion. There were some bone chips all the way down her spine, and a broken hand. Another doctor was going to do something to fix the hand but we just wanted to give the Lord time. And it's not because I'm against surgery. Both of my sons have experienced surgery, so that's not an issue. But it seemed like something was going on here that was really remarkable— that God was restoring everything as the healing process was sovereignly controlled by His power.

PATRICIA: You can call it a miracle or say it's over and above nature's process, but the two therapists who were taking care of me said they had seen a lot of injuries such as mine and that I was a "walking miracle." My therapist, Dr. Sam Britten, said I had an unusual healing. Then I went to the dentist recently because one of my crowns was knocked out from the fracture of my jaw, and he took a complete facial X-ray. He could not even find where my jaw had been fractured. That's unbelievable because they had wanted to do plastic surgery. The fracture was so obvious. The only thing you can say is that

God did a complete healing on my jaw. Even my neurologist could not explain why the feeling returned to my extremities and the paralysis left my arm. There is no way to humanly explain it. I can tell you that people in the medical field have said that I'm a walking miracle, that I'm very unusual in my recovery.

DICK: Has the severity of the accident and the completeness of the recovery changed your view of how God deals with our physical lives? For example, how He heals, whether He heals, when He heals, and to what extent He heals?

JOHN: No, it really doesn't change my theology. I've always believed that God heals. I've never questioned the power of God to heal. I've never questioned the power of God to do anything consistent with His nature. Healing must be consistent with His nature because when Jesus was here, He healed. God has healed in the past and there is no reason to assume that God doesn't choose to heal in the present. So the accident never really changed anything, but it sure personalized the reality of God's healing. In one sense it was kind of wonderful to go through this and to see this constant evidence of God's grace. We lived out our theology that says, "Yes, God does heal." He heals according to His own will and His own purpose. In this case it was His purpose and His will to providentially control Patricia's situation and perhaps even intervene in supernatural ways that we don't understand in order to give her complete health for His glory and honor. He has demonstrated His ability to answer prayer in the physical realm.

DICK: What lessons are there to learn for people who read this interview? For example, I'm thinking about those who are in the hospital with a terminal illness, or husbands whose wives have suffered some kind of a severe trauma.

JOHN: First of all, the one thing you want to be aware of is that nothing happens outside the purposes of God. There are no surprises in heaven. He knows the end from the beginning and every detail of our lives. Second, He is intimately concerned about every one of those details. Third, He can providentially overrule all the bad that happens to us. Those truths are found all through the Scriptures. Start reading the Psalms. Over and over again you see that God rescues and delivers and protects. You also see that in the character of Jesus as He came into the world. The attributes of God that He demonstrated most clearly prior to the cross were God's mercy and compassion and grace toward suffering people. We also know that we can pray for the physical area of life and we can pray for God to heal. In His grace, in His mercy, and in complete harmony with His sovereignty, He will answer that prayer.

PATRICIA: The accident affirmed that our days are numbered and God is in charge. That is what I kept emphasizing to our daughter who was in the accident with me—one, that God is in control of our lives and, two, that He is totally sovereign. Whatever He allows to come into our lives, He has a purpose for it which is for our good and His glory. And three, it made me realize how temporary this life on earth is. Sometimes we are incapacitated and inconvenienced, and we all have to go sometime. In this particular instance, God demonstrated His grace.

People asked me, "Why do you think God allowed this to happen?" or, "What did you learn through it?" I've learned again that God is sovereign; He will go through any circumstance with us. The verse that kept going through my mind is, "Thou wilt keep him in perfect peace, whose mind is stayed on thee" [Isaiah 26:3 KJV]. I used to sing that a lot in the morning. I know His salvation, and I have come to know His healing powers in a personal way. Certainly our prayer is not necessarily answered according to our spiritual state. I think it's what He sees as best for everybody involved. In my situation, there were so many people aware of the accident and praying for my healing and recovery. Because of the effect it would have had on His ministry, He saw fit to answer the prayers according to the way they were asked—not because I was deserving of this particular kind of healing.

DICK: Patricia, some of the great saints in the Old Testament walked through the valley of the shadow of death and despaired, even to the point of wanting God to take them. We remember men like Moses, Job, Jeremiah, and Elijah. Did you have any moments like those, or similar to those?

PATRICIA: I really didn't. I was so thankful that another song often entered my mind. It's from Scripture: "I will sing of the mercies of the Lord forever." I saw Him demonstrate His mercy in my life. I enjoy my life here and pray that the Lord will use my influence on my grandchildren and by coming alongside my husband to be his helpmate. I feel the Lord has given me the heart of service and I enjoy and love it. That's my role in life. But if the outcome had been different, I probably would have prayed differently.

DICK: What did you receive from friends around the world that encouraged you most?

PATRICIA: I was really moved by the concern and prayers of the people. It wasn't just a get-well card, it was a heartfelt, prayerful note they would send me. That was another way the Lord used this accident—to show me the caring and loving support of the people in the church and around the world.

DICK: I remember that after they moved you out of the intensive-care unit, your whole family made a big wall poster for the hospital room.

JOHN: The kids made a bunch of posters and put them on the wall because she couldn't see anything with her head propped back. Eventually the cards ended up on the ceiling. There were all kinds of love notes and get-well cards hanging from the ceiling. Of course, the kids were also hanging stuff all over the walls—everywhere. The hospital staff had never seen anything like this loving support. We have a big family—my side, Patricia's side, and all the church family, and all our friends, and our kids. The little babies, our grandkids, were crawling all over her halo; we got some great pictures of that. Everyone close to us just got together and started hanging posters to encourage her. I remember sometimes the cards would fall down from the ceiling and we would be up there taping them back so she could see them.

DICK: I recall the 2 Corinthians 4:17 poster: "For momentary, light affliction is producing for us an eternal weight of glory far beyond all comparison." How would you describe what has happened here? Your recovery wasn't just by mere medical means, nor was it an instant miraculous intervention. How would you describe what happened that led to an unexpected and complete recovery, certainly ahead of any time expectation?

JOHN: It was a situation where she had a life-threatening injury; and there were certain healing processes which God in His sovereign power superintended, accelerated, and made complete. There is no reason not to believe that. Why fall off on the side of not believing this when it's clear that God has the power to do that and she is living proof of a total restoration? Even unconverted people say she is a walking miracle. The fact is that her health was restored as if nothing had happened.

PATRICIA: There is no question that God orchestrated these things to bring glory to Himself. I'm just thankful that He chose me to be a recipient of His undeserved and unexplained grace.

18

Your Healing Promise

C an you imagine visiting your doctor for a minor problem, only to have him diagnose your ailment as a potentially terminal disease? As disappointing as such news could be, it is far better to discover life-threatening ailments while you can still receive treatment.

In the early 1930's my Grandfather Lee complained of a skin irritation on his left ear. At my grandmother's insistence, he scheduled a doctor's appointment.

Much to my grandfather's shock, his physician discovered a cancerous inflammation. Surgery followed the next day, and although they amputated his ear, the operation prevented the cancer from spreading to his brain. The good news overshadowed the bad.

The Unexpected

Two thousand years ago a certain man found himself in a similar situation. He suffered from obvious paralysis, but Jesus announced that he carried a far more serious problem—

the terminal disease of sin, which would take his life eternally unless he experienced a miraculous cure (Mark 2:1-12).

During His ministry Jesus had earned a reputation for the unexpected, and this occasion was no exception. When the paralytic was brought before Him, instead of saying, "Arise and walk," the Savior shockingly proclaimed, "Your sins are forgiven."

The disabled man perceived paralysis to be his most serious defect, but Jesus diagnosed his deepest problem as *sin*. Paralysis is temporal; it ceases at death. But sin is eternal; it results in separation from God forever. Jesus dealt with the man's sin first because of its eternal consequences.

Many people see the paralytic's physical healing as the main point of the Bible passage, but God intended it to be only the illustration. The primary healing here involved the forgiveness of the paralytic's sins, which brought him into eternal fellowship with God.

The Elements of Spiritual Healing

Healed of Eternal Death

Not until the Pharisees challenged Christ's authority to forgive sin (Mark 2:6-8) did Jesus actually heal the paralytic. He healed only so that the eyewitnesses would know that the Son of Man had authority on earth to forgive sins. And note this carefully: Although the man eventually lost his newfound health through death, this very day he experiences eternal life because Christ forgave his sins.

It could be that you, like the paralytic and his faithful friends, have been focusing exclusively on the physical. Yet Christ reminds us that God's concern lies chiefly in the spiritual realm. Sin presents our greatest problem, not sickness. Even though the mortality rate of every generation eventually reaches 100 percent, which ensures that we will all fail in preserving our physical health, it doesn't have to be that way eternally.

Romans 3:9-18 pictures sin as an ugly cancer that spreads throughout the body. It affects our mind (verse 11), mouth (verse 14), throat (verse 13), feet (verse 15), tongue (verse 13), eyes (verse 18), and lips (verse 13).

Unfortunately, no one has immunity from this disease; sin afflicts us all. "There is none righteous, not even one; there is none who understands, there is none who seeks for God" (Romans 3:10-11). "For all have sinned and fall short of the glory of God" (Romans 3:23). Sin affects our soul as cancer affects our body. Dr. Paul Brand and Philip Yancey picture sin as cancer in the physical body.

> Like many Indian beggars, the woman was emaciated, with sunken cheeks and eyes and bony limbs. But, paradoxically, a huge mass of plump skin, round and sleek like a sausage, was growing from her side. It lay beside her like a formless baby, connected to her by a broad bridge of skin. The woman had exposed her flank with its grotesque deformity to give her an advantage in the rivalry for pity. Though I saw her only briefly, I felt sure that the growth was a lipoma, a tumor of fat cells. It was a part of her and yet not, as if some surgeon had carved a hunk of fat out of a three-hundred-pound person, wrapped it in live skin, and deftly sewed it on this woman. She was starving; she feebly held up a spidery hand for alms. But her tumor was thriving, nearly equaling the weight of the rest of her body. It gleamed in the sun, exuding health, sucking life from her.[1]

Like the tumor which sucked life from the beggar woman in India, sin snatches life from the spiritually impoverished. Jesus Christ provides the only cure. Jesus said, "I am the way, and the truth, and the life; no one comes to the Father, but through Me" (John 14:6). Peter preached Christ as the only Savior: "There is salvation in no one else; for there is no other name under heaven that has been given among men, by which we must be saved" (Acts 4:12).

Perhaps you fully understand that sin presents your greatest problem, but you don't know what to do about it. If so, consider Paul's words:

If you confess with your mouth Jesus as Lord, and believe in your heart that God raised Him from the dead, you shall be saved; for with the heart man believes, resulting in righteousness, and with the mouth he confesses, resulting in salvation. . . . For "Whoever will call upon the name of the Lord will be saved" (Romans 10:9-10,13).

By grace you have been saved though faith; and that not of yourselves, it is the gift of God; not as a result of works, that no one should boast. For we are His workmanship, created in Christ Jesus for good works, which God prepared beforehand, that we should walk in them (Ephesians 2:8-10).

In Matthew 11:28-30 Jesus personally gives this gracious invitation for you to be healed of your sins: "Come to Me, all who are weary and heavy-laden, and I will give you rest. Take My yoke upon you, and learn from Me, for I am gentle and humble in heart; and you shall find rest for your souls. For My yoke is easy, and My load is light."

Christ extends salvation to you. If you are weary and heavy-laden with sin, He offers you eternal rest. But you must lay down your sin and come to Christ as your Savior (11:28). Submit yourself to His lordship by entering the yoke with Him (verse 29). He will take away your burden of guilt and shame; eternal life will be yours; you will be truly healed for all eternity—just like the paralytic.

If that is your present need, bow your head right now, wherever you are, and receive Jesus Christ as your Savior and Lord (John 1:12-13). Pray in your own words—He will understand.

When you receive Christ, the promise of John 5:24 will be yours to cherish. "Truly, truly, I say to you, he who hears My Word, and believes Him who sent Me, has eternal life, and does not come into judgment, but has passed out of death into life." You will be healed of eternal death by salvation unto eternal life.

Healed of Sin's Bondage

Eternal salvation, however, does not eliminate the experience of sin in a believer's present life. The ravage of sin on the human race far surpasses the worst epidemics in all of human history. While the *penalty* of eternal separation from God is removed through salvation in Jesus Christ, the *practice* of sin does not immediately cease, as evidenced by Paul's lament in Romans 7:18-25.

However, the *enslavement* to sin has been broken by salvation. Sin no longer has mastery over the Christian (Romans 6:17-22).

As Christians we have been healed of sin's enslavement by sanctification unto holiness. To help us understand this in practical terms, J.I. Packer puts this truth in both a present and an eternal perspective.

> We are all invalids in God's hospital. In moral and spiritual terms we are all sick and damaged, diseased and deformed, scarred and sore, lame and lopsided, to a far, far greater extent than we realize. Under God's care we are getting better, but we are not yet well.
>
> ... The old saying that the church is God's hospital remains true. Our spiritual life is at best a fragile convalescence, easily disrupted. When there are tensions, strains, perversities, and disappointments in the Christian fellowship, it helps to remember that no Christian, and no church, ever has the clean bill of spiritual health that would match the total physical well-being for which today's fitness seekers labor. To long for total spiritual well-being is right and natural, but to believe that one is anywhere near it is to be utterly self-deceived.[2]

Sin's effects in this world still batter us even though Christ has freed us from sin's bondage. In this life we can expect to know the fellowship of Christ's sufferings (Philippians 3:10) even though we are spiritually on the mend. But because sin no longer weighs us down, we can effectively live above life, even though we have not yet been removed from it. Also, spiritual healing in this life should produce amazing responses to life-threatening situations. Patient endurance, not escape, in one sense exemplifies a higher form of healing in this life.

> Real healing is experienced by people with an incurable illness who find it possible to face it without despair precisely because they are Christians, by people who cope with daily pain as they depend on Christ for strength, by those who remain healthy people even though they live in the midst of irresolvable family problems, and by those whose faith enables them to endure oppression and injustice without becoming victims of destructive hatred.[3]

Healed from Physical Death

As we well know, healing from eternal death and sin's bondage does not prevent physical death. As the old adage goes, "Only two things in life are certain—taxes and death." While death solves our tax problem, what solves the death dilemma? Answer: God's promise of resurrection. As Christians we will be healed, even from death's sting.

> We ourselves, having the first fruits of the Spirit, even we ourselves groan within ourselves, waiting eagerly for our adoption as sons, the redemption of our body (Romans 8:23; *see also* Philippians 3:20-21; 1 Thessalonians 4:13-18).

In a real sense, resurrection culminates the ultimate healing. Everything that Adam experienced before the Fall will be ours because of resurrection for eternity. We will no longer be separated from fellowship with God by sin. We will no longer have the prospect of eternal alienation from God in hell. We will no longer live in a perishable body so that physical death can separate the body from our soul.

We will live forever, without sin and without the curse brought about by sin. We will live in the presence of our holy God because we have been healed from physical death by resurrection unto eternal glorification (Revelation 22:1-5).

Your Healing Promise

Now let's go back and look once more at God's healing promise. Hopefully it makes more sense than it did when we first began this study.

> He Himself bore our sins in His body on the cross, that we might die to sin and live to righteousness; for by His wounds you were healed. For you were continually straying like sheep, but now you have returned to the Shepherd and Guardian of your souls (1 Peter 2:24-25).

God has provided spiritual healing in Christ's salvation sacrifice at Calvary. Christ bore our sins so that we could be healed of eternal death, of bondage to sin, and of physical death. Salvation, sanctification, and resurrection restore those who have received Jesus Christ as Savior and Lord (John 1:12-13). That is God's healing promise to us. We deserve far less; we could ask for no more; we should hope for this alone!

A Final Prayer

These thoughts, penned by an unknown Puritan centuries ago, best express the faith and hope of those who possess and understand God's healing promise from an eternal perspective.[4] I can identify with this prayer. What about you?

"The Broken Heart"

O Lord,
No day of my life has passed
   that has not proved me guilty in thy sight.
Prayers have been uttered from a prayerless heart;
Praise has been often praiseless sound;
My best services are filthy rags.
Blessed Jesus, let me find a covert in thy appeasing
     wounds.
Though my sins rise to heaven thy merits soar above
     them;
Though unrighteousness weighs me down to hell,
   thy righteousness exalts me to thy throne.
All things in me call for my rejection,
All things in thee plead my acceptance.
I appeal from the throne of perfect justice
   to thy throne of boundless grace,
Grant me to hear thy voice assuring me:
     that by thy stripes I am healed,
     that thou wast bruised for my iniquities,
     that thou hast been made sin for me
       that I might be righteous in thee,
     that my grievous sins, my manifold sins,
       are all forgiven
       buried in the ocean of thy concealing blood.
I am guilty, but pardoned,
   lost, but saved,
   wandering, but found,
   sinning, but cleansed.
Give me perpetual broken-heartedness,
Keep me always clinging to thy cross,
Flood me every moment with descending grace,
Open to me the springs of divine knowledge,
   sparkling like crystal,
   flowing clear and unsullied
   through my wilderness of life.

A FINAL WORD

Your Healing Ministry

A fter all of your reading you may be wondering, "Where do I fit in?"

Health does not come through our own goodness, but rather by God's grace and mercy. Because we have freely received, let me show you from Scripture how we can also freely give to the sick and suffering. Here is where you fit in. You can have a healing ministry.

God's Compassion

It all begins with a desire to be like God. Nothing models God's character more than compassion.[1] (*See* Exodus 34:6; Psalm 86:15; 112:4; 116:5; 145:8; Joel 2:13; James 5:11.)

> The LORD's lovingkindnesses indeed never cease, For His compassions never fail. They are new every morning; great is Thy faithfulness (Lamentations 3:22-23).

Christ embodied compassion throughout His earthly ministry (Matthew 9:36-38; Mark 6:34). Some of Scripture's most memorable teachings embrace compassion—for example, the prodigal son (Luke 15:11-32), the forgiven slave (Matthew 18:21-35), and the good Samaritan (Luke 10:25-37). The New · Testament continually prods Christians to reach new levels of compassionate ministry (Galatians 6:2; Colossians 3:12; 1 Peter 3:8; 1 John 3:11-17).

Compassion cannot remain optional for Christians if we are to be like God. Someone once defined compassion as "your pain in my heart, which moves me to deeds of comfort and mercy on your behalf." That's healing ministry at the core—when we serve the suffering with God's compassion.

Compassion's Call

Why does compassion rate such importance? Consider these biblical commendations.

First, service to the suffering symbolizes the epitome of Christianity.

> This is pure and undefiled religion in the sight of our God and Father, to visit orphans and widows in their distress, and to keep oneself unstained by the world (James 1:27).

Authentic believers relieve the pressures of life that squeeze such helpless people as orphans and widows. The Greek word translated "distress" in James 1:27 portrays life painfully closing in on all sides—trouble that presses people dry. These dear folks are chief candidates for Christ's comforting love applied through us.

Second, service to the suffering epitomizes godliness. David was a man after God's heart because he did all of God's will (Acts 13:22). A part of God's will caused David to care for Mephibosheth, the crippled son of Jonathan (2 Samuel 9:3-10). Like David, we need to manifest the kindness of God.

Next, service to the suffering follows the example of our Lord Jesus Christ.

> The Son of Man did not come to be served,
> but to serve, and to give His life as a ransom for
> many (Matthew 20:28).

Just as doctors do not attend to the healthy, neither did Christ minister to the righteous, according to Mark 2:17. Instead, He cared for sinners and the sick. While we cannot serve by direct healing like Christ did, we can serve by sharing the gospel and by caring for the suffering.

Fourth, service to the suffering illustrates the ways of God. Comfort begins with the Father of mercies and God of all comfort (2 Corinthians 1:3), which He dispenses to us in our hour of need (2 Corinthians 1:4). Then God extends His comfort through us to others in need . . . "so that we may be able to comfort those who are in any affliction with the comfort with which we ourselves are comforted by God" (2 Corinthians 1:4).

Remember, comfort never runs out and never wears thin. The Father of mercies expects us to pass it on.

Finally, service to the suffering obeys the exhortation of Scripture.

> Now there are many members, but one body.
> And the eye cannot say to the hand, "I have no
> need of you"; or again the head to the feet, "I
> have no need of you." On the contrary, it is much
> truer that the members of the body which seem
> to be weaker are necessary; and those members
> of the body, which we deem less honorable, on
> these we bestow more abundant honor, and our
> unseemly members come to have more abundant
> seemliness, whereas our seemly members have
> no need of it. But God has so composed the body,
> giving more abundant honor to that member
> which lacked, that there should be no division in
> the body, but that the members should have the
> same care for one another. And if one member

suffers, all the members suffer with it; if one member is honored, all the members rejoice with it. Now you are Christ's body, and individually members of it (1 Corinthians 12:20-27).

The weaker, the less honorable, and the unseemly should not be neglected. *All* members of Christ's church need to suffer with those other members who suffer. Without such service, the body of Christ really suffers.

Compassion in Action

Paul called the church to compassion in 1 Thessalonians 5:14:

We urge you, brethren, admonish the unruly, encourage the fainthearted, help the weak, be patient with all men.

How then does all this translate into a healing ministry? Let me outline some major elements of such a ministry:

1. Extend salvation's hope by sharing the gospel with unbelievers. They will be healed of eternal death, sin's bondage, and physical death when they receive Jesus Christ as their personal Lord and Savior. This constitutes the most effective form of testimony.

2. Show compassion to the suffering by coming alongside them with the ministry of mercy. This might be in home or hospital visitation; it could be caring for a widow or orphan; perhaps you could spend time with a hurting person by being a friend when the rest of the world has walked out; you can even help deal with sin in the life of a fellow believer.

3. Solicit God's grace through prayer. Appealing to God for help on behalf of the helpless constitutes the highest form of worship, ministry, and potential healing.

If you would like a useful resource and reference tool that includes the entire healing record of the Bible, you can request a copy of *The Biblical Pattern for Divine Healing* by Richard L. Mayhue from BMH Books, Winona Lake, IN 46590.

Recommended Reading

Colin Brown, *That You May Believe,* Grand Rapids, MI: Eerdmans, 1985.

Walter J. Chantry, *Signs of the Apostles: Observations on Pentecostalism Old and New,* 2d ed., Edinburgh: The Banner of Truth Trust, 1976.

Henry Frost, *Miraculous Healing,* reprint, London: Evangelical Press, 1972.

Hank Hanegraaff, *Christianity in Crisis,* Eugene, OR: Harvest House Publishers, 1993.

Michael Horton, *The Agony of Deceit,* Chicago: Moody Press, 1990.

André Kole, *Miracles or Magic?* Eugene, OR: Harvest House Publishers, 1987.

John F. MacArthur, Jr., *The Charismatics,* Grand Rapids, MI: Zondervan Publishing House, 1978.

John F. MacArthur, Jr., *Charismatic Chaos,* Grand Rapids, MI: Zondervan Publishing House, 1992.

Peter Masters, *The Healing Epidemic*, London: The Wakeman Trust, 1988.

Richard L. Mayhue, *The Biblical Pattern for Divine Healing*, Winona Lake, IN: BMH Books, 1979.

D.R. McConnell, *A Different Gospel,* Peabody, MA: Hendrickson Publishers, 1988.

Michael G. Moriarity, *The New Charismatics,* Grand Rapids, MI: Zondervan Publishing House, 1992.

John Napier, *Charismatic Challenge,* Homebush West, Australia: Anzea Publishers, 1991.

William A. Nolen, *Healing: A Doctor in Search of a Miracle,* Greenwich, CT: Fawcett Publications, 1976.

C. Samuel Storms, *Healing and Holiness,* Phillipsburg, NJ: Presbyterian and Reformed Publishing Company, 1990.

Joni Eareckson Tada and Steve Estes, *A Step Further,* Grand Rapids, MI: Zondervan Publishing House, 1990.

R.A. Torrey, *Divine Healing,* reprint, Grand Rapids, MI: Baker Book House, 1974.

Benjamin B. Warfield, *Counterfeit Miracles,* reprint, Edinburgh: The Banner of Truth Trust, 1972.

Notes

CHAPTER 1—God's Healing Promise

1. "Praise, My Soul, the King of Heaven" (stanza 1) written by Henry F. Lute.
2. "Jesus, I Come" (stanza 1) written by William T. Sleeper.
3. These questions have been asked by David Allen Hubbard in Lewis B. Smedes, ed., *Ministry and the Miraculous* (Pasadena, CA: Fuller Theological Seminary, 1987), 9; Richard Mayhue, *Divine Healing Today* (Chicago: Moody Press, 1983), 11; and Jonathan Graf, ed., *Healing: The Three Great Classics on Divine Healing* (Camp Hill, PA: Christian Publications, 1992), 2.
4. R.A. Torrey, *Divine Healing* (Grand Rapids, MI: Baker Book House, reprinted 1974).
5. *Ibid.*, 10.
6. *Ibid.*, emphasis added, 5.
7. Joni Eareckson Tada and Steve Estes, *A Step Further* (Grand Rapids, MI: Zondervan Publishing House, 1990), 108.
8. This section has been modeled after William C. Moore, "Nine Half-Truths on Healing," *Eternity* (May, 1983), 36-38.
9. C. Everett Koop, "Faith-Healing and the Sovereignty of God" in *The Agony of Deceit*, ed. by Michael Horton (Chicago: Moody Press, 1990), 179-80.
10. Hank Hanegraaff, *Christianity in Crisis* (Eugene, OR: Harvest House Publishers, 1993).
11. Charles R. Swindoll, *Flying Closer to the Flame* (Dallas: Word Publishing, 1993), 180.

CHAPTER 2—Contemporary Confusion

1. "The Exorcist," *Newsweek* (September 10, 1973), 31.
2. Francis Schaeffer, *The New Super Spirituality* (Downers Grove, IL: InterVarsity Press, 1972), 16.
3. David F. Wells, *No Place For Truth* (Grand Rapids, MI: Eerdmans, 1993), is a classic work on this subject.
4. Since the history of healing is not the central focus of this volume, I point the reader to three volumes by Frank C. Darling: *Biblical Healing* (Boulder, CO: Vista Publications, 1989); *Christian Healing in the Middle Ages and Beyond* (Boulder, CO: Vista Publications, 1990); and *The Restoration of Christian Healing* (Boulder, CO: Vista Publications, 1992). Also consult Keith M. Bailey, *Divine Healing: The Children's Bread* (Harrisburg, PA: Christian Publications, 1977), 199-210; J. Sidlow Baxter, *Divine Healing of the Body* (Grand Rapids, MI: Zondervan Publishing House, 1979), 29-105; and B.B. Warfield, *Counterfeit Miracles* (Edinburgh: The Banner of Truth Trust, reprinted 1972), 33-69.
5. *See* Michael G. Moriarity, *The New Charismatics* (Grand Rapids, MI: Zondervan Publishing House, 1992), 20-86, for a good overview of this time period. Also Donald W. Dayton, *Theological Roots of Pentecostalism* (Grand Rapids, MI: Francis Asbury Press, 1987), 115-41, comments on the late-nineteenth century.
6. F.F. Bosworth, *Christ the Healer* (Old Tappan, NJ: Fleming H. Revell, reprinted 1973). This volume originally appeared in 1924.
7. For a survey of this period, *see* the definitive work by David E. Harrell, Jr., *All Things Are Possible: The Healing and Charismatic Revivals in Modern America* (Bloomington, IN: Indiana University Press, 1975).

8. David E. Harrell, Jr. chronicles the life of Oral Roberts up through 1985 in *Oral Roberts: An American Life* (Bloomington, IN: Indiana University Press, 1985).

9. Hobart Freeman, *Faith* (Claypool, IN: Faith Publications, n.d.), 11. Dr. Freeman's strong stance against physicians and medicine and consequent practice by his congregation eventually led to over 85 documented deaths in his church. Freeman, widely recognized at one time as a reputable Old Testament scholar, eventually died after refusing to seek medical treatment for pulmonary and heart disease.

10. William Caldwell, *Meet the Healer* (Tulsa, OK: Front Line Evangelism, 1965), 5.

11. Oral Roberts, *Seven Divine Aids for Your Health* (Tulsa, OK: Oral Roberts, 1960), 35.

12. *See* Peter Masters, *The Healing Epidemic* (London: The Wakeman Trust, 1988), 21-35. Masters charges Cho with incorporating occultic elements in his ministry.

13. For an in-indepth analysis of this movement and its leaders, *see* Bruce Barron, *The Health and Wealth Gospel* (Downers Grove, IL: InterVarsity Press, 1987); Gordon D. Fee, *The Disease of the Health and Wealth Gospel* (Costa Mesa, CA: The Word for Today, n.d.); Hank Hanegraaff, *Christianity in Crisis* (Eugene, OR: Harvest House Publishers, 1993); Michael Horton, ed., *The Agony of Deceit* (Chicago: Moody Press, 1990); Dave Hunt, *Beyond Seduction* (Eugene, OR: Harvest House Publishers, 1987); John F. MacArthur, Jr., *Charismatic Chaos* (Grand Rapids, MI: Zondervan Publishing House, 1992); Douglas Moo, "Divine Healing in the Health and Wealth Movement," *Trinity Journal* (1988), 191-209; Michael G. Moriarity, *The New Charismatics*.

14. For a succinct theological analysis, read Ken L. Sarles, "A Theological Evaluation of the Prosperity Gospel," *Bibliotheca Sacra* (October-December, 1986), 329-52.

15. Extensive documentation to support the charge of cultic origins has been provided by D.R. McConnell, *A Different Gospel* (Peabody, MA: Hendrickson Publishers, 1988) and H. Terris Neuman, "Cultic Origins of Word-Faith Theology Within the Charismatic Movement," *Pneuma* (Spring, 1990), 32-55.

16. *See* Richard Mayhue, "Job: A Righteous Victor" in *A Christian's Survival Guide* (Wheaton, IL: Victor Books, 1987), 120-31.

17. This label finds its popularization in the MC510 "Signs, Wonders and Church Growth" course taught by C. Peter Wagner, John Wimber, and Charles Kraft in the early 1980s. A whole issue of *Christian Life* magazine (October, 1982) explained this unusual course offered by Fuller Theological Seminary. Sufficient doubt, questions, and confusion surfaced over the course, causing Fuller to suspend continued offerings of the course in order to allow a panel of faculty representatives to evaluate the course content and address varying charges. The written conclusions of this task force appear in Lewis B. Smedes, ed., *Ministry and the Miraculous* (Pasadena, CA: Fuller Theological Seminary, 1987).

18. C. Peter Wagner coined the term "Third Wave." By this he means that the early-1900s Pentecostal outpouring represented the "First Wave," followed by the charismatic renewal of the 1960s and 1970s, which served as the "Second Wave." Now the "Third Wave" comes with broad-based, ecumenical support for signs and wonders. *See* C. Peter Wagner, *The Third Wave of the Holy Spirit* (Ann Arbor, MI: Vine Publications, 1988).

19. Until recently, Wimber's writings constituted the major, biblical expressions of the movement. They include John Wimber and Kevin Springer, *Power Evangelism* (San Francisco: Harper and Row, 1986). A second, revised and expanded edition has been released in 1992. Also, John Wimber and Kevin Springer, *Power Healing* (San Francisco: Harper and Row, 1987). The most ambitious attempt to biblically substantiate "Vineyard theology" has been offered by Gary S. Greig and Kevin N. Springer, eds., *The Kingdom and the Power* (Ventura, CA: Regal Books, 1993).

20. *See* Jack Deere, *Surprised by the Power of the Spirit* (Grand Rapids, MI: Zondervan Publishing House, 1993).

21. Evaluations of the signs and wonders movement have been offered by John H. Armstrong, D.A. Carson, and James M. Boice in Michael Horton, ed., *Power Religion* (Chicago: Moody Press, 1992), 61-136; John F. MacArthur, Jr., *Charismatic Chaos*, 128-51; Thomas D. Pratt, "The Need to Dialogue: A Review of the Debate on the Controversy of Signs, Wonders, Miracles, and Spiritual Warfare Raised in the Literature of the Third Wave Movement," *Pneuma* (Spring, 1991), 7-32; Ken L. Sarles, "An Appraisal of the Signs and Wonders Movement," *Bibliotheca Sacra* (January-March, 1988), 57-82. I personally listened to John Wimber make the following assessment of the Vineyard movement at the annual Evangelical Theological Society meetings held at San Diego, California in November, 1989. A cassette tape containing Wimber's comments made during the question-and-answer portion of Dr. Gary Breshear's workshop "Third Wave of the Holy Spirit: What Is It?" can be ordered from Mobiltape Company, Inc., 25061 W. Avenue Stanford, Suite 70, Valencia, CA, 91355. These words express Wimber's assessment of the Vineyard movement up to 1989: "[O]ur thought is not very mature; we're not very reflective; we're not very objective; we're not sophisticated. . . ."
22. John Wimber and Kevin Springer, *Power Healing*, 137.
23. *Ibid.*, 162.
24. *Ibid.*, 166.
25. For a well-documented summary of Hinn's ministry and teachings, read Hank Hanegraaff, *Christianity in Crisis*, 33-34, 339-45.
26. Benny Hinn, *The Anointing* (Nashville, TN: Thomas Nelson Publishers, 1992), 59-60.
27. Benny Hinn, *Lord, I Need a Miracle* (Nashville, TN: Thomas Nelson Publishers, 1993), 63.
28. *Ibid.*
29. *Ibid.*, 74-75.
30. *Ibid.*, 79, 81, 83-84.
31. *Ibid.*, 85-87.
32. *Ibid.*, 58-62.
33. *Ibid.*, 67, 72.
34. *Ibid.*, 100-02.
35. Benny Hinn, *The Anointing*, 146-47.
36. Stephen Strang, "Benny Hinn Speaks Out," *Charisma* (August, 1993), 28.
37. John F. MacArthur, Jr., *Charismatic Chaos*, 203-04. It's interesting to note that Frank Darling, in *The Restoration of Christian Healing*, includes Mary Baker Eddy (Church of Christ, Scientist), Charles and Myrtle Fillmore (Unity School of Christianity), Ernest Holmes (Church of Religious Science), and the Roman Catholic Church along with other Christian healing ministries. This further makes the point that contemporary healing ministries could not be distinctively biblical in their healings or they would not be like or be associated with healings that are alleged by cults and false religions.
38. Charles R. Swindoll, *Flying Closer to the Flame* (Dallas: Word Publishing, 1993), 197.
39. Larry and Alice Parker have published their story in *We Let Our Son Die* (Irvine, CA: Harvest House Publishers, 1980). Larry has given permission to quote this letter. In so doing, the Parkers are not endorsing all of the conclusions reached in this volume.

CHAPTER 3—Are Faith Healers for Real?

1. James Randi, *The Faith Healers* (Buffalo: Prometheus Books, 1987).
2. Robert Lee Whitworth, *God Told Me to Tell You* (Green Forest, AR: New Leaf Press, 1989), 109.

3. William Nolen, "In Search of a Miracle," *McCall's* magazine (September, 1974), 107. An expanded rendition appeared in William A. Nolen's *Healing: A Doctor in Search of a Miracle* (Greenwich, CT: Fawcett Publications, 1976), 93-94.
4. Taken from a transcribed conversation with Benny Hinn on February 6, 1992.
5. Benny Hinn, *Lord, I Need a Miracle* (Nashville, TN: Thomas Nelson Publishers, 1993).
6. Taken from a transcribed conversation with Benny Hinn on February 6, 1992.
7. *Ibid.*

CHAPTER 4—Understanding Reported Healings

1. Harry Swofford, "Miracles," *National Courier* (April 29, 1977), 36. Experience-oriented, religion-based healing episodes usually carry much more weight in those discussions which attempt to make the case for contemporary healing ministries than any careful use of Scripture. For example, Benny Hinn, *Lord, I Need a Miracle* (Nashville, TN: Thomas Nelson Publishers, 1993) employs about 105 pages of experiences (out of 166 total pages) to convince people that his 53 pages of attempted biblical discussion is correct. While other sources do not have the same imbalance, one gets the distinct impression that experience at least equals Scripture in Jack Deere, *Surprised by the Power of the Holy Spirit* (Grand Rapids, MI: Zondervan Publishing House, 1993) and John Wimber and Kevin Springer, *Power Healing* (San Francisco: Harper & Row, 1987). Edith L. Blumhofer made this same observation in "Dispensing with Scofield," *Christianity Today* (January 10, 1994), 57, where she reviews Deere's work. For all three, "religion works," but the same testimonies could be given by people in other world religions and cults.
2. "Science Takes New Look at Faith Healing," *U.S. News & World Report* (February 12, 1979), 68.
3. Lewis B. Smedes, ed., *Ministry and the Miraculous* (Pasadena, CA: Fuller Theological Seminary, 1987), 58. This careful statement has been taken from a faculty-authored report written in response to the perceived excesses of the MC510 course "Signs, Wonders and Church Growth" taught by John Wimber, C. Peter Wagner, and Charles Kraft. The report's point, simply made, is twofold: 1) there are more healings outside of Christianity than within, and 2) to be declared miraculous and truly from God, Christian healings must be clearly verified as substantially distinct from other religious-based healings.
4. John F. MacArthur, Jr., *Charismatic Chaos* (Grand Rapids, MI: Zondervan Publishing House, 1992), 210. Later, in Chapter 17 of *The Healing Promise*, John and Patricia MacArthur will relate their perspectives on Patricia's remarkable survival and complete recovery from extensive injuries suffered in a life-threatening automobile accident during the summer of 1992.
5. Charles R. Swindoll, *Flying Closer to the Flame* (Dallas: Word Publishing, 1993), 198-200. Used by permission.
6. Lonnelle Aikman, *Nature's Healing Arts: From Folk Medicine to Modern Drugs* (Washington, D.C.: The National Geographic Society, 1977) presents an interesting survey of this worldwide field.
7. Irving Wallace, David Wallechinsky, and Amy Wallace, "Doctors May Be Harmful," *Parade* (October 4, 1981), 27.
8. Doug Podolsky and Rita Reuben, "Heal Thyself," *U.S. News & World Report* (November 22, 1993), 64.
9. Dr. D. Martyn Lloyd-Jones, *Healing and the Scriptures* (Nashville, TN: Oliver-Nelson Books, 1988), 29-31. *See also* Dr. Franklin E. Payne, Jr., *Biblical Healing for Modern Medicine* (Augusta, GA: Covenant Books, 1993), 153.
10. Dr. Verna Wright, "A Medical View of Miraculous Healing" in Peter Masters, *The Healing Epidemic* (London: The Wakeman Trust, 1988), 210.

11. Kenneth Pelletier, "Mind as Healer, Mind as Slayer," *Christian Medical Society Journal*, 11:1 (1980), 8.

12. William A. Nolen, *Healing: A Doctor in Search of a Miracle* (Greenwich, CT: Fawcett Publications, 1976), 253-55.

13. Dr. Verna Wright, "A Medical View of Miraculous Healing," 211. Also, read C. Samuel Storms, *Healing and Holiness* (Phillipsburg, NJ: Presbyterian and Reformed Publishing Company, 1990), 43-46.

14. Doug Podolsky, "No Place For Sick People," *U.S. News & World Report* (August 5, 1991), 39.

15. George W. Peters, *Indonesian Revival* (Grand Rapids, MI: Zondervan Publishing House, 1973), 80-83. Used by permission.

16. Dr. Verna Wright, "A Medical View of Miraculous Healing," 205-06.

17. Rita Reuben, "Placebos' Healing Power," *U.S. News & World Report* (November 22, 1993), 78.

18. Dr. Franklin E. Payne, Jr., *Biblical Healing for Modern Medicine,* 152-53.

19. Cited by Dr. Verna Wright, "A Medical View of Miraculous Healing," 211-13. David C. Lewis, an anthropologist by training, attempted a follow-up study of attendees of John Wimber's November, 1986 Harrogate, England, conference. He reports the results in *Healing: Fiction, Fantasy or Fact?* (London: Hodder and Stoughton, 1989). While Lewis's conclusions sympathetically affirm Wimber's ministry, neither the medical community nor the Christian community have been convinced by either the assumptions of the study or the interpretation of the data.

20. *Ibid.*

21. "Retraction," *Moody Monthly* (February, 1977), 53.

22. James Randi, *The Faith Healers* (Buffalo: Prometheus Books, 1987), 99-181, chronicles his successful efforts to expose these men as frauds. Mike Hertenstein and Jon Trott document the fraud of Christian celebrity, author, and musician Mike Warnke in *Selling Satan* (Chicago: Cornerstone Press, 1993).

23. William A. Nolen, *Healing: A Doctor in Search of a Miracle*, 272.

24. To explore the medical details that exalt God's creative order in the human body, *see* Dr. Paul Brand and Philip Yancey, *Fearfully and Wonderfully Made* (Grand Rapids, MI: Zondervan Publishing House, 1980).

CHAPTER 5—Before the Cross

1. John Wimber and Kevin Springer, *Power Healing* (San Francisco, CA: Harper & Row, 1987), 244. Appendix C, "Healing in the Old Testament," needs to be used with great caution and careful study lest one be left with erroneous impressions. Of the 75 texts cited, only 15 deal with a particular incident of physical healing. Most deal with spiritual, national, or millennial restoration, not physical healing. It is a bit ironic, considering the book's emphasis, that three of the texts listed contain the message that "there is no healing" (Jeremiah 46:11; 51:8-9; Hosea 5:13). Surprisingly, the list does not include six of the 20 Old Testament occurrences of specific healing (Genesis 21:1-2; 29:31; 30:22; Numbers 25:1-9; 1 Samuel 1:19-20; 2 Samuel 24:1-17; and Job 42).

CHAPTER 6—Jesus and the Multitudes

1. Norris McWhirter and Ross McWhirter, *Guinness Book of World Records* (New York: Bantam, 1977), 1.

2. This chart conforms to the synoptic chronology according to Robert L. Thomas and Stanley N. Gundry, *A Harmony of the Gospels* (Chicago: Moody Press, 1979).

CHAPTER 7—The Apostolic Legacy

1. This section has been adapted from Richard Mayhue, *How to Interpret the Bible for Yourself* (Winona Lake, IN: BMH Books, 1988), 145-51. *See also* Colin Brown, "The Other Half of the Gospel?" *Christianity Today* (April 21, 1989), 26-29.

CHAPTER 8—Is There Healing in the Atonement?

1. I have been greatly surprised by the deficiency of attention given to Isaiah 53 by some of the most recent, highly visible volumes advocating a contemporary healing ministry. For instance, Jack Deere, *Surprised by the Power of the Spirit* (Grand Rapids, MI: Zondervan Publishing House, 1993) devotes only one paragraph (169) in a 299-page book on healing. John Wimber and Kevin Springer, *Power Healing* (San Francisco: Harper & Row, 1987) devote less than four full pages (152-56) out of 269 pages, but use most of the space discussing what men have said rather than what the Scriptures teach. Benny Hinn, *Lord, I Need a Miracle* (Nashville, TN: Thomas Nelson Publishers, 1993) provides less than two pages (55-56). Jeffrey Niehaus in *The Kingdom and the Power* (Ventura, CA: Regal Books, 1993) devotes less than three full pages (48-50). For a complete exegetical discussion of Isaiah 53, *see* Edward J. Young, *The Book of Isaiah*, Vol. 3 (Grand Rapids, MI: Eerdmans, 1972), 340-54.
2. The New Testament consistently presents Christ as the Christian's substitutionary sinbearer in His atonement. *See* Matthew 20:28; John 1:29; Romans 4:25; 5:6-8; 8:3; 1 Corinthians 15:3; 2 Corinthians 5:21; Galatians 1:4; 3:13; 4:4-5; Hebrews 9:28; 1 Peter 3:8; and 1 John 2:2; 4:10.
3. D.A. Carson, *Showing the Spirit* (Grand Rapids, MI: Baker Book House, 1987), 156-57.
4. It seems more biblically precise to say, "There *will* be physical healing *through* the atonement" rather than, "There *is* physical healing *in* the atonement." I agree with Doug Moo, "Divine Healing in the Health and Wealth Gospel," *Trinity Journal*, 9 (1988), 204: "We would prefer, then, to say that physical healing is one *effect* of the atoning death of Christ." *See* also W. Kelly Bokovay, "The Relationship of Physical Healing to the Atonement," *Didaskalia* (April, 1991), 35: "It is misleading for anyone to suggest that healing is 'in' the Atonement without major qualifications; sickness is only dealt with in the sense that it is an *effect* of sin and its eventual eradication is guaranteed because our sin has been atoned for."
5. J. Sidlow Baxter, *Divine Healing of the Body* (Grand Rapids, MI: Zondervan Publishing House, 1979), 136-37. Baxter minces no words here in utterly denying that the atonement provides any basis for present physical healing.
6. John Wimber and Kevin Springer, *Power Healing*, 154, cite R.A. Torrey, *Divine Healing* (Grand Rapids, MI: Baker Book House, reprinted 1974), 53 (actually on page 43), writing on Isaiah 53 as meaning ". . . that based on what Jesus experienced on the cross we as a consequence may experience one hundred per cent healing here on earth." At best, this is an overstatement of Torrey's discussion (43-46); at worst, a misrepresentation. Let the reader be cautious when reading quotes from other writers, especially when the cited literature is not immediately available for verification.
7. James I. Packer, "Poor Health May Be the Best Remedy," *Christianity Today* (May 21, 1982), 15.

CHAPTER 9—Is James 5 for Me?

1. I have been surprised to see how many works that deal with healing will cite James 5:13-20 in whole or in part, but never interpret the passage. For example, Benny Hinn's *Lord, I Need a Miracle* (Nashville, TN: Thomas Nelson Publishers, 1993) cites this text several times in seven short chapters which purpose to develop a

theology of miracles. In *The Kingdom and the Power* (Ventura, CA: Regal Books, 1993), edited by Gary S. Greig and Kevin N. Springer, James 5 is cited on at least 33 occasions, but the most extensive treatments of the passage extend for only one paragraph (118, 125, 409). Jack Deere's *Surprised by the Power of the Spirit* (Grand Rapids, MI: Zondervan Publishing House, 1993) refers briefly to James 5 on at least three occasions, but never gives any exposition to validate his points. John Wimber and Kevin Springer, *Power Healing* (San Francisco: Harper & Row, 1987), cite James 5 on several occasions but never deal with the text. With only two teaching passages about physical healing in the New Testament epistles (1 Corinthians 12:8,29,30 being the other), we would expect more than mere passing references if a person's theology is to have biblical credence. On the other hand, each of the works listed above abound in detailed, anecdotal support for their opinions on healing. In contrast, Ralph P. Martin, *James* in *Word Biblical Commentary*, Vol. 48 (Dallas: Word Publishing, 1988), 197-216, provides the most informed, evenhanded, and convincing treatment of James 5:12-18 known to this writer along with Peter Davids, *Commentary on James* (Grand Rapids, MI: Eerdmans, 1982), 191-98.

2. The word group, *astheneō, astheneia, asthenēs* occurs about 83 times in the New Testament. With rare exceptions, the Gospels translate it in reference to physical sickness. Six out of seven occurrences in Acts refer to sickness. Even in the epistles, where "weak" is the majority use, it is used of Epaphroditus (Philippians 2:26-27), Trophimus (2 Timothy 4:20), and the Corinthians (1 Corinthians 11:30) to speak of physical infirmities. Since James was written before the Gospels and earlier than Acts, the sense of *astheneia* would best be taken as physical weakness, especially if other textual factors point in this direction also.

3. *See* Carl Armerding, "Is Any Among You Afflicted?" *Bibliotheca Sacra* (April-June, 1938), 195-201 and Daniel R. Hayden, "Calling the Elders to Pray," *Bibliotheca Sacra* (July-September, 1981), 258-66. I'm not convinced by Hayden's discussion because 1) he really doesn't do justice to the illustration in James 5:17-18; 2) he unacceptably tries to interpret James with the majority (but not exclusive) Pauline use of *astheneō, astheneia, asthenēs*; and 3) he effectively ignores the fact that 24 out of the 25 gospel usages of *iaomai* (used in James 5:16) refer to physical sickness. Thus, his proposal lies at the low end of the grammatical possibility scale.

4. Doug Moo, *James* in *Tyndale New Testament Commentaries* (Grand Rapids, MI: Eerdmans, 1985), 184. C. Samuel Storms, *Healing and Holiness* (Phillipsburg, NJ: Presbyterian and Reformed Publishing Company, 1990), 111 also provides an exegetically convincing discussion.

5. *See* Merrill Unger, "Divine Healing," *Bibliotheca Sacra* (July-September, 1971), 234-44 and Henry Frost, *Miraculous Healing* (London: Evangelical Press, reprinted 1972), 68 for a defense of this hyperdispensational view.

6. Lewis B. Smedes, *Ministry and the Miraculous* (Pasadena, CA: Fuller Theological Seminary, 1987), 32-33. Based on James 5, Jack Deere, *Surprised by the Power of the Spirit*, writes, "We let our church know that from now on we would be applying this passage in our services and also in our private counseling appointments. From now on, the elders and the pastors of the church would be willing to visit homes whenever called on and would pray for the sick in their homes" (30). Deere goes way beyond the authorial intent of this passage in his application.

7. Benny Hinn, in *Lord, I Need a Miracle*, asserts, "Again, when the Lord forgives sin, He always includes healing . . . (James 5:14-15)" (68). The logical conclusion to this unbiblical statement is that anyone who gets saved also gets healed. Nowhere does the Bible teach this—especially not in James 5.

8. A.J. Gordon, *The Ministry of Healing* in *Healing: The Three Great Classics on Divine Healing* (Camp Hill, PA: Christian Publications, reprinted 1992), 140-41

and A.B. Simpson, *The Gospel of Healing* in *Healing: The Three Great Classics on Divine Healing*, 294, both connect the two texts without any contextual or exegetical warrant. This also appears to be the case with Jack Deere, *Surprised by the Power of the Spirit*, 164-65.

9. *See* Gary S. Shogren, "Will God Heal Us—A Re-examination of James 5:14-16a," *The Evangelical Quarterly* (April, 1989), 99-108. This article subsequently appeared in J.I. Packer, gen. ed., *The Best of Theology*, Vol. 4 (Carol Stream, IL: Christianity Today, Inc., 1990), 75-83. It contains a full discussion of the interpretive possibilities for "anoint."

10. John Wimber and Kevin Springer, *Power Healing,* err when they state, concerning James 5:14-15, "This passage assumes that healing is a gift of God given freely to his people, not simply a means for winning new converts" (161). This passage refers to elders only, not to Christians at large.

11. *Ibid.*, 152. Wimber and Springer also err when explaining why some people are not healed: "Some people do not have faith in God for healing (James 5:15)." The faith spoken of in this text is that of the elders, not the person who is ill.

12. Roger Barrier, in *The Kingdom and the Power*, states, "Without a word from God it is not possible to pray the prayer of faith (Compare James' use of Elijah as an example in James 5:14-18 and 1 Kings 18:1, 41-44)" (226). However, God's word to Elijah in 1 Kings 18 is not the point of the illustration in James 5:17-18. To import this historical example from the Old Testament and then impose it on James 5:14-16 is to greatly exceed and misinterpret the text.

13. "If he has committed sins" (verse 15) is a complex clause (third class condition—periphrastic perfect). It carries the idea of persistence and probability. Even though a person has openly, knowingly, recklessly, and rebelliously persisted in sin, those sins will be forgiven him. This implies that 1) the person has confessed his sins, and 2) he has asked for forgiveness, and God grants healing based on the repentance, just as Elijah's day (verses 17-18).

The last clause in verse 15 is "they will be forgiven him." The Greek text actually says "*it* will be forgiven him"; that is, the state of sin will be forgiven. So, this passage concerns a believer who has recklessly involved himself in sin without repentance. Perhaps he succumbed to dishonesty, immorality, or some other pattern of sin in his life. But now he repents and confesses his sin, asking God's forgiveness.

J.B. Mayor, who has written one of the most scholarly and complete commentaries on the book of James, suggests that this passage ought to read, "If he has committed sins, which have given rise to the sickness." This latter part of verse 15 gives the *condition* that helps us understand its absolute promise. The condition explains the limitation of the passage. James 5 applies only to people who persist in a pattern of sinful living and become physically ill as a result of divine chastisement.

According to Anointing and Pastoral Care of the Sick (Washington: U.S. Catholic Conference, 1973, 5, "The sacrament of the anointing of the sick is administered to those who are dangerously ill, by anointing them on the forehead and hands with olive oil or if opportune, with another properly blessed vegetable oil." This was a radical change for the Roman church. For centuries they had used

14. The Roman Catholic sacrament of extreme unction (or more commonly called "last rites"), known in Christendom only since the ninth century, supposedly rests on James 5. However, the Catholic understanding of this passage runs contrary to James' intention. James 5 speaks of restoring a seriously ill person to life, while the sacrament proposes to prepare a person for death. James 5:15 actually promises recovery both spiritually and physically in this particular situation (5:14a) when the corrective process (5:15b) is followed.

James 5 to support the sacrament of Extreme Unction, or removal of sin as preparation for death. The major changes came in the omission of any mention of the danger of death as a condition for the anointing. The Roman church finally recognized that the content of James 5 depicts the experience of a Christian who is seriously ill and needs to be restored to health, not prepared to die.

15. Following A.B. Simpson, *The Gospel of Healing*, 295, Gary S. Greig and Kevin N. Springer, *The Power and the Kingdom*, assert that James 5:16 commands the church to pray for healing (30-31). Jack Deere, *Surprised by the Power of the Spirit*, on pages 129-30 states, "God commissioned the whole church to heal. . . ." A careful reading of the text points to the believer's obligation to ". . . confess your sins to one another, and pray for one another . . ." (5:16). The emphasis is on the spiritual, not the physical. It primarily deals with sin, not sickness. Whether there is a link between the two, it seems best to see 1) the healing only as a possibility, not a certainty, and 2) the infirmity as a result of sin. This does not constitute a mandate for the church to deal with all physical problems and suffering, but rather, to deal with sin.

16. Charles R. Swindoll, *Flying Closer to the Flame*, (Dallas: Word Publishing, 1993), 208-09.

CHAPTER 10—Demons and Sickness

1. John MacArthur, Jr., *How to Meet the Enemy* (Wheaton, IL: Victor Books, 1992), 103-04.

2. For example, Jack Deere, *Surprised by the Power of the Spirit* (Grand Rapids, MI: Zondervan Publishing House, 1993); Michael Green, *Exposing the Prince of Darkness* (Ann Arbor, MI: Servant Publications, 1991); Gary S. Greig and Kevin N. Springer, eds. *The Kingdom and the Power* (Ventura, CA: Regal Books, 1993); John Wimber and Kevin Springer, *Power Healing* (San Francisco: Harper & Row, 1987).

3. For example, Mark I. Bubeck, *The Adversary* (Chicago: Moody Press, 1975) and *Overcoming the Adversary* (Chicago: Moody Press, 1984); C. Fred Dickason, *Demon Possession & the Christian* (Chicago: Moody Press, 1987); Merrill F. Unger, *What Demons Can Do to Saints* (Chicago: Moody Press, reprinted, 1991).

4. I have previously written on the subject of Satan, but not demons. *See Unmasking Satan* (Wheaton, IL: Victor Books, 1988).

5. C. Fred Dickason, *Demon Possession & the Christian*, 325, explains: "We have come to the conclusion that neither the Bible itself nor any logical or theological extrapolation of biblical truth can finally solve the question. We have also considered the wealth of clinical evidence available and have concluded that there is good basis for holding that believers may have inhabiting demons." For a clear analysis of the error in Dickason's logic, *see* Brent Grimsley, "Can a Christian be 'Demonized'?" *Christian Research Journal* (Summer, 1993), 19, 37.

6. Frank E. Peretti, *This Present Darkness* (Westchester, IL: Crossway Books, 1986), set the standard, along with his sequel *Piercing the Darkness*. We could only wish that the recent appearance of Christian fiction was as oriented to the Scriptures as John Bunyan's classics—*Pilgrim's Progress* and *The Holy War*.

7. J.I. Packer, *Rediscovering Holiness* (Ann Arbor, MI: Servant Publications, 1992), 9.

8. For a comprehensive discussion of this passage in relationship to Satan and demons, *see* Richard L. Mayhue, "False Prophets and the Deceiving Spirit," *The Master's Seminary Journal* (Fall, 1993), 135-63.

9. The Gospel material in this section conforms to the synoptic chronology according to Robert L. Thomas and Stanley N. Gundry, *A Harmony of the Gospels* (Chicago: Moody Press, 1979). Peter's sifting by Satan (Luke 22:31-32) has not

been included because the Scriptures give no evidence of demonic activity, even though John Wimber and Kevin Springer, *Power Healing*, 117, suggest this possibility.

10. John Wimber and Kevin Springer, *Power Healing*, 117, erroneously include Judas among their examples of true believers who encountered demons.

11. I have not included the Ananias and Sapphira incident (Acts 5:1-11) because the phrase "Satan has filled your heart to lie" does not constitute being invaded by demons. Nor have I included the unrepentant fornicator in 1 Corinthians 5:1-13 because 1) there is no evidence of demon involvement, and 2) there is a strong possibility that he was a counterfeit believer (cf. "so-called brother" [5:11] and "wicked man" [5:13] as indicators). David responded to the pressures of Satan (2 Samuel 24:1; 1 Chronicles 21:1), but there is no evidence of demons or Satan indwelling David. For a fuller treatment of this episode, *see* Richard Mayhue, *Unmasking Satan*, 136-44.

12. For the sake of clarity, I am speaking here in the biblical sense of being "demon possessed" (*daimonizomai*). This verb occurs 13 times in the Gospels and is uniformly translated in the NIV as "demon possessed." To be precise, "ownership" is not the point, but "occupancy" is in view. Biblically, *daimonizomai* means to possess in the sense of spatially reside/indwell with the need for the demon to be evicted or cast out. While Dickason, *Demon Possession and the Christian*, 33-40, prefers the term "demonization" rather than "demon possessed," he correctly identifies the phenomenon associated with *daimonizomai* as a demon "residing in a person" (40). John Wimber and Kevin Springer, *Power Healing*, 109-10, confuse the issue by translating *daimonizomai* with "demonize" and then redefining the term in English to mean "influenced, afflicted or tormented in some way by demonic power" (109). By this, they mean either demonic activity externally or internally to either a believer or an unbeliever. While both Dickason (325) and Wimber (114) conclude that Christians can have demons residing within who need to be expelled, they arrive at that conclusion by different routes— Dickason being accurate with the biblical text but going beyond with experience, and Wimber being inaccurate with the biblical text.

13. I have not included 1 Corinthians 12:1-3, since it seems clear that those who curse Christ are unbelievers without the Holy Spirit (Romans 8:9).

14. The God-rejecting, rich man in Luke 16:24 cried out from Hades for "Father Abraham." The unbelieving Pharisees considered themselves "sons of Abraham" (Luke 3:8; John 8:33). Jesus affirmed this to be true (John 8:37).

15. *See* I. Howard Marshall, *The Epistles of John* in *New International Commentary on the New Testament* (Grand Rapids, MI: Eerdmans, 1978). The essential idea of "touch" (*haptomai*) in the context of Satan/demons is "fasten onto with the intent to harm." This passage does not teach that Christians will never encounter Satan and demons; but it surely must mean that once we have been delivered from the domain of darkness and transferred to the kingdom of God's beloved Son (Colossians 1:13), we will never have to be delivered again. Certainly, 1 John 5:18 rules out being subjected to indwelling demons. This wonderful text, which extols Christian liberation from death, sin, and Satan, could mean nothing less.

16. In light of this biblical conclusion, I must state that, in my opinion, the following men have misunderstood the Scriptures on this point and widely teach a major error which potentially has serious consequences. They all believe that true Christians can be indwelt by demons with the need for demons to be expelled: Jack Deere, *Surprised by the Power of the Spirit*, 26-28; C. Fred Dickason, *Demon Possession & the Christian*, 325; Lloyd D. Fretz, in *The Kingdom and the Power*, 248-52; D. Martyn-Lloyd Jones, *Healing and the Scriptures* (Nashville, TN: Thomas Nelson Publishers, 1988), 165-67; Ed Murphy, *The Handbook for Spiritual Warfare* (Nashville, TN: Thomas Nelson Publishers, 1992), 286-87; Merrill F. Unger,

What Demons Can Do to Saints, 97-109; John Wimber, *Power Healing*, 114.

On the other hand, Brent Grimsley, "Can a Christian Be 'Demonized'?" 19, 37; Edward Gross, *Miracles, Demons, & Spiritual Warfare* (Grand Rapids, MI: Baker Book House, 1990), 163-67; Thomas Ice and Robert Dean, Jr., *Overrun by Demons* (Eugene, OR: Harvest House Publishers, 1993), 119-29; John MacArthur, Jr., *How to Meet the Enemy* (Wheaton, IL: Victor Books, 1992), 135-36; and Robert Morey, *Satan's Devices* (Eugene, OR: Harvest House Publishers, 1993), 94-95, all agree that true believers cannot ever be indwelt by demons.

The reader might be surprised to learn that the historic Pentecostal position of the Assemblies of God church (Springfield, MO) agrees with this "no possession/residency" conclusion. *See* W. Duane Collins, "An Assemblies of God Perspective on Demonology, Part 1" in *Paraclete* (Fall, 1993), 29, and L. Grant McClury, Jr. in *Wrestling with Dark Angels*, ed. by C. Peter Wagner and F. Douglas Pennoyer (Ventura, CA: Regal Books, 1990), 207.

17. Thomas Ice and Robert Dean, Jr., *Overrun by Demons* and John MacArthur, Jr., *How to Meet the Enemy*, have been written in our time. In addition, I highly recommend the Puritan classic by Thomas Brooks, *Precious Remedies Against Satan's Devices* (Edinburgh: The Banner of Truth Trust, reprinted, 1984).

18. An alternate way to understand the resurrection of the Antichrist in Revelation 13:3-12 is "apparent resurrection." The appearance of death and subsequent appearance of resurrection deceived the whole world. In my opinion, Ed Gross, *Miracles, Demons, & Spiritual Warfare*, 96-107, mistakenly gives Satan credit for miraculous power without effectively substantiating his assertion with a strong biblical defense. The passages he cites, Exodus 7–12 and 2 Thessalonians 2, would be better understood as very convincing, deceitful illusions rather than truly miraculous. J. Sidlow Baxter, *Divine Healing of the Body* (Grand Rapids, MI: Zondervan Publishing House, 1979), 19, also attributes miraculous power to Satan. Robert Morey, *Satan's Devices*, 72-73, 77-78, has a helpful discussion.

CHAPTER 11—Answers to "What About . . . ?" Questions

1. Bruce M. Metzger, *A Textual Commentary on the Greek New Testament* (New York: United Bible Society, 1971), 126.

2. A.T. Robertson, *Word Pictures in the Greek New Testament*, Vol. 1 (Nashville, TN: Broadman, 1930), 405.

3. Gary Greig and Kevin N. Springer, *The Kingdom and the Power* (Ventura, CA: Regal Books, 1993), 399-403. Andrew Murray, *Divine Healing* (Fort Washington, PA: Christian Literature Crusade, reprinted 1971), 11, also reasoned this way almost 100 years ago.

4. J. Sidlow Baxter, *Divine Healing of the Body* (Grand Rapids, MI: Zondervan Publishing House, 1979), 116, who is sympathetic to Greig and Springer's conclusion, warns of the danger in treating Mark 16 this way by assuming that something is a positive potential if it has not been expressly condemned or prohibited.

5. Colin Brown, *That You May Believe* (Grand Rapids, MI: Eerdmans, 1985), 192.

6. J. Sidlow Baxter, *Divine Healing of the Body*, 118.

7. C. Samuel Storms, *Healing and Holiness* (Phillipsburg, NJ: Presbyterian and Reformed Publishing Company, 1990), 77. Gary Greig and Kevin N. Springer, *The Kingdom and the Power*, 393-97, fall way short of convincing me that believers today can do greater physical miracles than Christ because 1) they fail to allow the parallel passage in John 5:20-21 help to interpret John 14:12, and 2) they fail to identify "greater works" with the miracle of salvation.

8. J. Sidlow Baxter, *Divine Healing of the Body*, 174-77.

9. *See* Robert L. Thomas, *Understanding Spiritual Gifts* (Chicago: Moody Press, 1978), 40-42, 82-83, for a complete discussion.

10. J. Sidlow Baxter reached essentially this same conclusion in *Divine Healing of the Body* (Grand Rapids, MI: Zondervan, 1979), 281-83, as has D.A. Carson, *Showing the Spirit* (Grand Rapids, MI: Baker Book House, 1987), 39-40.

11. *Ibid.*, 123.

12. *Ibid.*, 155-80.

13. *Ibid.*, 157.

14. Jack Deere, *Surprised by the Power of the Spirit* (Grand Rapids, MI: Zondervan Publishing House, 1993), 64-68.

15. *Ibid.*, 18-19, 99-115.

16. *Ibid.*, 58.

17. Peter H. Davids, "Sickness and Suffering in the New Testament," in *Wrestling with Dark Angels*, ed. by C. Peter Wagner and F. Douglas Pennoyer (Ventura, CA: Regal Books, 1990), 215-37, argues that the categories of "sickness" and "suffering" should be considered separately and do not overlap in experience. I take issue with this theory, as did Walter R. Bodine's response in the same volume (238-47).

18. Jack Deere, *Surprised by the Power of the Spirit*, 235, 287. Dr. Deere *never* tells his reader that the word translated "miracle" can just as easily be translated "power" and refer to the power of God in salvation (Romans 1:16; 1 Corinthians 1:18; 2 Corinthians 6:7; 1 Thessalonians 1:5; 2 Timothy 1:8).

19. John A. McLean, "Galatians 3:5: A Change in Nature or a Change of Nature?" (unpublished paper delivered at the 44th Annual Meetings of the Evangelical Theological Society, November 19-21, 1992). Dr. McLean presents a very convincing case for this possibility.

20. Dennis J. DeHaan, "Running to Heaven," *Our Daily Bread* (Grand Rapids, MI: Radio Bible Class) September 4, 1981.

21. D. Edmond Hiebert, "An Exposition of 3 John 1-4," *Bibliotheca Sacra* (January-March 1987), 60-62, provides an excellent, comprehensive exposition.

CHAPTER 12—What About Miracles?

1. Jack Deere, *Surprised by the Power of the Spirit* (Grand Rapids, MI: Zondervan Publishing House, 1993), 114 (also 54, 99).

2. I have followed Millard J. Erickson, *Christian Theology* (Grand Rapids, MI: Baker Book House, 1986), 365-410, in the basic twofold breakdown of God's work into 1) orginating creation and 2) continuing providence.

3. C. Everett Koop, "Faith Healing and the Sovereignty of God," in *The Agony of Deceit*, ed. by Michael Horton (Chicago: Moody Press, 1990), 169-70. Rex Gardiner, *Healing Miracles* (London: Darton, Longman and Todd, 1986), does not consider the inexplicable phenomena of natural healing in his understanding of "miracles": "By miraculous healing I mean the healing of organic disease by means, or at a speed, inexplicable medically and preceded by prayer in the name of Jesus Christ."

4. John particularly notes seven signs that Jesus performed in order to authenticate Himself as the One in whom people should believe for salvation (20:30-31). They included 1) turning water to wine (2:1-11); 2) healing the royal official's son (4:46-53); 3) healing a sick man (5:1-9); 4) feeding the multitudes (6:9-14); 5) walking on water (6:16-21); 6) healing a blind man (9:1-34); and 7) raising Lazarus from the dead (11:1-46).

5. The Scriptures warn about 1) false prophets (Deuteronomy 13:1-5; 18:14-22; 1 John 4:1-4); 2) false apostles (2 Corinthians 12:12); 3) false believers (Matthew 7:13-23; 2 Corinthians 11:26; Galatians 2:4); and 4) false signs (2 Thessalonians 2:9; Revelation 13:13; 16:14; 19–20).

6. At least 20 miracles associated with Elisha are recorded in 2 Kings 2–13. This concentration approaches the intensity experienced in the times of Moses and Christ.

7. B.B. Warfield, *Counterfeit Miracles* (Edinburgh: The Banner of Truth Trust reprinted 1972), 10.

8. Philip Schaff, *History of the Christian Church*, 8 vols. (Grand Rapids, MI: Associated Publishers & Authors, n.d.), 3:191-92.

9. B.B. Warfield, *Counterfeit Miracles*, 6. Jack Deere, *Surprised by the Power of the Spirit* (Grand Rapids, MI: Zondervan Publishing House, 1993), 49-56, 253-66, takes great issue with Warfield's cessationist view. In so doing, he claims to base his argument on Scripture alone (22-23), but, in fact, argues primarily from experience: "There is one basic reason why Bible-believing Christians do not believe in the miraculous gifts of the Spirit today. It is simply this: *they have not seen them*" (55). Then in Appendix C (253-66), he repeatedly castigates John MacArthur's view of miracles through men. Deere's discussion not only unfairly misrepresents MacArthur's position, but also shows serious theological deficiency in that Deere does not clearly distinguish between the miraculous or supernatural directly from God and the miraculous from God through human agency.

10. Jack Deere, *Surprised by the Power of the Spirit*, 229-52, argues that the miraculous gifts of the Holy Spirit experienced in the apostolic church did not cease with the apostolic era; he further claims that B.B. Warfield popularized the notion of gifts ceasing (229). Dr. Deere did *not* tell his readers that throughout church history, while there has been debate, the majority view on the subject has always been the cessation view. *See* Walter J. Chantry, *Signs of the Apostles*, 2nd ed. (Edinburgh: The Banner of Truth Trust, 1976) 140-46, for a survey of cessationist proponents from Chrysostom to A.W. Pink.

CHAPTER 13—God Heals Today!

1. Philip Yancey, *Where Is God When It Hurts?* (Grand Rapids, MI: Zondervan, 1977), 13.

2. *Ibid.*, 15.

3. R.A. Torrey, *Divine Healing* (Grand Rapids, MI: Baker Book House, reprinted, 1974), 51-54.

4. James Randi, *The Faith Healers* (Buffalo: Prometheus Books, 1987), 25.

5. John F. MacArthur, Jr., *The Charismatics* (Grand Rapids, MI: Zondervan Publishing House, 1978), 150-51.

6. William A. Nolen, *Healing: A Doctor in Search of a Miracle* (Greenwich, CT: Fawcett Publications, 1974), 258.

7. *Ibid.*

8. *Ibid.*

9. *Ibid.*, 267.

10. John Wimber and Kevin Springer, *Power Healing* (San Francisco: Harper and Row, 1987), 133.

CHAPTER 14—What About Faith, Prayer, and Doctors?

1. Dr. James Boyer first suggested this insightful outline to me.

2. John R. Rice, *Healing in Answer to Prayer* (Murfreesburo, TN: Sword of the Lord Publishers, 1944), 20.

3. For an unabridged discussion of what the Bible says about physicians, *see* Franklin E. Payne, Jr., *Biblical Healing for Modern Medicine* (Augusta, GA: Covenant Books, 1993), 195-97.

4. Loraine Boettner, "Christian Supernaturalism," *Studies in Theology* (Phillipsburg, NJ: Presbyterian and Reformed Publishing Company, 1976), 74-75.

CHAPTER 15—Joni Eareckson Tada on Sickness

1. To learn more about Joni and her struggles to be victorious, read her account in *A Step Further* (Grand Rapids, MI: Zondervan Publishing House, 1990). To find out more about her ministries, write to JAF Ministries, P.O. Box 3333, Agoura Hills, CA 91301, or call (818) 707-5664.

CHAPTER 16—On My Back by Divine Design

1. Harold S. Kushner, *When Bad Things Happen to Good People* (New York: Avon Books, 1981).
2. O. Hallesby, *Prayer* (Minneapolis: Augsburg Publishing House, reprinted 1975), 129-30.
3. Benny Hinn, *Lord, I Need a Miracle* (Nashville, TN: Thomas Nelson Publishers, 1993), 63.
4. C. Everett Koop, "Faith Healing and the Sovereignty of God," in *The Agony of Deceit*, ed. by Michael Horton (Chicago: Moody Press, 1990), 176.
5. C.S. Lewis, *The Problem of Pain* (New York: Macmillan Publishing Company, 1962), 93.
6. Written by the author's mother in mid-1986 after she was paralyzed by a stroke. This testimony was shared at Washington Bible College and Capitol Seminary.
7. Charles R. Wood, "We Learned to Pray for Healing," *Moody Monthly* (November, 1976), 157.

CHAPTER 17—When Suffering Arrives

1. John F. MacArthur, Jr., *Faith Works* (Dallas: Word Publishing, 1993), 17-19. Used by permission.

CHAPTER 18—Your Healing Promise

1. Paul Brand and Philip Yancey, *Fearfully and Wonderfully Made* (Grand Rapids, MI: Zondervan Publishing House, 1980), 57-58.
2. J.I. Packer, *Rediscovering Holiness* (Ann Arbor, MI: Servant Publications, 1992), 40-41.
3. Donald E. Gowan, "Salvation as Healing," *Ex Auditu*, 5 (1989), 15-16. *See also* Paul Brand with Philip Yancey, "And God Created Pain," *Christianity Today* (January 10, 1994), 18-23.
4. Arthur Bennett, ed., *The Valley of Vision* (Edinburgh: The Banner of Truth Trust, 1975), 83.

A FINAL WORD—Your Healing Ministry

1. For a more complete discussion of what the Bible means when it exhorts Christians to be like God, *see* Richard Mayhue, *Spiritual Maturity* (Wheaton, IL: Victor Books, 1992), 43-61.

Scripture Index